TRANSCENDENTAL
UTOPIAS

TRANSCENDENTAL UTOPIAS

Individual and Community at

Brook Farm, Fruitlands,

and Walden

RICHARD FRANCIS

Cornell University Press

ITHACA AND LONDON

First published 1997 by Cornell University Press.

Printed in the United States of America

TCF This book is printed on Lyons Falls Turin Book,
a paper that is totally chlorine-free and acid-free.

Library of Congress Cataloging-in-Publication Data

Francis, Richard, 1945–
    Transcendental utopias : individual and community at Brook Farm,
Fruitlands, and Walden / Richard Francis.
        p.   cm.
    Includes index.
    ISBN 0-8014-3093-3 (cloth : alk. paper)
    1. Utopias—Massachusetts—Case studies.   2. Brook Farm Phalanx
(West Roxbury, Boston, Mass.)   3. Fruitlands (Harvard, Mass.)
4. Walden Woods (Mass.)   5. Transcendentalism (New England)
I. Title.
HX655.M4F73   1997
355'.02'09744—dc21   96-46314

Cloth printing   10   9   8   7   6   5   4   3   2   1

TO JO, WILLIAM, AND HELEN

Contents

Preface

In the introduction to *The American Renaissance*, F. O. Matthiessen writes that his subject is the artistic achievement of the mid-nineteenth century in America, particularly the way in which the great practitioners fused form and content. As if worried that his monumental study might not be regarded as adequate, he goes on to confess that there were two other books that he might have written but had not. The first of these would have been called *The Age of Swedenborg*, and it would have dealt with the way the midcentury had "embraced the subjective philosophy that 'the soul makes its own world.'" That subjective philosophy, however, had objective repercussions. The individual's sense of self-worth made him conscious of his social rights, and this awareness in turn made possible Orestes Brownson's extraordinary anticipation of "some of the Marxist analysis of the class controls of action." The unwritten book necessary to explore these and related issues Matthiessen calls *The Age of Fourier*. These two (non)titles point to what Sacvan Bercovitch has more recently termed, in his discussion of Emerson in *The Puritan Origins of the American Self*, "the paradox of a literature devoted at once to the exaltation of the individual and the search for a perfect community."

This paradox is the central problem one encounters when confronting the thought of the New England Transcendentalists. The most obvious way to view it is in terms of the duality of subjective and objective worlds, of the internal vis-à-vis the external. This dichotomy manifests itself in many of the actual titles of works devoted to participants in the movement, classic studies such as Stephen Whicher's *Freedom and Fate:*

An Inner Life of Ralph Waldo Emerson, for example, or Sherman Paul's
Shores of America: Thoreau's Inward Exploration. Everywhere we look there
seems to be a dialectic between liberty and restriction, the me and the
not-me, the one and the totality.

The dialectic can be bypassed, of course, if we simply concentrate on
one of its terms. David Van Leer points out that scholars have tended
to write one or the other of Matthiessen's unwritten books. His own
rigorously analytical contribution, *Emerson's Epistemology: The Argument
of the Essays,* is on the Swedenborgian, that is to say the subjective or
inward, side of the argument, investigating Emerson's contribution to
American idealism. Another commentator has shown great ingenuity
in transferring the conflict from the Transcendentalists themselves to
the scholars who in modern times have endeavored to analyze their
thinking. Anne C. Rose, in *Transcendentalism as a Social Movement,* tracks
a development from Perry Miller's emphasis on romantic individualism, through W. R. Hutchison's study of Transcendentalist efforts at
institutional reform, to a modern understanding that the movement
was "a matter of social consciousness and action." Her book is a valuable one, though her transference of the axis from its nineteenth-
century setting to our own time is not wholly convincing. In any
case, the Fourieristic emphasis did not supplant the Swedenborgian
one; the two approaches were available simultaneously and comple-
mented each other. Emerson himself remarked, in an essay in the *Dial*
that later became the basis for his "Historic Notes of Life and Letters
in New England," that during the Transcendentalist period "mechanics were pushed so far as fairly to meet spiritualism. One could not
but be struck with strange coincidences betwixt Fourier and Swedenborg."

One of those strange coincidences was that both Fourier and Swedenborg had formulated serial philosophies. Fourier attempted to impose "order and series" on all things by means of a "system which was
coherent and comprehensive of facts to a wonderful degree"; Swedenborg had a "doctrine of Series and Degrees," and, "like a musical com-
poser, goes on unweariedly repeating a simple air or theme, now high,
now low, in solo, in chorus, ten thousand times reverberated, till it fills
earth and heaven with the chant." There was a connection between the
two precisely because, in being philosophers of seriality, both took connection as their very subject matter. They may have been situated at
opposite ends of a spectrum, but their principal interest was in defining and describing that spectrum. (I am talking, of course, about the

Emersonian apprehension of Swedenborg and Fourier—as Matthiessen also was—not of those thinkers per se.)

I have written this book in the belief that the Transcendentalists were essentially bridgers of duality rather than victims of it. Their basic mission was to solve the very problem that they are frequently taken to embody. And nowhere was the nature and significance, not to mention the success and failure, of this endeavor more apparent than in their efforts to inaugurate utopia.

The Transcendentalist social experiments—Brook Farm, Fruitlands, Walden—serve to bring the movement into sharp focus better than any other achievement. We can analyze the major writings that were produced, but to do so turns Transcendentalism into a two-horse race. Other characteristic phenomena are the controversy about miracles and some second-rate philosophizing, neither of which accounts for the impact the movement made (in its own time and since), or provides an adequate context for the literary achievement of its two geniuses, Emerson and Thoreau.

One's sense that these communities were somehow the key issue is confirmed by the folklore, for, despite their transitoriness and relatively small scale, anyone with even the most cursory knowledge of the period has heard of them. But this assessment is also justified by the fact that utopia itself, as a concept, inevitably brought the problems faced by the Transcendentalists onto center stage. Utopian communities juxtapose freedom and social organization; they exalt the individual and represent a search for communal perfection. To put it another way, they connect the eternal world of nature and natural law—the world, in that pre-Darwinian, prerelativistic period, of stability and pattern—with the dynamic world of history and contingency. They connect subjective and objective, inward and outward, contemplation and action. Utopias provide the bridge the Transcendentalists were seeking, for they are situated exactly halfway between the ideal and the real.

I began my study of Transcendentalist utopian thought many years ago, and it culminated in two substantial articles, one on the ideology of the Fruitlands community, the other on that of Brook Farm. Then I let the matter rest. It is not always easy to reconstruct one's own past motives, as I now know, having devoted a book to reconstructing those of other people. Perhaps I felt that I had said all I could on the topic. Perhaps, like Thoreau, I simply decided that I had other lives to lead. Then a few years ago I had the good fortune to meet Lyman Tower

Sargent, that great authority on utopianism, at a conference at Exeter University, and he suggested to me that I should revisit the topic and write a book on it.

The more I thought about his suggestion, the more it seemed like good advice. Important work had, of course, been done in the intervening period: Rose's book on the social dimensions of the movement, Frederick Dahlstrand's intellectual biography of Bronson Alcott, and Carl J. Guarneri's brilliant study of American Fourierism are obvious examples. Much detailed scholarship had appeared in the learned journals, particularly in the pages of the yearbooks edited by Joel Myerson, *Studies in the American Renaissance* (it has been a continuing source of pride to me that my article on Brook Farm was the first piece in the first volume of that series). None of this work, though, seemed to preempt my own task. Indeed, so far as I am aware, no one has attempted a coordinated view of the Transcendentalist utopian project, despite its centrality to the movement's concerns, and despite the fact that each community in itself constituted a claim by its members that a coordinated view of human behavior was both possible and indeed necessary. And of course such seriality was precisely what my own earlier forays into the topic had lacked.

To my relief I found that it was not necessary to repudiate most of my earlier analysis. Indeed, turns of phrase from that work, sentences, arguments flit ghostlike in and out of this book, and I am most grateful to the editors of *American Quarterly* and *Studies in the American Renaissance* for permission to draw on that material. But the context in which it now appears is both more detailed and more extensive, and needless to say the discourse in which it participates has been transformed by developments in literary and cultural theory. Above all, the book overcomes the structural inconsistency implicit in producing separate and incomplete explorations of the Transcendentalist search for completeness and structural consistency.

A fellowship from the American Council of Learned Societies enabled me to pursue my research as a visiting scholar at Harvard University, as did a sabbatical leave granted by Manchester University. I am grateful to many libraries and archives for the opportunity to study, quote from, and in some cases reproduce material held by them: the Houghton and Widener Libraries of Harvard University, the Boston Public Library, the Fruitlands Museums, the Massachusetts Historical Society, the John Rylands University Library of Manchester, the Manchester Public Library, the Portico Library, and the British Library.

I am indebted to the people who have given me advice and/or hospitality during the writing of this book: Roberta Bienvenu, Jinx Bohstedt, John Bohstedt, Jean Day, Clio and Anthea Harrison, the late William Henry (Pat) Harrison, Jim and Carol Hoopes, W. R. Hutchison, Joel Myerson, Tom Quirk, Lyman Tower Sargent, Michael Schmidt, and Ian Walker. Other friends have given me help that is not so direct but equally important. And I want to take this opportunity to give thanks, for everything, to my late father, Leslie; my mother, Marian; and my dedicatees, my wife, Jo, who has shared this project—and all my projects—from the beginning, and my children, William and Helen.

NOTE: I capitalize Transcendentalism and its variants when referring to the New England movement, and use lowercase on the relatively few occasions when the words have a purely philosophical sense.

RICHARD FRANCIS

Manchester

TRANSCENDENTAL
UTOPIAS

1

Nature versus History

N ew England Transcendentalism was a many-sided phenomenon. From a parochial point of view, it can be seen as the product of a doctrinal argument within the Unitarian Church of
Boston; from an international one, as the American accommodation of
European romanticism. As a movement it had literary, religious, philosophical, and social ramifications. Its proponents wrote essays on topics
ranging from circles to civil disobedience, and in addition produced
political articles, sermons, and manifestos, kept journals, wrote poems,
edited magazines and newspapers, conducted conversations, gave lectures; they started communities, lived in huts, were feverishly active,
deeply withdrawn, joined churches, left churches, founded churches,
taught school, farmed, fished, waited at table. No medium of discourse,
area of knowledge, or field of activity seemed closed to them.

The broad explanation for such breadth of interests is that the movement was a manifestation of the American cultural project. It was a
new(ish) country, and there was still a great deal to do on all fronts.
Benjamin Franklin in the previous century had organized street-clean-
ing and fire-fighting services, studied lightning, built stoves, drawn up
constitutions. The Transcendentalists, while starting from a different
set of premises (though, as we shall see, not necessarily so different as
all that) had a similarly crowded agenda. But one can argue that it was
not simply the nature of the world they inhabited which determined
the range of their activities, but also the perspective on that world—
indeed on any world—which Transcendentalism by its very nature generated. In fact, one of the preoccupations of the movement was to

1

analyze the relationship between the world and its knower. Because such analysis is of a fundamental kind, its ramifications can be tracked in every direction. The circle, as described in Emerson's essay on the subject, symbolizes the "Unattainable, the flying Perfect," which may "conveniently serve us to connect many illustrations of human power in every department."[1]

My purpose is to consider one department in particular, the utopian aspiration which is one of the most famous manifestations of the Transcendental afflatus. Even this department can be divided into subdepartments, however: the large-scale enterprise of Brook Farm, the "consociate family" at Fruitlands, and Thoreau's "community of one." Moreover, the interdisciplinary nature of Transcendentalist thinking means that this exploration will involve trying to come to terms with other themes and preoccupations. Indeed, it has to begin with an attempt to grapple with the basic epistemology of the movement, a search for that maddening "Unattainable . . . around which the hands of man can never meet."[2] If the deepest concern of the New England Transcendentalists—perhaps of anybody—is to locate humankind within the world, then a quest for the basis of their utopian ideology must take us very directly to that preoccupation, since this mission inevitably involves problems of the relation between contingent and absolute, past and future, the singular and the totality, and above all, between history and nature. I explore these issues in this chapter as the essential basis for confronting, or rather for monitoring how the Transcendentalists confronted, the central paradox of utopianism: that it acknowledges disorder (in its dissatisfaction with the status quo) while affirming order (in offering a millennial prospect). The Transcendentalists' most important task was to find a law that somehow reconciled mutability with permanence, and thereby to come to terms with the ambivalence embodied in that phrase "the flying Perfect."

1. Ralph Waldo Emerson, "Circles," in *Essays: First Series,* vol. 2 of *Collected Works of Ralph Walso Emerson,* ed. Alfred R. Ferguson et al., 5 vols. (Cambridge: Belknap Press of Harvard University Press, 1971– © President and Fellows of Harvard College), 179. All subsequent references to this volume will be to *Essays 1;* subsequent references to this edition will be to *Collected Works.* For a stimulating account of the relationship between this essay's handling of "a strange, shimmering illusive truth" and modern deconstruction, see Leonard N. Neufeldt and Christopher Barr, "'I Shall Write Like a Latin Father': Emerson's 'Circles,'" *New England Quarterly* 59 (March 1986): 92–108. In this and the following chapters on Brook Farm, I have made use, where appropriate, of material originally published in my essay "The Ideology of Brook Farm," in *Studies in the American Renaissance, 1977,* ed. Joel Myerson (Boston: Twayne Publishers, 1978), 1–48.
2. Emerson, "Circles," 179.

One possible explanation for Transcendentalism's scale and eclecticism is simply that it was vague and diffuse. Hawthorne suggests a paradoxical combination of bulk and intangibility when he portrays "Giant Transcendentalist" in "The Celestial Railroad" as "a heap of fog and duskiness."[3] Half a century later H. C. Goddard referred to "the popular definition of transcendental, 'transcending commonsense.'"[4] But the opposite possibility is just as plausible. In Emerson's "Divinity School Address," one of the great defining documents of the movement, it is worth noting that the word "law" appears more than twenty times. An alternative explanation for the remarkable range of Transcendentalist concerns is that at the heart of them lies a preoccupation with what might hold the full range of the world's phenomena, and of the individual's experiences, together, and link them to one another: a preoccupation with the principle of consistency, with the tissue of connectiveness, with the nature of law itself. A movement asserting the unity of all things can test that faith only by the criteria of variety and heterogeneity. It is true that Emerson said he proposed to write the word "*Whim*" on the lintels of his doorpost, but that may be construed as an assertion of confidence in the stability and permanence of the doorpost. In the same essay, "Self-Reliance," he claims that perception is not whimsical but fatal. He also says, of course, that "a foolish consistency is the hobgoblin of little minds," but that can be taken as an attack on a specific category of consistency, to wit, the foolish sort, rather than on the principle of order itself. At the opening of the essay he suggests that it is the task of Transcendentalism to advance "on Chaos and the Dark."[5]

Perhaps we should start our inquiry where New England Transcendentalism, as a specific intellectual movement with a particular membership, is usually held to begin: with the issue of the authenticity of the gospel miracles, the central subject of Emerson's "Address."

During the early part of the nineteenth century the Unitarian Church in New England subsisted on a doctrinal minimum. Its development had been toward a liberal, open-ended alternative to the more enthusiastic and elaborately formulated dogmas of the New Calvinists. The law

3. Nathaniel Hawthorne, "The Celestial Railroad," in *Mosses from an Old Manse*, vol. 10 of *Centenary Edition of the Works of Nathaniel Hawthorne*, ed. William Charvat et al., 23 vols. (Columbus: Ohio State University Press, 1960–94), 197. All subsequent references to this edition will be to *Centenary Edition*.
4. H. C. Goddard, *Studies in New England Transcendentalism* (New York: Columbia University Press, 1908), 10.
5. Ralph Waldo Emerson, "Self-Reliance," *Essays 1*, 30, 38, 33, 28.

of equilibrium, however, required that the one positive element in an otherwise unassertive theology should be firmly stressed; and for the Unitarians the sticking point was the gospel miracles. These provided an essential guarantee of the truth and relevance of the Christian message. As Andrews Norton, former Dexter Professor of Sacred Literature at Harvard and leading proponent of the orthodox Unitarian position, put it in his *Discourse on the Latest Form of Infidelity*: "Nothing is left that can be called Christianity, if its miraculous character be denied. Its essence is gone; its evidence is annihilated. Its truths, involving the highest interests of man, the facts which it makes known, and which are implied in its very existence as a divine revelation, rest no longer on the authority of God."[6]

The trouble is that the miracles which provide this essential guarantee happened so long ago that we are left with what Norton likes to call "belief on testimony," but which he acknowledges could be called "belief on authority." Obviously anticipating objections to his putting so much faith in the supernatural—and in the secondhand supernatural at that—Norton claims that belief in miracles passes the test of rational scrutiny and affirms, by discreet use of negatives, that our knowledge of Christianity can be equated with our knowledge of anything else: "In maintaining . . . that the thorough investigation of the evidences and character of our religion requires much knowledge and much thought, and the combined and continued labor of different minds, we maintain nothing that gives to Christianity a different character from what belongs to all the higher and more important branches of knowledge, and nothing inconsistent with its being in its nature a universal religion."[7] The gospel miracles, by an accident of history, took place in the past, so that our knowledge of them can be achieved only by recourse to secondary sources. Scholars therefore need to establish the provenance of documents and interpret their contents just as they would if they were researching the life of Julius Caesar. But a parallelism in the tasks of the historian does not imply a parallelism in the status of the historical subject. Whether as a historian or as a contemporary witness, one "knows" that Christ changed the water into wine in quite a differ-

6. Andrews Norton, *Discourse on the Latest Form of Infidelity* (Cambridge: J. Owen, 1839), 22, excerpted in Perry Miller, ed., *The Transcendentalists: An Anthology* (Cambridge: Harvard University Press, 1950), 211. Miller's book remains the best source of material on the miracles controversy, and indeed in conjunction with his later anthology *The American Transcendentalists: Their Prose and Poetry* (New York: Anchor Books, 1957) and George Hochfield's *Selected Writings of the American Transcendentalists* (New York: New American Library, 1966) provides the most convenient access to the movement as a whole.
7. See Miller, *Transcendentalists*, 213.

ent way from that in which one "knows" that Caesar conquered Gaul.
Norton's curious hybrid of rationalism and revelation is the direct legacy of John Locke, who, in the words of Bertrand Russell, will at one
time claim that "the bare testimony of revelation is the highest certainty," and at another that "revelation must be judged by reason."[8]

It is fascinating to see how the Transcendentalists react to this incon-
gruity. If they are to be defined by their capacity to transcend common
sense—if, for example, the characteristic Transcendentalist stance is
that adopted by Jones Very, who, while a temporary patient at the
McLean asylum, took down an essay on Shakespeare which was dictated to him from above—then the assumption must be that in any
two-horse race between reason and revelation, their money would inevitably be on revelation.[9] But this was not the case. Indeed, they showed
that they were capable of subjecting the orthodox position to a strin-
gent critique. The fact that when Theodore Parker entered the fray he
chose to assume the no-nonsense persona of Levi Blodgett is almost as
significant as the arguments he put forward. The name evokes an almost depressing degree of Yankee common sense. "You make us rest
our moral and religious faith, for time and eternity," Blodgett informs
Norton—with rather more of a rhetorical surge than one might expect
from a farmer with mud on his boots—"on evidence too weak to be
trusted in a trifling case that comes before a common court of law."[10]
George Ripley goes further, asserting that "we know of no unerring
test, by which to distinguish a miracle of religion from a new manifestation of natural powers, without a previous faith in the divinity of
the performer. The phenomena of electricity and magnetism exhibit
wonders surpassing the ordinary agencies of nature. Upon their first
discovery, they presented all the characteristics by which we designate
miracles, except their application to religious purposes."[11] Interestingly
enough, this is precisely the point that Hume fails to make satisfactorily
in his "Essay on Miracles." Anthony Flew points out that the great skeptic mars his attack on Locke by defining the laws of nature as "merely
numerical universal propositions," therefore necessarily conceding that

8. Bertrand Russell, *History of Western Philosophy* (London: Allen & Unwin, 1946), 631.
For the influence of Locke on the Unitarians, see W. R. Hutchison, *The Transcendentalist
Ministers* (New Haven: Yale University Press, 1959), 18–20.
9. See Edwin Gittleman, *Jones Very, The Effective Years, 1833–1840* (New York: Columbia
University Press, 1967), 235.
10. Levi Blodgett, *The Previous Question Between Mr. Norton and His Alumni* (Boston:
Weeks, Jordan & Co., 1840), excerpted in Miller, *Transcendentalists*, 230–31.
11. George Ripley, "Review of Martineau's Rationale of Religious Enquiry . . . ," *Christian
Examiner* 21 (November 1836): 253; excerpted in Miller, *Transcendentalists*, 131.

a new occurrence would have to be a miracle.[12] We thus have the intriguing spectacle of a Transcendentalist out-Humeing Hume.

Ripley advocates skepticism, but he does not completely rule out the
possibility of miracles. In his pamphlet *An Essay on Transcendentalism*,
published anonymously in 1842, Charles Mayo Ellis restates Ripley's
argument that a sudden encounter with hitherto unanticipated natural
phenomena could be mistaken for a miracle. He points out that "were
we all in a state of ignorance, and should one come among us, such as
we now consider a mere common man, the wonders he would work
merely from his knowledge of astronomy, the sciences, arts, mechanics,
would seem to us only to be ascribed to miraculous power." Half a
century early (or a thousand years late) we have a glimpse of Mark
Twain's Connecticut Yankee forecasting an eclipse and blowing up
Merlin's tower before an open-mouthed rabble of King Arthur's subjects. Moreover, Ellis's main argument is not that the dividing line between nature and the supernatural is a difficult one to trace, but that
miracles cannot occur at all: "Now Christ had all the knowledge that
man can possess. Consequently, his works must always, to all men, so
long as they remain imperfect, appear miraculous; though in themselves they were no violation of God's laws, but the result of his knowledge and perfect observance of those laws."[13]

Four years earlier, in "The Divinity School Address," Emerson had
made the same assertion, but with more elegance. By his second paragraph he is already evoking the comprehensiveness of the laws of the
universe, a comprehensiveness that at the present stage of our development we cannot fully comprehend: "Behold these outrunning laws,
which our imperfect apprehension can see tend this way and that, but
not come full circle. Behold these infinite relations, so like, so unlike;
many, yet one." And later in the address he memorably disposes of the
conception of miracle in favor of a belief in the consistent ordering of
the world of nature: "But the very word Miracle, as pronounced by the
Christian churches, gives a false impression; it is Monster. It is not one
with the blowing clover and the falling rain."[14]

Not all the New England Transcendentalists were prepared to go
quite as far as Emerson and Charles Mayo Ellis, but leading members
of the movement were certainly prepared to go far enough. Ripley in-

12. Anthony Flew, *Hume's Philosophy of Belief* (London: Routledge, 1961), 204–5.
13. [Charles Mayo Ellis], *An Essay on Transcendentalism* (Boston: Crocker & Ruggles,
1842), 82.
14. Ralph Waldo Emerson, "The Divinity School Address," in *Nature, Addresses, and Lectures,
Collected Works*, 1:76–77, 81. All subsequent references to this volume will be to *NAL*.

sists that, though he believes in miracles as much as the next person, he simply is not prepared to rest the weight of his Christian commitment on them. Parker meanwhile generously takes on board not merely Christ's miracles but those of "other religious teachers" too. But, really, the two of them are doing no more than making polite gestures in the direction of orthodoxy; for both of them the supernatural is a bit of unnecessary decoration on the surface of the hard and commonsensical substance of Christianity. "I need no miracle to convince me that the sun shines," says Parker, "and just as little do I need a miracle to convince me of the divinity of Jesus and his doctrines, to which a miracle, as I look at it, can add just nothing."[15]

The wheel has turned full circle. Parker, like Norton, emphasizes that knowing the central truths of Christianity is no different from knowing anything else, but instead of using this argument to substantiate the gospel miracles, he dismisses them as irrelevant to his basic point. The Transcendentalists, in short, whatever their reputation for transcending common sense, have developed a more consistent position than their opponents. Indeed, they have developed a position in which consistency itself, far from being the hobgoblin of little minds, is perceived to have an intrinsic value. This does not mean that they had a perverse ambition to achieve a more arid logic than Norton. On the contrary, by bringing Christ into the light of common day—indeed, by comparing him with the sun—they hoped to redeem the day. The Transcendentalists were attempting to pit law against legalism. "Any distrust of the permanence of laws," Emerson warns in *Nature*, "would paralyze the faculties of man." Fortunately their "permanence is sacredly respected, and his faith therein is perfect."[16]

The outcome of this argument with Unitarian orthodoxy is two-edged. On the one hand, the common day has been redeemed; on the other, Christ has been demystified. In Emerson's loaded phrase, he turns out to have been a "true man." Christ's contribution was an act of perception: "He saw that God incarnates himself in man." In this respect his achievement can be emulated: "A true conversion, a true Christ, is now, as always, to be made, by the reception of beautiful sentiments."[17] In short, the truest, most outstanding of men can be characterized by his qualities as perceiver and receptacle. This precept is worth bearing in mind, since the Transcendentalists are often pic-

15. Ripley, "Review of Martineau," 253; Theodore Parker, "The Previous Question," in Miller, *Transcendentalists*, 229.
16. Ralph Waldo Emerson, *Nature*, in *NAL*, 29–30.
17. Emerson, "The Divinity School Address," 81, 83.

tured as aggressive, indeed idiosyncratic, individualists. The exceptionalism and mysticism that unsympathetic observers have attributed to their view of nature has also been applied to their perspective on mankind. After all, the fog and duskiness that Hawthorne claimed characterized the movement were embodied in the form of a giant. In this respect—as a study in, so to speak, comparative giganticism—it is illuminating to compare Emerson's *Representative Men* with the book that was in some respects its source, Carlyle's *On Heroes, Hero-Worship, and the Heroic in History*, published nearly a decade previously.[18] It is a testimony to our expectation of Transcendentalist arrogance that we take it for granted that great men inevitably provide the yardstick by which members of the movement would prefer to be judged. But, as it happens, Emerson's main concern is with precisely the legitimacy and relevance of this yardstick.

For Carlyle the topic of great men is an "illimitable" one, since they are "the modellers, patterns, and in a wide sense creators, of whatsoever the general mass of men contrived to do or to attain."[19] The great man, in Carlyle's scheme of things, is so inordinately great that the rest of us hardly get a look in. Great men pull the strings and the puppets dance. Great men embody the history of the world and transmit the radiance of heaven.

Emerson can be warm in his admirations also, though he is capable of a sudden rectifying caution which holds him back from Carlylean excesses. In the final analysis, his model of the cause and effect which operates between great men and common humanity works in precisely the opposite direction from Carlyle's. For Emerson the great man "stands where all the eyes of men look one way, and their hands all point in the direction where he should go."[20] He is, after all, great only to the extent that he is representative. Sacvan Bercovitch distinguishes between Carlyle's "titan born to master the multitude, . . . the Frankenstein's monster of leftwing Protestantism," and Emerson's true American, undertaking "a battle against 'mere antinomianism.' "[21] Shakespeare and Dante, for Carlyle, are "*canonised*, so that it is impiety to

18. Ralph Waldo Emerson, *Representative Men* (1850), vol. 4 of *Collected Works*. All subsequent references to this volume will be to *RM*. Thomas Carlyle, *On Heroes, Hero-Worship, and the Heroic in History* (1841), 4th ed. (London: Chapman and Hall, 1852).
19. Carlyle, *Heroes*, 1–2.
20. Ralph Waldo Emerson, "Shakespeare, or the Poet," *RM*, 109.
21. Sacvan Bercovitch, "Emerson the Prophet: Romanticism, Puritanism, and Auto-American Biography," in *Emerson: Prophecy, Metamorphosis, and Influence*, ed. David Levin (New York: Columbia University Press, 1975), 17.

meddle with them." They are, in short, "a peculiar Two."[22] For Emerson, by contrast, Shakespeare has "no peculiarity." Shakespeare "was the farthest reach of subtlety compatible with an individual self,—the subtilest of authors, and only just within the possibility of authorship." His abilities did not heighten his stature but instead blurred his individuality. He is (just) distinguishable by his almost complete indistinguishability. By the same token, Napoleon "almost ceases to have a private speech and opinion." Emerson relishes Napoleon's claim to be merely the creature of circumstances and, in explaining his hero's ability to hold sway over so many others, displays his own kind of intellectual daring and panache: "It is Swedenborg's theory that every organ is made up of homogeneous particles, or, as it is sometimes expressed, every whole is made of similars; that is, the lungs are composed of infinitely small lungs, the liver of infinitely small livers, the kidney of little kidneys, &c. Following this analogy, if any man is found to carry with him the power and affections of vast numbers, if Napoleon is France, if Napoleon is Europe, it is because the people whom he sways are little Napoleons."[23]

Swift's remark about big fleas having little fleas upon their backs to bite 'em comes to mind, though in this case it is more a matter of little Napoleons having bigger Napoleons over their heads to rule them. When Emerson deals with Swedenborg himself, he is also keen to demonstrate that scale is, as it were, only relative. Swedenborg is to be admired because he is "vast," a "colossal soul," "one of the missouriums and mastodons of literature." In a rush of enthusiasm Emerson claims that this stature provides a perspective that cannot be achieved on a smaller scale: "A drop of water has the properties of the sea, but cannot exhibit a storm." Two pages later, however, he is backtracking rapidly. Swedenborg achieved "that native perception of identity which made mere size of no account to him," and possessed "the fine secret that little explains large, and large little." It is as though a mastodon should stand for election to the assembly of heroes on an anti-mastodon ticket. In the light of such short-circuiting, Emerson's oxymoron about Plato—"He is a great average man"—seems hardly provocative at all.[24] In sum, whereas for Carlyle a great man is "a flowing light-fountain," Emerson prefers to watch him disappear in a puff of smoke: "I find

22. Carlyle, *Heroes*, 133.
23. Emerson, "Shakespeare," 121; idem, "Napoleon, or the Man of the World," *RM*, 131, 129.
24. Ralph Waldo Emerson, "Swedenborg, or the Mystic," *RM*, 58, 60; idem, "Plato, or the Philosopher," *RM*, 34.

him greater, when he can abolish himself and all heroes, by letting in this element of reason, irrespective of persons, this subtilizer, and irresistible upward force, into our thought, destroying individualism;—the power so great, that the potentate is nothing."[25]

An analysis made many years ago by Woodbridge Riley might be relevant here. In his book *American Thought*, published in 1915, Riley identifies a paradoxical by-product of Transcendentalist individualism: "The rights of man were no longer to be measured merely in public documents, in measured terms, but each man was to follow his own private inclinations, to break down the trammels of society, to rely upon himself. Seldom before had individualism reached such heights. Indeed by a sort of paradox it led to a degree of detachment that was at times indifference."[26] He gives us here, it seems to me, a beautifully compact account of what was a complex and ironic cultural development: first, the withdrawal from the "measured terms" of public authority, and its replacement by the anarchic doctrine (potentially at least) of self-reliance; then the intensification of this condition until it reached a point of detachment or even "indifference." Nobody was more aware of this paradox than Emerson himself: "In youth we are mad for persons. Childhood and youth see all the world in them. But the larger experience of man discovers the identical nature appearing through them all. Persons themselves acquaint us with the impersonal."[27]

The logic of this situation is as follows: a structure that connects all phenomena cannot itself be phenomenal; ergo, it is "transparent"; if the pattern is indeed not merely consistent but also comprehensive, then it must include humankind; individuals must therefore share an identical nature, and persons must be impersonal.

Perhaps nowhere is this paradoxical connection between external and internal, world and knower, more powerfully and more beautifully expressed than in the first chapter of Emerson's *Nature*. His opening remarks on the significance of season and setting come into sharp and memorable focus when he gives us this vignette of himself: "Crossing a bare common, in snow puddles, at twilight, under a clouded sky, without having in my thoughts any occurrence of special good fortune, I have enjoyed a perfect exhilaration. Almost I fear to think how glad I am."[28] One can recognize the experience Emerson describes without at

25. Carlyle, *Heroes*, 2; Ralph Waldo Emerson, "Uses of Great Men," *RM*, 14.
26. Woodbridge Riley, *American Thought from Puritanism to Pragmatism and Beyond* (1915; rpt. Gloucester, Mass.: Peter Smith, 1959), 145–46.
27. Ralph Waldo Emerson, "Self-Reliance," *Essays I*, 164.
28. Emerson, *Nature*, 10.

first consciously noting the oddness of the circumstances that have generated it. What we have is a series of self-canceling pairings: the common that provides the setting is bare, the snow has melted into puddles, the light is dim, the sky is obscured. Each itemized feature, in short, proves to be in actuality absent, or at least diminished. And so far as the observer of these ambivalences is concerned, he enjoys his exhilaration while lacking thoughts of any special good fortune. His gladness seems to be canceled out by fear. Cause and effect have become unglued.

Emerson then proceeds, in his memory or his imagination, into woods. Here, too, the blanking out of the external world continues. Instead of being covered by trees and undergrowth, the ground is "bare," and the observer is conscious of "infinite space." The precision of these reversals is reminiscent of Wordsworth's sonnet "Composed Upon Westminster Bridge," where it is an urban environment that folds back into itself, as Wordsworth rhymes "wear" with "bare": "This city now doth, like a garment, wear / The beauty of the morning; silent, bare . . ." If Emerson finds exhilaration frightening, so Wordsworth finds majesty "touching," and his experience culminates in the perception of a heart that has, in fact, stopped beating: "And all that mighty heart is lying still."[29]

Like Wordsworth, Emerson is trying to achieve a glimpse of the deeper structure of the world, a perspective that unifies the jostling contradictions of daily life: "I become a transparent eye-ball. I am nothing. I see all. The currents of the Universal Being circulate through me; I am part or particle of God."[30] In this bare environment where there is nothing to see, the eye becomes infinitely perceptive. A transparent eyeball is an eyeball that cannot be seen, and therefore establishes the observer as literally self-effacing: an indifferent Transcendentalist par excellence. The reticence of the image can be contrasted with the conventionally romantic depiction of the artist's relation to his surroundings in Asher B. Durand's painting *Kindred Spirits* (1849), in which William Cullen Bryant and Thomas Cole are shown standing on a high ledge, with the wild landscape of the Catskills at their disposal, so to speak. At the same time, however, the phrase in this context also suggests an eyeball that can *perceive* transparency. As James M. Cox has put it, "There is outside the perimeter of the eye the negative world of

29. William Wordsworth, "Composed Upon Westminster Bridge," in *The Poetical Works of Wordsworth*, ed. Thomas Hutchinson (London: Oxford University Press, 1964), 214.
30. Emerson, *Nature*, 10.

the vanished ego."[31] The question of priority between man and the world does not arise, therefore, since ultimately both are zeroes and balance each other out.

It seems to me essential for an understanding of Emerson's outlook, and indeed of Transcendentalist philosophy as a whole, to realize that this equation does not leave us with nothing, however contentless it seems. What we have before us is the structure of the equation itself, a structure that connects the individual and the world, the one and the many. Once we have been liberated in this algebraic fashion from the particular and the specific, we are able to concentrate on the connective tissue in which they are found: "The name of the nearest friend sounds then foreign and accidental. To be brothers, to be acquaintances,—master or servant, is then a trifle and a disturbance. I am the lover of uncontained and immortal beauty."[32]

This experience is, inevitably, intermittent, requiring a special set of circumstances, or rather noncircumstances, to come about. The difference between the human angle of vision and the Almighty's is well brought out in a couple of sentences in "Circles": "Our globe seen by God, is a transparent law, not a mass of facts. The law dissolves the fact and holds it fluid." God, as a transparent being, is able consistently to view the transparent nature of the world. The second sentence, however, captures the fleeting nature of such experiences from where we stand, as the woods dissolve around us. It is not clear (and this is a significant ambiguity) whether the fluidity is a function of the process of perception, as the eye has a sense of traveling through the fact toward the underlying law, or whether the characteristic of that law itself is to be dynamic and "fluid." Whatever its basis, the nature of the experience is likely to be that of a pattern on the move. "The natural world," we are told, "may be conceived of as a system of concentric circles, and we now and then detect in nature slight dislocations, which apprize us that this surface on which we now stand, is not fixed, but sliding."[33]

One such dislocation was observed by Thoreau as he walked from Walden Pond to Concord along the railroad cutting. One of its banks has begun to thaw in the warming sun, and the unlocking of the frost unlocks in turn a whole sequence of associations in his mental perception. In an exuberant passage he compares the configurations of the

31. James M. Cox, "R. W. Emerson: The Circles of the Eye," in Levin, *Emerson*, 63. This essay provides a close and interesting reading of the "transparent eye-ball" passage in *Nature*, though I disagree with some of its conclusions.
32. Emerson, *Nature*, 10.
33. Emerson, "Circles," 179, 186.

thawing sand with lava, lichen, coral, leopards' paws, birds' feet, brains, lungs, bowels, excrements, rivers, the liver, fatty tissue, feathers, wings, the grub and butterfly, and the great globe itself, not to mention various aspects of the human form: the ball of the finger, the skeleton, fingers, toes, the hand, the ear, the lip, the nose, the chin, the cheeks. All these apparently diverse phenomena resemble one another; all are reducible to one basic shape, which Thoreau nominates as that of the leaf. This one hillside can illustrate "the principle of all the operations of Nature": "The Maker of this earth but patented a leaf."[34]

The most obvious manifestation of the consistency of law is to be found in the phenomenon of seriality; and, I want to suggest, the search for a, or rather *the*, serial component of the universe is one of the most important elements in the Transcendentalists' mission. They wish to emulate the poet who "turns the world to glass, and shows us all things in their right series and procession."[35] The quest for the law of series is replete with paradoxes, ironies, complications. There is no more reason to identify the leaf as the primitive form than (presumably) the bowels or the butterfly, though it is true that we associate leaves with repetitiveness, as is testified by Whitman's choice of a title for his own epic of seriality, *Leaves of Grass.* While Thoreau's spirits ride high on the tensions created by such similarity in difference, in another mood, or when one's energy is low, the effect can be vertiginous, as Emerson testifies in "Experience": "Where do we find ourselves? In a series, of which we do not know the extremes, and believe that it has none. We wake and find ourselves on a stair: there are stairs below us, which we seem to have ascended; there are stairs above us, many a one, which go upward and out of sight. . . . All things swim and glimmer. Our life is not so much threatened as our perception." Ralph L. Rusk describes the aged Emerson, his mind failing, pathetically floundering in a world where objects slide into one another: "He arrived at hen only after zigzagging from cat to fish, fish to bird, and bird to cock."[36]

34. Henry David Thoreau, *Walden,* in *The Writings of Henry D. Thoreau,* ed. Walter Harding et al., 7 vols. (Princeton: Princeton University Press, 1971–), 304–8. All subsequent references to this edition will be to *Writings.*
35. Ralph Waldo Emerson, "The Poet," in *Essays, Second Series, Collected Works,* 3:12. All subsequent references to this volume will be to *Essays 2.* As Lawrence Buell has written: "The Transcendentalist literati were not merely committed as Yeats was to the principle that the secrets of the universe could be discovered through poetry; they also believed it." Lawrence Buell, *Literary Transcendentalism: Style and Vision in the American Renaissance* (Ithaca: Cornell University Press, 1973), 143.
36. Ralph Waldo Emerson, "Experience," in *Essays 2,* 27; Ralph L. Rusk, *The Life of Ralph*

Roman Jakobson divides aphasia into two broad categories: similarity disorder and contiguity disorder. The disability that clouded Emerson's final years belongs to the first type, which is characterized by difficulty in the selection of words. In such a case a word that is taken out of context ceases to have meaning: it becomes, as Jakobson puts it, "nothing but *blab*." In other words, the patient's language develops a sort of invisibility. Jakobson describes how key words can be superseded by abstract anaphoric substitutes, so that a French patient, as Freud recorded, used terms such as *machin* and *chose* instead of more specific nouns. Eventually "only the framework, the connecting links of communication, is spared by this type of aphasia at its critical stage."[37] In short, all that is left is grammar itself. In Emerson's philosophy—which gave priority to the principle of connectivity over what was connected, which advocated the transparency of the eyeball and celebrated the poet's capacity to turn the world into glass—such a medical condition could almost be regarded as an occupational hazard. The facts of men and chickens dissolve into one another. The philosopher maintains his status for as long as he is able to discern that beneath the zeroes lies the equation itself. The patient is someone who has lost the ability to handle the abstract structures that are revealed by the process of verbal emaciation: "Told to repeat the word 'no,' [the] patient replied 'No, I don't know how to do it.' While spontaneously using the word in the context of his answer ('No, I don't . . .'), he could not produce the purest form of the equational predication, the tautology a $=$ a: «no» is «no»." Jakobson goes on to explain that the problem in the case of this patient results from an inability to use a meta-language: "The examples of equational predication sought in vain from the patients cited above, are metalinguistic propositions referring to the English language."[38]

Strictly speaking, if the law of series is coextensive with the universe as a whole, then the philosopher should also be denied a meta-language to speak of it. This problem does not worry Thoreau, however—at least not in the passage under discussion. The seriality of the universe is manifested in the structure of language as in the structure of

---

Waldo Emerson (New York: Scribner's, 1949), 491. Another example of the Transcendentalist habit of climbing phenomenological staircases occurs in Bronson Alcott's 1849 MS "Tablets in Colours: Disposed on Twelve Tables," Houghton Library, 59M-306 (11), 91 (page out of order), where he quotes "Oken's Skeleton reproduced in the Head": "The Brain is the . . . *Spinal Marrow* / The Cranium is the *vertebrae column or Spine* / The Mouth is the *intestine* & *abdomen* / The Nose is the *lungs* & *thorax* / The Jaws are *the limbs* . . . ," and so on.
37. Roman Jakobson, "Two Aspects of Language and Two Types of Aphasic Disturbance," in *Selected Writings*, 8 vols. (The Hague: Mouton, 1962–88), 2:245–46.
38. Ibid., 247–48.

everything else. Philip F. Gura has used the phrase "epistemological etymology" to describe the kind of analysis Thoreau undertakes here:

> *Internally*, whether in the globe or animal body, it [the leaf] is a moist thick *lobe*, a word especially applicable to the liver and lungs and the *leaves* of fat, (λείβω, *labor, lapsus,* to flow or slip downward, a lapsing; λοβός, *globus*, lobe, globe; also lap, flap, and many other words,) *externally* a thin dry *leaf*, even as the *f* and *v* are a pressed and dried *b*. The radicals of *lobe* are *lb*, the soft mass of the *b* (single-lobed, or B, double lobed,) with the liquid *l* behind it pressing it forward. In globe, *glb*, the guttural *g* adds to the meaning the capacity of the throat.[39]

The exuberance and resourcefulness of this analysis notwithstanding, Thoreau is perfectly well aware that the divide between man and nature cannot be bridged so easily. The history of the human race is out of step with the serene permanence of the laws of the universe. We may echo the language of nature, but we still cannot interpret it aright. "What Champollion," Thoreau asks, "will decipher this hieroglyphic for us, that we may turn over a new leaf at last?"[40] In keeping with the general tone, the appeal he makes here is jocular and ingenious, playing on the various associations of the word *leaf*, the intellectual (as in page) and the spiritual, as well as the structural. Nevertheless, however optimistic and positive he and the other Transcendentalists may be, they cannot gloss over or ignore the doctrine of the Fall of Man, the separation of human history from natural order. One of the recurring concerns of this book will be to explore their efforts to come to terms with the issues raised by that separation.

Meanwhile, it is interesting to watch Emerson undertake the same sort of serial analysis as his friend Thoreau. In his essay "The Method of Nature," written more than ten years before the publication of *Walden*, he too suggested the leaf as creation's building block, and went on to point up the irony of this sameness in diversity by referring to the "catholic character [of nature] which makes every leaf an exponent of the world."[41] Some years later he expanded and enriched this idea in "Swedenborg, or the Mystic" in *Representative Men*.

39. Philip F. Gura, *The Wisdom of Words: Language, Theology, and Literature in the New England Renaissance* (Middletown, Conn.: Wesleyan University Press, 1981), 118; Thoreau, *Walden*, 306.
40. Thoreau, *Walden*, 308.
41. Ralph Waldo Emerson, "The Method of Nature," in *NAL*, 125. The Brook Farmer John Sullivan Dwight also tended to seize on the leaf as a prime example of nature's method, as this claim from his pamphlet *Association in Its Connection with Education and Religion* (Boston: B. H. Greene, 1844) indicates: "The universe of mind and

We have already seen how Emerson used Swedenborg's ideas to bolster his claim that Napoleon was able to rule so successfully because we are all little Napoleons. The origin of such a paradox lies in Swedenborg's "doctrine of Series and Degrees," which insists that "Nature iterates her means perpetually on successive planes." This idea, Emerson stresses, was not peculiar to Swedenborg but "dates from the oldest philosophers, and derives perhaps its best illustration from the newest," one of whom is obviously Emerson himself.[42] Many of the philosophers Emerson is thinking of were no doubt among the writers discussed in Lovejoy's famous series of lectures called "The Great Chain of Being," since we are obviously dealing with a particularly concrete and literal version of that powerful metaphor whose persistence Lovejoy traces from classical times to the early nineteenth century. What Emerson finds in Swedenborg, significantly, is an extension of the chain into the interior of consciousness, where it can anchor the individual psyche to what Emerson himself would call the over-soul, and which the Stoic philosophers he admired identified as the universal pneuma.

On the vegetative plane of natural iteration the Maker, Emerson tells us, has but patented a leaf: "In the plant, the eye or germinative point opens to a leaf, then to another leaf, with a power of transforming the leaf into radicle, stamen, pistil, petal, bract, sepal, or seed." In the higher forms of life the leaf has toughened into a vertebra: "In the animal, nature makes a vertebra, or a spine of vertebrae, and helps herself still by a new spine, with a limited power of modifying its form—spine on spine, to the end of the world." Emerson goes on to describe how the human body and indeed the human mind have been constructed out of these building blocks:

> Manifestly, at the end of the spine, nature puts out smaller spines, as arms; at the end of the arms, new spines as hands; at the other end, she repeats the process, as legs and feet. At the top of the column, she puts out another spine, which doubles or loops itself over as a spanworm into a ball, and forms the skull,—with extremities again; the hands being now the upper jaw, the feet the lower jaw, the fingers and toes being represented this time by upper and lower teeth. This new spine is destined to high uses. It is a new man on the shoulders of the last. It can almost shed its trunk, and manage to live alone, according

---

matter is one great harmony; every planet, every leaf, every atom, every action, has a destined place in which, (however small,) it is of infinite significance and worth" (9).
42. Emerson, "Swedenborg," 60.

to the Platonic idea in the Timaeus. Within it, on a higher plane, all that was done in the trunk, repeats itself. Nature recites her lesson once more in a higher mood.[43]

The immediacy of the language here, and in particular the busy present tense of the verbs, gives one a sense of structure being transformed into process: "Nature puts out . . . repeats . . . puts out another spine, which doubles or loops itself over . . . forms the shell . . . recites her lesson once more." The vision, however, is essentially static, not Darwinian; the process involved is that of consciousness, as it makes the discovery of the connections between all things. Indeed, the only part of the system where some sort of variable seems at least conceivable is the area of consciousness itself, connected to the rest of the edifice by that poignant adverb "almost," as mankind is aware of not quite belonging in nature's continuum, but not successfully achieving independence from it either.

Similarly, though it was the *thaw* of the railroad bank that caught Thoreau's attention, providing the spectacle of a pattern on the move, his emphasis is on his own capacity for cross-referencing rather than on the phenomenon of dynamic improvisation in the external world. These mental juxtapositions have been brought about by the special circumstances of this particular location, although Thoreau does celebrate the creative energy of nature—and of God. He writes: "When I see on the one side the inert bank,—for the sun acts on one side first,—and on the other this luxuriant foliage, the creation of an hour, I am affected as if in a peculiar sense I stood in the laboratory of the Artist who made the world and me,—had come to where he was still at work, sporting on this bank, and with excess of energy strewing his fresh designs about."[44] Perhaps there is some intuition here of the possibility that nature's own reproductive energies could offer the spectacle of an organic, developing pattern. Nevertheless, at this stage in his career Thoreau sees nature's dynamics as operating within strict boundaries.[45] The grub might go through its set mutations, finally turning into a butterfly, just as the seasons go through their annual cycle, but in this universal ordering it is only the human leaves that are likely

43. Ibid., 61.
44. Thoreau, *Walden*, 306.
45. The Transcendentalists' interest in the precursors of the doctrine of evolution, and their receptiveness to the theory itself when it came along, is illuminatingly discussed in Frederick L. Dahlstrand, "Science, Religion, and the Transcendentalist Response to a Changing America," in *Studies in the American Renaissance, 1988*, ed. Joel Myerson (Charlottesville: University Press of Virginia, 1988), 10–14.

to be turned over, through the shift in consciousness brought about by the discoveries of some Champollion. Similarly, the coalescing forms in this passage from Emerson's "Compensation" are the product not of evolutionary generation but of lateral cross-references in a world of "appearances":

> These appearances indicate the fact that the universe is represented in every one of its particles. Every thing in nature contains all the powers of nature. Every thing is made of one hidden stuff; as the naturalist sees one type under every metamorphosis, and regards a horse as a running man, a fish as a swimming man, a bird as a flying man, a tree as a rooted man. Each new form repeats not only the main character of the type, but part for part all the details, all the aims, furtherances, energies and whole system of every other.[46]

The somewhat absurd ramifications of looking at the world in this way are reminiscent of the excesses of the eighteenth-century French philosophe J. B. Robinet, who, Lovejoy tells us, pushed his faith in the chain of being to such lengths that he asserted the existence of "fish-men and fish-women (human with respect to the upper part of their bodies)" and who, in "the quest of these adumbrations of the human form in the lower orders of creation, . . . was unhappily led to find similitudes of faces, as well as of arms and legs, in the radish and other plants, and to publish drawings of these vegetable anthropoids." After all, Emerson himself suggests in *Nature* that there is an "occult relation between man and the vegetable."[47] But for Emerson there is a sudden energy, as of friction, to be derived from such species juxtapositions and, more important, an implication of an elaborate process of exploration, of inventiveness, of patterned movement lying behind them. Nature, viewed phenomenologically, may be ranked and static, but the fact of consciousness gives it fluidity, airiness, abstract scope.

At the end of his essay on Swedenborg, Emerson complains that the great man's system "wants central spontaneity" and, as a result, "there is no individual in it." For Swedenborg, we now discover, "the Universe is a gigantic crystal, all whose atoms and laminae lie in uninterrupted order, and with unbroken unity, but cold and still." Whereas previously Emerson has described the inability of consciousness be autonomous as a defining and tantalizing fact of the human condition (a chronic

46. Ralph Waldo Emerson, "Compensation," in *Essays 1*, 59.
47. Arthur O. Lovejoy, *The Great Chain of Being* (Cambridge: Harvard University Press, 1936), 271, 281; Emerson, *Nature*, 10.

condition of almostness, as it were), he now diagnoses this problem as specific to Swedenborg himself: "With a force of many men, he could never break the umbilical cord which held him to nature and he did not rise to the platform of true genius. It is remarkable that this man who by his perception of symbols saw the poetic construction of things and the primary relation of mind to matter, remained entirely devoid of the whole apparatus of poetic expression, which that perception creates."[48]

Given the doctrine of the sameness of all things, it is not wholly surprising that Emerson's account of Goethe is at times almost indistinguishable from his account of Swedenborg. Goethe too "suggested the leading idea of modern Botany, that a leaf or the eye of a leaf is the unit of botany, and that every part of the plant is only a transformed leaf to meet a new condition." Moreover, by references to tapeworm and caterpillar, the leaf is promoted into a series of vertebrae, with the head and all it contains, "only the uppermost vertebra transformed." Once again, though, at the very moment when he makes the connection between human consciousness and the natural continuum, Emerson seems to recoil. He admires Goethe as a savant because contemplation is superior to action: "Men's actions are too strong for them," with the result that "what they have done, commits and enforces them to do the same again." Since this outcome would seem to imitate the imitative processes of nature itself, one might expect it to be welcomed, but no. Here too, then, the problem of a static or crystalline structure is paramount. In *Nature*, as we have seen, contemplation provides access to transcendent law; here, conversely, activity is castigated for leading to reductive pattern. Emerson evokes the context of social radicalism and utopianism to make the point: "The fiery reformer embodies his aspiration in some rite or covenant, and he and his friends cleave to the form, and lose the aspiration. The Quaker has established Quakerism, the Shaker has established his monastery and his dance, and, although each prates of spirit, there is no spirit, but repetition, which is anti-spiritual."[49] Emerson criticizes institutional Christianity in his "Divinity School Address" on the grounds that "the idioms of his [Christ's] language, and the figures of his rhetoric, have usurped the place of his truth; and churches are not built on his principles, but on his tropes." The imaginative power of language has been short-circuited by an over-literal response to metaphor and symbol, and the freedom of con-

48. Emerson, "Swedenborg," 74–75, 80.
49. Ralph Waldo Emerson, "Goethe; or, the Writer," in *RM*, 158, 154.

sciousness to move from the crystalline to the fluid has been denied. As a result, Christianity has fossilized into a "Mythus."[50]

I think we have come here to the most confusing problem in Transcendentalist philosophy. But though it is impossible to offer a watertight solution—partly because the movement was complex and manifold, partly perhaps because the confusion was never squarely confronted—it is important for an understanding of the Transcendentalists' utopian thought and practice to get some sort of grip on the issues involved. At one and the same time the Transcendentalists believe in a unifying structure but reject static patterning or crystallization; they think poetically but are suspicious of tropes; they celebrate their glimpses of the serene laws of nature but accept that they themselves are part of a historical and contingent reality; they assert the existence of a serial chain but suspect that the links that connect us to it are not secure.

George Santayana has probably come closer than anyone else to providing an account of the inner tensions of Transcendentalist thought in "The Genteel Tradition in American Philosophy," which began life as a lecture delivered before the Philosophical Union of the University of California on August 25, 1911. He identifies two forces, pulling in opposite directions, at the very heart of the movement. The distinction is between, on the one hand, philosophical or methodical transcendentalism and, on the other, a mythic variety that is characterized by a fundamentally different stance toward the external world.[51]

The first sort of transcendentalism is fundamentally empirical in its orientation. It is curious about and engaged with the external world, which indeed it transcends only to the extent of establishing for itself an a priori vantage point from which that world can be perceived. It is a transcendentalism of form, not of content, one that does no more than acknowledge the existence of mental categories to act as receptacles for external reality. The second sort, self-indulgent rather than receptive, is characterized by an undervaluing or even a complete ignoring of objective reality in favor of a subjective, ultimately solipsistic alternative. On the one hand, we have a group of transcendentalists with their eyes wide open; on the other, a group with their heads buried in the sands of a phenomenological desert. Both kinds of tran-

50. Emerson, "The Divinity School Address," 81. Philip Gura discusses the claim by Emerson and others that a preoccupation with tropes has led to the neglect of the laws of "nature and God" in "The Transcendentalists and Language: The Unitarian Exegetical Background," *Studies in the American Renaissance, 1979*, ed. Joel Myerson (Boston: Twayne, 1979), 10–11.
51. George Santayana, "The Genteel Tradition in American Philosophy," in *Winds of Change* (New York: Scribner's, 1913), 186–215.

scendentalism, Santayana claims, found a place within the American philosophical tradition. The second sort, transcendental myth, provided a refuge for the now toothless remnants of the Calvinistic faith of an earlier and sterner generation. The first sort, transcendental method, suited the outlook of the young republic: "It was autonomous, undismayed, calmly revolutionary."[52]

Perhaps this distinction—and in particular the way in which transcendental myth can be associated with outmoded patterns of thought and behavior—can be clarified by reference to Lévi-Strauss's analysis of the difference between mythical and scientific modes of thought in *The Savage Mind.* Lévi-Strauss compares mythical thinking with the activities of the *bricoleur,* the jack-of-all-trades. The *bricoleur* brings to bear on each task the ragbag of tools and bits and pieces (Lévi-Strauss goes to the trouble of quoting the English expression "odds and ends") which he has accumulated during his previous tasks. Thus, "it might be said that the engineer questions the universe, while the 'bricoleur' addresses himself to a collection of oddments left over from human endeavours, that is, only a sub-set of the culture."[53]

Santayana is talking in broader terms than Lévi-Strauss, but this basic outline of the two possible stances toward the external world seems to shed light on some aspects of the distinction he is making. The methodical transcendentalist, like Lévi-Strauss's engineer, brings to his experience a particular intellectual structure, but one unencumbered as far as possible by ideological baggage. The result is an openness to experience (his "concepts thus appear like operators *opening up* the set being worked with"), while the myth-making transcendentalist brings to bear the full "treasury" of what he has accumulated (so that his "signification [is] like the operator of that set's reorganization, which neither extends nor renews it and limits itself to obtaining the group of its transformations").[54]

In his lecture Santayana points the way in which these methodical and mythic tendencies in American Transcendentalism interacted, almost alternated. Emerson, for example, "had no system" but "opened his eyes upon the world every morning with a fresh sincerity." At the same time, he was drawn to the "very verge of system-making; but he stopped short." His "notions of compensation, or the over-soul, or spiritual laws" were counteracted by his return "to experience, to history, to

52. Ibid., 196.
53. Claude Lévi-Strauss, *The Savage Mind* (London: Weidenfeld and Nicholson, 1972), 22, 20.
54. Ibid., 20.

poetry, to the natural science of his day," and therefore were never given the sustained attention that would have made them into "thin and forced" constructions like "other transcendental systems."[55]

One can see Emerson wrestling with these contradictory tendencies, and from a certain point of view actually reconciling them, in one of his most mysterious and problematic poems, "The Sphinx," which was written in 1840 and accorded the status of first poem in the collection of 1846.[56] In this poem the stable domain of nature is contrasted with the world of change inhabited by the human race. After all, in our culture the most powerful utopian vision is retrospective, not prospective: it is of the golden age, the Garden of Eden, the world of nature that existed before history began and that can still be conceived of apart from its processes. There we perceive harmony:

> Sea, earth, air, sound, silence,
>   Plant, quadruped, bird,
> By one music enchanted,
>   One deity stirred . . .

Sadly, we have been exiled from that condition: "But man crouches and blushes . . ." By contrast with the rest of the animal kingdom which remains stable, entranced by the Lethe of nature, man is a restless, striving creature who lives within the medium of time simply because he is conscious that he does. He takes chances, makes mistakes, commits sins, all in the search for progress: "The fiend that man harries / Is love of the Best." And when he arrives at the end of the rainbow, he promptly sets off once again:

> The heavens that now draw him
>   With sweetness untold,
> Once found,—for new heavens
>   He spurneth the old.

Man, in short, has repudiated nature for history, being for becoming.

The Sphinx tells the poet-protagonist that their relationship is not adversarial after all. It cannot be, since the Sphinx turns out to be not

55. Santayana, "Genteel Tradition," 197.
56. Ralph Waldo Emerson, "The Sphinx," in *Poems*, vol. 9 of *Complete Works of Ralph Waldo Emerson*, ed. Edward Waldo Emerson, 12 vols. (Boston: Houghton Mifflin, 1903–6), 21–25. All subsequent references to this edition will be to *Works*.

a being in her own right but simply an aspect of the poet's psyche.[57] The poet incorporates the Sphinx since he asks questions continually—questions that, whatever their ostensible purport, must be variations on the theme of "Who am I?," the most basic inquiry of all. What is consistent is the ongoing quest. The answer to the question what is man is that man is the creature who asks that question—and is perpetually dissatisfied by the answers he gets:

> So take thy quest through nature,
> It through thousand natures ply;
> Ask on, thou clothed eternity;
> Time is the false reply.

At this point the Sphinx begins to ply through a thousand natures herself. This development presents a difficulty only if one loses sight of the fact that merely two stanzas previously she has claimed to be the poet's very spirit and yoke-fellow. She embodies the dynamic and questing part of his nature, the eyebeam of his roving eye. But an eyebeam has two ends, one attached to the subject (and, as Lewis Leary has pointed out, Emerson enjoys punning on eye/I),[58] the other to the world which he perceives. Since the poet is committed to a philosophy of change, he cannot be expected to see nature as the manifestation of a serene and static order. Just as Thoreau, a few years later, was to see a pattern on the move as he made his way to Concord beside the thawing sand bank, so Emerson's poet perceives the outside world to manifest his own state of flux. The Sphinx becomes Proteus.

Part of the surrealism of this stanza derives from the fact that although the mythology of the poem clearly originates with the Greek Sphinx, Emerson pictures her as the Egyptian one, a vast stone statue which, like that of Hermione in *The Winter's Tale*, finally comes to life. In doing so the Sphinx keeps faith with her portmanteau identity—

57. Part of the problem that critics have experienced with this poem is caused by their tendency to see it in dramatic terms, as a dialogue between two characters, rather than in philosophical terms, as a conflict between two aspects of the poet's own nature. R. A. Yoder, for example, in *Emerson and the Orphic Poet in America* (Los Angeles: University of California Press, 1978), agrees with an earlier commentator, Thomas Whittaker, that "the poet is rebuked and the poem dramatizes ultimate skepticism," going on to claim that the riddle is necessarily unsolved because "one cannot understand the part before he fully understands the whole" (119). David Porter, in *Emerson and Literary Change* (Cambridge: Harvard University Press, 1978), comments that "it is unclear whether or not the poet solves the Sphinx's riddle"; the poet seems, Porter tells us, to defeat the Sphinx and then in turn to be defeated by her (80).

58. Lewis Leary, *Ralph Waldo Emerson: An Interpretative Essay* (Boston: Twayne, 1980), 5.

woman's head, lion's body, serpent's tail, and eagle's wings, a concrete manifestation if ever there was one of unity in diversity, and a potent image in a pre-evolutionary cultural milieu of nature as process. The verbs tell the story: melted, silvered, spired, flowered, flowed. The words themselves almost merge into one another. Wherever he looks, Emerson's poet sees order in transience, a pattern of change. And his Sphinx identifies herself with the phenomena that most obviously represent this redemptive process (that is to say, the redemptiveness implicit in the very concept of process): cloud, moon, flame, blossoms, wave.[59]

Finally and paradoxically, she who was once stone herself stands at the end of her cavortings on top of Mount Monadnock with no intention whatever of dashing herself to pieces in the valley below: "She stood Monadnock's head." The elision of the preposition emphasizes that this is the triumphant solution of both the Sphinx's riddle and the human dilemma. Verb modulates directly into noun; poet-Sphinx becomes mountain; man and nature, subject and object, become one.[60] The name itself, that of an actual New Hampshire mountain, is perhaps significant. In "History" Emerson adopts Leibniz's vocabulary to monitor "the monad through all his masks as he performs the metempsychosis of nature," and here we are able to penetrate through the series of masks to that ultimate monad.[61] Emerson has achieved, within the lines of a poem, his synthesis of crystal and fluid, pattern and process.

At this point nature chimes in again to confirm this reading. The truth, after all, is everywhere; diversity is possible because of the inward connection of things, and successive answers are not lies after all but versions of the truth: "'Who telleth one of my meanings / Is master of all I am.'" The recognition of one meaning represents the revelatory experience of that transcendentalist method described by Santayana,

---

59. Something of the same effect is achieved in this rapt sentence from Dwight's *Association in Its Connection with Education and Religion*, in which he evokes the universal harmony: "Like the lines and curves of a landscape; like the whole perspective of the sky and clouds; like the graceful symmetry of the human form; like the musical fugue and its types in running waves of water, and in uproaring, flickering tongues of flame . . . " (17).

60. Ivy Schweitzer has said of *Nature* that Emerson converts nature into spirit partly by stylistic means, "the effect of turning nouns, the signifiers of rooted and bounded phenomena, into verbs, which perform the action they signify." See Ivy Schweitzer, "Transcendental Sacramentals: 'The Lord's Supper' and Emerson's Doctrine of Form," *New England Quarterly* 61, no. 3 (September 1988): 415. What I have traced here is the opposite process, but since my point is that for the Transcendentalists spirit and nature are simply different manifestations of the same law, priority hardly matters.

61. Ralph Waldo Emerson, "History," in *Essays 1*, 10.

the insight of Lévi-Strauss's engineer. The consequent mastery of the totality establishes faith in a preexisting mythic architecture, the treasury of the *bricoleur*.

The issues raised by the poem can be crudely summarized: nature is the manifestation of the law of the universe, whereas the human world is temporal—that is, historical—and therefore in a state of flux. But, as a result of this division, mankind is able to see a deeper, dynamic pattern in the universe. The very act of perception transforms crystal into fluid, providing the "central spontaneity" and individual presence that Swedenborg's static system lacked. The poem builds a bridge over the structural divide—between a revolutionary capacity to see the world afresh and a conservative need to believe in ongoing systems or myths—which Santayana identifies at the heart of the transcendentalist worldpicture, and establishes man as a composite being, that "empirico-transcendental doublet" described by Michel Foucault.[62] Emerson's poem manages to grasp the "flying Perfect."

This is, in its way, a remarkable solution to the problem, but one that convinces only on an aesthetic level. When Emerson tackles the conflict between nature and history from the other point of view, highlighting the question of history itself, it proves far more intractable. His essay "History" was written at roughly the same time as the poem, and it too received pride of place in the collection in which it was featured, the *Essays: First Series*. But, perhaps appropriately, it bears the marks of Emerson's struggle with the structural dilemma he faced, leaving the issue unresolved.

Emerson begins by asserting the solidarity of the human race— "There is one mind common to all individual men"—and therefore the principle of historical continuity: "All the facts of history preëxist in the mind as laws." Thus, "Belzoni digs and measures in the mummypits and pyramids of Thebes, until he can see the end of the difference between the monstrous work and himself."[63] The example is a revealing one. For one thing, it is drawn from the realm of culture rather than from political, military, or social history. Indeed, the whole essay testifies to the editing out of history's less palatable facts. Moreover, there is an evident preoccupation with artifacts that embody the intention of

62. Michel Foucault, *The Order of Things* (London: Tavistock, 1970), 318.
63. Emerson, "History," 3, 7. Jonathan Bishop provides an interesting analysis of the basis of Emerson's argument here in *Emerson on the Soul* (Cambridge: Harvard University Press, 1964), 59–66. He also offers a trenchant dismissal of some of its ramifications: "Thus when he says, 'All that Shakespeare says of the king, yonder slip of a boy that reads in the corner feels to be true of himself,' we are free to say, no" (63).

achieving the closest approximation to permanence. The Egyptian "mummy-pits" and pyramids, however alien and "monstrous" they might seem, were designed by their makers specifically to enact the principle of continuity through time. In another mood Emerson would find such structures wanting in "central spontaneity"; all that he can pit against decline and decay are examples of what he could equally well excoriate as embodiments of inertia and fossilization. The Tartar tent has solidified into the Chinese pagoda, the primeval mound dwelling into the Egyptian temple, the forest into a cathedral, the flower into stone.[64]

Petrification offers itself as one possible source of historical continuity and patterning; another, more suitable for the accommodation of "winged facts," involves a kind of organic analogy, the postulation of a racial equivalent of biological growth. Thus, Xenophon's troops are "a gang of great boys with such a code of honour and such lax discipline as great boys have."[65] The biological rule that ontogeny recapitulates phylogeny—that the life of the individual reenacts that of the species or race—is effectively put into reverse, so that phylogeny proves to be merely an enormous extrapolation of ontogeny. This idea can be tracked back at least to Adam Ferguson, one of the Scottish moral philosophers, who claimed in his *Essay on the History of Civil Society* (1767) that "not only the individual advances from infancy to manhood, but the species itself from rudeness to civilization."[66] In short, as Emerson tells us, "the student interprets the age of chivalry by his own age of chivalry, and the days of maritime adventure and circumnavigation by quite parallel miniature experiences of his own."[67]

The inadequacy of this model of historical development hardly needs comment; nor does it support Emerson's attempt at optimism through much of the essay, since it must predict decline and disintegration as surely as it does progress and maturity. As he approaches the end, he forces his rhetoric into a millennial crescendo, endeavoring to delineate the spirit of time itself, a being with the power to bring the historical process to a utopian conclusion: "I shall find in him the Foreworld; in his childhood the Age of Gold; the Apples of Knowledge; the Argonautic Expedition; the calling of Abraham; the building of the

64. Emerson, "History," 11–12.
65. Ibid., 15.
66. Adam Ferguson, *Essay on the History of Civil Society* (Edinburgh, 1767), 2, quoted in Ernest Lee Tuveson, *Millennium and Utopia: A Study in the Background of the Idea of Progress* (Gloucester, Mass.: Peter Smith, 1972), 195.
67. Emerson, "History," 15.

Temple; the Advent of Christ; Dark Ages; the Revival of Letters; the Reformation; the discovery of new lands, the opening of new sciences, and new regions in man. He shall be the priest of Pan, and bring with him into humble cottages the blessing of the morning stars and all the recorded benefits of heaven and earth." Then his confidence abruptly evaporates: "Is there somewhat overweening in this claim? Then I reject all I have written, for what is the use of pretending to know what we know not? But it is the fault of our rhetoric that we cannot strongly state one fact without seeming to belie some other." He has already informed us that, although man "is the compend of time[,] he is also the correlative of nature."[68] The uneasy synthesis he has tried to establish between the dynamic world of history and the patterned one of nature, expressed in terms of the biological curve, here collapses, separating out into its individual components.

The failure is hardly surprising. Ernest Lee Tuveson, in his seminal work *Millennium and Utopia*, claims that one of the great projects in the intellectual history of modern times has been to transfer the operations of Providence to nature. He tracks the process back to Thomas Barnett's *History of the Earth* (1684–90), and claims that it reaches its completion with nineteenth-century positivism. The distinction is between the chaotic and contingent operations of human history on the one hand, and on the other the coherent sequence of cause and effect which was determined and set in motion by God at the outset of creation.[69] The culmination of the process eliminated "Providence as a factor openly operating historically, although it was present in its disguised form, being called 'natural law.'" What Emerson is trying to unite, a century and a half of historical thought had been busily engaged in putting asunder.[70] In the end, at least in this essay, he has to admit defeat: "Hear the rats in the wall, see the lizard on the fence, the

68. Ibid., 22, 20.

69. The Transcendentalists' Puritan forefathers had an easier task because their notion of election, as Sacvan Bercovitch has pointed out in *The Puritan Origins of the American Self* (New Haven: Yale University Press, 1975), permitted a distinction between "soteriology and secular history, where secular history designates the providential view . . . and soteriology the mode of identifying the individual, the community, or the event in question within the scheme of salvation." In short, Providence did not have to provide utopia for all but simply had to establish the salvation of the saved, and this could be achieved "however dismal the repetitive course of human, subordinate affairs, no matter how ominous the signs of secular time" (43).

70. Tuveson, *Millennium and Utopia*, 119. Of course, this tendency did not stop with Emerson. G. S. Kirk points out, in *The Nature of Greek Myths* (Harmondsworth: Penguin, 1974), that early twentieth-century psychologists, including even Freud, were guilty of falling into this "absurd kind of genetic fallacy" (73).

fungus under foot, the lichen on the log. What do I know sympathet-
ically, morally, of either of these worlds of life?" Our "so-called history"
is a "village-tale," reflecting our provincialism of spirit. "What does
Rome know of rat and lizard?" In "The Divinity School Address" he had
made an equation between the law of gravitation and the human heart
which particularly aroused the ire of Andrews Norton.[71] Now he has to
concede that there is a dichotomy between the natural order and human behavior.[72] The former is characterized by consistency and stability, whatever intimations Emerson may feel of the evolutionary breakthrough to come. Meanwhile, the historical domain where we humans
live our lives is obstinately resistant to pattern, since it represents nothing more than an accumulation of contingencies.

This state of affairs is clearly an unsatisfactory one, as the staccato
shifts and changes of the concluding paragraphs of "History" testify.
The one thing a philosophy of consistency cannot brook is (of course)
inconsistency. If the law of series is any sort of law at all, it must be in
some way discernible in the field of human behavior. And yet we are
left with a curious discontinuity between the inward, spiritual dimension of humankind and the external evidence of our transitoriness and
mutability.

One way of solving this problem would be to establish a theory of
social amelioration whereby the pattern apparently visible in the static
world of nature could be shown to be slowly disclosing itself in the
world of human affairs. This approach would have the added advantage of exemplifying the notion of a pattern on the move that seems
such an integral part of the Transcendentalist apprehension of serial
law. In "On the Progress of Civilization," published in the *Boston Quarterly Review* for October 1838, George Bancroft, who hovered on the
fringes of the Transcendentalist movement for a time, asserts such a
solution, though he fails to support his claim with anything like evidence: "The world cannot retrograde; the dark ages cannot return.

71. Emerson, "History," 22; idem, "The Divinity School Address," 93; Andrews Norton,
"The New School in Literature and Religion," *Boston Daily Advertiser*, August 27, 1838, 43,
quoted in Miller, *The Transcendentalists*, 196.
72. Many years later Emerson playfully slides over this dichotomy in "Historic Notes of
Life and Letters in New England": "The German poet Goethe . . . proposed . . . in
Botany, his simple theory of metamorphosis;—the eye of a leaf is all. . . . The revolt
became a revolution. Schelling and Oken introduced their ideal natural philosophy,
Hegel his metaphysics, and extended it to Civil History. The result in literature and the
general mind was a return to law; in science, in politics, in social life; as distinguished
from the profligate manners and politics of earlier times. The age was moral. Every
immorality is a departure from nature, and is punished by natural loss and deformity."
Ralph Waldo Emerson, *Lectures and Biographical Sketches*, in *Works*, 10:338.

Dynasties perish; cities are buried; nations have been victims to error, or martyrs for right; Humanity has always been on the advance; its soul has always been gaining maturity and power."[73]

Much more convincingly, in a review on the subject of social progress published in the *Christian Examiner* several years before Bancroft's piece (March 1834), Frederic Henry Hedge provides an analysis of the historical process that anticipates the solution subsequently adopted in the utopian ideologies of the Transcendentalists. Hedge concedes that on the face of it there is no evidence of consistent progressive development, that indeed "alternate civilization and barbarism make up the apparent history of man." But he goes on to say that although specific peoples and civilizations may founder, society as a whole has never actually gone backwards, though its forward motion may become imperceptible—or actually come to a halt—from time to time. The conception he puts forward is one of intermittent evolutionary development. He makes an analogy between intellectual progress and the action of the heart: "The human mind, the source of this progress, has acted like the animal heart, not by a constant effort, but by successive pulsations, which pulsations, however, unlike those of the animal heart, must be reckoned, not by seconds, but by ages."[74] This notion of "successive pulsations" provides us with a way of perceiving a regular—and moving—pattern in history. Moreover, a parallel with nature gives the theory its bona fides.

Intriguingly, this explanation of social evolution parallels the theory of biological evolution known as "punctuated equilibria" offered by the American paleontologists Niles Eldredge and Stephen Jay Gould in 1972. Just like historians, paleontologists have to cope with a record of jerky and incoherent development. Eldredge and Gould make the point that the problem has dogged evolutionism since it was formulated: Charles Darwin decided that the absence of the "'infinitely numerous transitional links' that would illustrate the slow and steady operation of natural selection" must be explained by the imperfection of the fossil record. Gould and Eldredge's theory constitutes an alternative explanation, the argument that "many breaks in the fossil record are real; they express the way evolution occurs, not the fragments of an

73. George Bancroft, "On the Progress of Civilization, or Reasons Why the Natural Association of Men of Letters Is with the Democracy," *Boston Quarterly Review* 1 (October 1838): 406–7, excerpted in Miller, *The Transcendentalists*, 429.
74. Frederic Henry Hedge, review of "An Address delivered before the Phi Beta Kappa Society in Yale College, New Haven, August 20, 1833, by Edward Everett," *Christian Examiner* 16, n.s. 11 (March 1834): 9–10.

imperfect record." Richard Dawkins, in his book on contemporary Dar-
winism, *The Blind Watchmaker*, summarizes their position: "Maybe . . .
evolution really did in some sense go in sudden bursts, punctuating
long periods of 'stasis,' when no evolutionary change took place in a
given lineage."[75]

Hedge elaborates his own theory of punctuated equilibria by explaining that the "pulsations" or "impulses" of the human mind are able to
advance the state of society as a whole by a process akin to the effect of
yeast on dough: "Each pulsation has sent forth into the world some
new sentiment or principle, some discovery or invention, which, like
small portions of leaven, have successfully communicated their quick-
ening energy to the whole mass of society."[76] What we have here is a
pattern on the move, or to put it another way, the reconciliation of
process (or history) with pattern (or nature). The way is open for the
transformation of society.

When Emerson attacks reformers, he accuses them of being unable
to offer, despite all their agitation and energy, any leverage whereby this process of transformation can take place. However many
converts they can attract to their cause, they are still trapped in the
historical world. They are incapable of creativity. Indeed, they pit themselves against the creative processes of nature. When he gives a list of
reforming fads in his lecture "New England Reformers," he significantly picks on the disapproval of the process of fermentation expressed by certain radicals: "It was in vain urged by the housewife that
God made yeast, as well as dough, and loves fermentation just as dearly
as he loves vegetation; that fermentation develops the saccharine element in the grain, and makes it more palatable and more digestible."
In taking up the cause of history, such reformers have actually alienated themselves from the creative cycles of nature. Instead they have
put their faith in the mechanism of consensual change, not understanding that "all the men in the world cannot make a statue walk and
speak, cannot make a drop of blood, or a blade of grass, any more than
one man can."[77]

It is easy to misunderstand this argument. Emerson's point is that
force of numbers, the inevitable goal of reformist agitation, is quite

75. Niles Eldredge and Stephen Jay Gould, "Punctuated Equilibria: An Alternative to
Phyletic Gradualism," in *Models in Paleobiology*, ed. Thomas J. M. Schopf (San Francisco:
Freeman Cooper, 1972), 87, 96; Richard Dawkins, *The Blind Watchmaker* (London: Long-
man, 1986), 229. It should be pointed out that Dawkins by no means endorses the
theory of Eldredge and Gould.
76. Hedge, review, 10.
77. Ralph Waldo Emerson, "New England Reformers," in *Essays* 2, 150, 157.

unnecessary: one is enough. Life, he tells us in "Fourierism and the Socialists," "scorns systems and system makers" and, eluding all conditions, "makes or supplants a thousand phalanxes and New-Harmonies with each pulsation. . . . The mistake is, that this particular order and series is to be imposed by force of preaching and votes on all men, and carried into rigid execution."[78] In "New England Reformers" he goes on to say: "But let there be one man, let there be truth in two men, in ten men, then is concert for the first time possible; because the force that moves the world is a new quality, and can never be furnished by adding whatever quantities of a different kind. . . . It is and will be magic."[79]

It is interesting to see how Emerson's expression, perhaps unconsciously, mimics the process that is being described. The first half of the sentence that begins "But let there be . . ." captures the development of the pulsation in its series of repetitive but progressive clauses and phrases; the second half, with its large and calm assertion, demonstrates the universal reach that the new force will have. Moreover, in true punctuationist fashion, the origin of the pulsation fails to leave a clear semantic track. One man will not start the process off simply by dint of *being* one man. "Truth" is the object of the verbal phrase "let there be," but that is not clear until we reach the second clause, with its retrospective apposition that sends the noun back. The truth is not visible until it begins to move. What we have is not an inert structure— "a gigantic crystal, all whose atoms and laminae lie in uninterrupted order and with unbroken unity, but cold and still"—but a pattern on the move, like Thoreau's thawing sand bank. "It is and will be magic." One thinks of the contempt for the word *miracle* that Emerson displays in his "Divinity School Address." Magic in this sense will be "one with the blowing clover and the falling rain," with nature transformed into process, with history revealed as pattern, with the law of series disclosing itself through time. The fluid world of consciousness, and the crystalline structure of the universe it inhabits, will have been reconciled.

In his essay "Resistance to Civil Government" Thoreau reverses Emerson's head count in order to make the same point: "I know this well, that if one thousand, if one hundred, if ten men whom I could name,—if ten *honest* men only,—aye, if *one* HONEST man, in this State of Massachusetts, *ceasing to hold slaves*, were actively to withdraw from this copartnership, and be locked up in the county jail therefor, it

78. Ralph Waldo Emerson, "Fourierism and the Socialists," *Dial* 3 (July 1842): 88–89.
79. Emerson, "New England Reformers," 157.

would be the abolition of slavery in America. For it matters not how small the beginning may seem to be: what is once well done is done for ever." Outside the punctuationist context this might pass as an example of rhetorical hyperbole; within it we have the blueprint of a pulsation. Elsewhere in the essay Thoreau uses the image of yeast—twenty years after Hedge's use of it in his review—to indicate the rapidity and completeness of potential transformation: "It is not so important that many should be as good as you, as that there be some absolute goodness somewhere; for that will leaven the whole lump."[80] One thinks of the distinction between Transcendentalist law and Unitarian legalism. In claiming that the spiritual emancipation and subsequent imprisonment of "one HONEST man" will transform American society at large, Thoreau is making a related assertion of the authority of law (in the absolute sense) over legalities. "All health and success does me good, however far off and withdrawn it may appear," he tells us in *Walden*, and goes on to suggest that "if . . . we would indeed restore mankind by truly Indian, botanic, magnetic, or natural means, let us first be as simple and well as Nature ourselves."[81]

Hedge was confident that there was nothing irregular or arbitrary about the occurrence of "pulsations." He was not, however, able to make out the details of the pattern himself. Instead, like a historiographical John the Baptist, he modestly awaited the coming of a "philosophic historian" who would be able to "trace and exhibit these successive impulses. He who can do this, and he only will be able to furnish a systematic history of Man; something very different from, and infinitely more important than the histories we now have of dynasties and tribes."[82]

For the Brook Farmers just such a "philosophic historian" came along in the person of the French utopian thinker Charles Fourier. A "systematic history of Man" was provided with great precision in his "Table of the Movement of Civilization, with its Four Ages or Phases," which showed how civilization reflected the fundamental law of nature, that of "groups and series." The Fruitlanders, meanwhile, found a similar savant in Bronson Alcott's English colleague Charles Lane, who carried in his baggage a precise and comprehensive punctuationist schema which had been devised by his recently deceased colleague James Pierre-

---

80. Henry David Thoreau, "Resistance to Civil Government," in *Reform Papers, Writings,* 75, 69.
81. Thoreau, *Walden,* 78.
82. Hedge, review, 10.

point Greaves. The "Circumstantial Law," as it was called, could be shown to manifest itself progressively in the "three dispensations" of human history.

Both Fourier and Lane were able to demonstrate, as we shall see, that although history was not an obvious sequence of cause and effect, it was nevertheless systematic and progressive. They both showed how fresh "pulsations" occurred just as a particular dispensation was petering out. They asserted that it was precisely when civilization was looking tired and purposeless that a new social order could come into being, like the phoenix—or indeed like America itself. In this way they were able to reconcile historical contingency with universal seriality. It is surely no coincidence that both these utopian blueprints originated on the other side of the Atlantic Ocean. Thus, George Ripley and the Brook Farmers, on the one hand, and Bronson Alcott, on the other, were able to have a spontaneous revelatory experience of a preexisting structure. Both the necessary elements in the "empirico-transcendental doublet" thereby come into play. The immediate and dynamic can be seen to merge with the universal and patterned. What becomes available in each case is not merely a theory of pulsations but the actual experience of one: a sudden apprehension of an overarching pattern. The invisible eye of the natural scientist (or poet) encounters the treasury of the mythmaker. The Americans opened their eyes with that "fresh sincerity" described by Santayana, and what they saw was a great edifice created by European romanticism.

Of course, the differences in the utopian ideologies developed by the Transcendentalists are as important as the similarities, and the most significant one is of scale. In "History" Emerson tells us that the universe is "represented in an atom." For the Brook Farmers and the Fruitlanders one might argue, though in terminology they would not have been able to understand, that the fundamental unit of serial law was a molecule, a cluster of individuals interlinked in a common cause and able to transmit its composite virtue to the social fabric as a whole. For the Brook Farmers the magic unit consisted of sixteen hundred and eighty persons (as Emerson sarcastically pointed out).[83] For the Fruitlanders it was the family, though as we shall see they had some difficulty defining what a family actually was.

In my next five chapters I discuss the ways in which the ideologies of these two utopian experiments provided practical and social manifesta-

---

83. Ralph Waldo Emerson, "Historic Notes of Life and Letters in New England," in *Lectures and Biographical Sketches*, 10:350.

tions of the law of series. I then turn my attention from these molecular versions of the law to an atomic one and consider Thoreau's "community of one." Like his friend Emerson, Thoreau had moments when
he could envisage a crossover between the harmonious world of nature
and the dynamic one of history, but he never succeeded in proposing a
structure that would make the bridge permanent. Indeed, like the
Emerson of "The Sphinx," he found art to be the most satisfactory way
of reconciling the daily contingencies of life with the absolute imperatives of natural law. In a sense he can be seen to have erected two huts,
one by Walden Pond, the other in the book called *Walden.*

My overall intention is to establish the depth and intensity of social
concern felt by members of the Transcendentalist movement, and to
shed light on the belief that underlies and unifies its apparent eclecticism, contradictoriness, and obscurity: the doctrine of repetitive order,
of the total consistency *of* consistency, of the universal sway of the law
of series. Obviously there are profound differences between the enterprises and achievements (not to mention the failures) under discussion; but there is nevertheless common ground underlying those differences, an invisible unifying landscape that lies buried beneath the
patchwork and multiform surface, like the charming one Emerson describes near the beginning of *Nature,* which transcends the twenty or
thirty farms that are positioned on it.[84] All these thinkers shared the
belief that we have to address ourselves to and perfect the microcosm,
though they disagreed about what that might be; and that when we
have done so, a new social order will crystallize around it. This doctrine
is the product of a synthesis between the conflicting forces Santayana
discerned within the movement as a whole.

As I track Transcendentalist communitarian and millennial thought
from the large-scale enterprise at Brook Farm to the more modest community at Fruitlands, and from there to the individual utopia of Thoreau's hut, it might not be too fanciful to suggest that these different
manifestations of the law of series fit together in a serial order of their
own.

84. Emerson, *Nature,* 9.

2

Brook Farm and Masquerade

T he Brook Farm community materialized on the scene so rapidly that it appears to have something of that "frolic architecture" celebrated by Emerson in his poem "The Snow-Storm," product of a "mad wind's night-work," though in this case the contributory weather was considerably better. In the summer of 1840 George Ripley, Unitarian minister of a church in Purchase Street, Boston, and leading participant in the Transcendentalist movement, and his wife, Sophia, went on a well-earned holiday. They found a "sweet spot" for a "tranquil retreat": a place called Brook Farm in what was then the village of West Roxbury. It had not only its inevitable brook but also woods, fields, birds aplenty, and great seclusion—though their friend Theodore Parker had the nearby ministry at West Roxbury, and other Transcendentalist colleagues such as Margaret Fuller, the "brilliant sibyl of the plains," were not far off. Still, time could be spent away from the hectic cut and thrust of Boston life, allowing Mrs. Ripley to doze under the nut trees and her husband to read Burns and whistle to the birds, who obligingly whistled back.[1] By the following spring the most famous communitarian experiment in American history had been established on the same spot.

There can be nothing more authentically Transcendentalist than a historical institution that appears on the scene with an air of having been produced suddenly out of a hat. Like the evolutionary transfor-

1. Sophia Ripley to John S. Dwight, August 1, 1841, quoted in Zoltan Haraszti, *The Idyll of Brook Farm* (Boston: Boston Public Library, 1937), 12–13. The original is Boston Public Library MS E.4.1 no. 26.

35

mations proposed by the punctuationists mentioned in the last chapter, the Brook Farm association came into existence so rapidly that it seems barely to have had time to leave behind a trace of its origins. Hedge emphasizes the speed of transformation when he describes historical pulsations in his *Christian Examiner* review, giving the example of the Reformation: "We need only to remind our readers, how suddenly, how almost immediately after the Reformation, society advanced to a state of civilization unknown in any former age."[2] On its own small scale Brook Farm also makes its appearance suddenly, thereby approaching the revelatory immediacy so beloved of those calm revolutionaries who, according to Santayana, opened their eyes "upon the world every morning with a fresh sincerity." It would not be fanciful to propose that during those idyllic summer weeks of 1840 Ripley did experience some sort of mystical connection between himself as an individual and the universe as a whole, a linkage between his dynamic consciousness and natural harmony. His wife, after all, describes such reciprocity in her account of his whistling and the birds whistling back. It is as a result of such a crossover between inner and outer environments that serial connections can be established.

This is not a flippant suggestion, however far-fetched it may seem under skeptical scrutiny. In any case, skepticism is inappropriate, since what matters is not what we think is possible but what the Transcendentalists themselves believed could—or did—happen. But their perspective tended to supplement the moment of insight or revelation, the fresh new concept that is the reward for open-minded inquiry, with consciousness of a larger historical context. Exhilaration and spontaneity were all very well, but there was also a need to confront historical imperatives—in Lévi-Strauss's words, to reorganize the cultural treasury. To return to Emerson's "Snow-Storm," the "north wind's masonry" is to be mimicked by painstaking human endeavor, "in slow structures, stone by stone, / Built in an age."[3] As a central—indeed as, in some ways, the definitive—Transcendentalist institution, Brook Farm should be a manifestation not merely of frolic architecture but also of slow structuring.

Ripley himself was aware that the enterprise might seem precipitate and self-indulgent, as we can see from a long letter to Emerson of November 9, 1840. Emerson was, naturally enough, the big fish he wanted to catch for his proposed community. "Your decision," he tells

2. Frederic Henry Hedge, review of "An Address delivered before the Phi Beta Kappa Society . . . ," *Christian Examiner* 16, n.s. 11 (March 1834): 14.
3. Ralph Waldo Emerson, "The Snow-Storm," in *Poems, Works*, 9:42.

him, "will do much towards settling the question with me, whether the time has come for the fulfillment of a high hope." If Ripley wanted to take the easy option, he says, he could rent Brook Farm for himself "at a rate, that with my other resources, would place me in a very agreeable condition, as far as my personal interests were involved. I should have a city of God, on a small scale of my own." But this kind of immediate and selfish gratification is not on his agenda. Instead, he envisages steady and prudent endeavor toward institutional self-sufficiency, with three or four families moving in on April 1, 1841, and a similar number the following autumn. "It would thus be not less than two or three years, before we should be joined by all who mean to be with us; we should not fall to pieces by our own weight; we should grow up slowly and strong; and the attractiveness of our experiment would win to us all whose society we should want." Emerson replies that though "of all the . . . philanthropic projects of which I have heard yours is the most pleasing to me," nevertheless it would suit neither him nor the community were he to join.[4]

Ripley's cautious—and disinterested—gradualism was not assumed just for Emerson's benefit. Brook Farm began on the small scale he envisaged. Mrs. Ripley wrote to John Dwight on May 6, 1841, that the "number assembled round the table in our large middle kitchen is thirteen," though she adds it will soon rise to sixteen.[5] These were accommodated in the main farm building, which became known as "the Hive." As the years passed, other buildings were added. A house across the narrow road leading to the farm, christened "the Nest" because of its diminutive size, was used as the school for some years, and also as guest accommodation. The Eyrie was built in 1842, a somewhat flimsy construction (apparently sound traveled right through it) on the higher of the farm's two low hills. The Ripleys themselves moved into it, along with many of the younger single members of the community, including the strange and reclusive Charles King Newcomb, who was much admired by Emerson. His one short story, "Dolon," vied with Bronson Alcott's "Orphic Sayings" as the most obscure contribution to be published by the *Dial* in its four-year history.[6] Two more buildings

4. George Ripley to Ralph Waldo Emerson, November 9, 1840, MS Houghton Library, bMS Am 1280 (2719); R. W. Emerson to George Ripley, December 15, 1840, in *The Letters of Ralph Waldo Emerson*, ed. Ralph L. Rusk, 6 vols. (New York: Columbia University Press, 1939), 2:371.
5. Reprinted in Haraszti, *Idyll of Brook Farm*, 18. For the original letter, see Boston Public Library MS E.4.1 no. 34.
6. Charles King Newcomb, "Dolon," *Dial* 3 (July 1842): 112–23; A. Bronson Alcott, "Orphic Sayings," *Dial* 1 (July 1840): 85–98; *Dial* 1 (January 1841): 351–61.

were erected during the early period of the community's history, the Cottage, which was also used as a residence until the changeover to Fourierism, when the school moved into it; and the Pilgrim House, a more substantial dwelling built in uncompromising New England style, which provided both lodgings and useful community functions, including a big parlor for amusements, the laundry and tailoring facilities, and ultimately the editorial offices of the *Harbinger*, the Fourierist newspaper that was edited in the community during its last years. In 1844 work began on the most ambitious building of all, the Phalanstery, which was intended to provide the basis of the community after Brook Farm became a phalanx (I shall maintain the Brook Farmers' habit of using these terms to distinguish a Fourierist dwelling from a Fourierist community). After nearly two years of work, the Phalanstery burned to the ground in March 1846 before it could be put to use, a catastrophe that was an important factor in bringing about Brook Farm's demise the following year.

There was at times pressure on accommodation (particularly because of the large numbers of curious visitors the community attracted), though this problem would have been eased without the bad luck of the fire.[7] Numbers rose rapidly during the second year, and by 1844, the midpoint of the community's trajectory, the account book was recording the work efforts of well over one hundred members (adults and older children).[8] The poor soil of the farm, and difficulties with the other "industries" caused by lack of appropriate skills, shortage of time and facilities for the proper seasoning of wood, and inadequate access to sales outlets in Boston and elsewhere, caused the community some headaches, though the school was a success story, and the production and distribution of the *Harbinger* in the final years of the farm was a remarkable achievement by any standard. The point that must be emphasized from the outset is that the farm was a well-grounded institution which lasted nearly six years, a respectable time for a utopian community. It was thoughtfully organized, even if it seemed to come out of nothing.

Nevertheless, partly because its founding followed so swiftly on the

7. See Lindsay Swift, *Brook Farm: Its Members, Scholars, and Visitors* (New York: Macmillan, 1900), 27–40.
8. See the Brook Farm Account Book for May 1844–April 1845 in the Houghton Library, fMS Am 931. Rebecca Codman Butterfield's MS account of Brook Farm, in the possession of the Massachusetts Historical Society, tells us that at the time she joined the community in 1843, there were about a hundred members (10). This document has been edited by Joel Myerson as "Rebecca Codman Butterfield's Reminiscences of Brook Farm," *New England Quarterly* 65 (December 1992): 603–30; see esp. 611.

heels of Ripley's summer holiday, it is frequently seen as a mere idyll, a "perpetual picnic," to use Emerson's phrase.[9] Part of the problem is quite simply that we lack adequate accounts of the thinking that led up to the establishment of the community and then propelled it along its course. This difficulty might seem an ironic one given the garrulity of the Transcendentalists in general. Whereas Coleridge spent years talking about the pantisocracy that never materialized, and Charles Fourier himself wrote at almost terrifying length about the associations to come but never did anything practical to bring them about, George Ripley seems to have grounded his institution on a minimal verbal foundation.

There is no personalist fallacy involved in giving Ripley that possessive pronoun. Brook Farm was very much—and the loading of this metaphor seems appropriate—his baby. It was his conception to start with, and although in the course of time he surrounded himself with varied and energetic talents, the testimony of his leadership, from those who lived in the community or visited it, is unequivocal. He was the father figure, the Archonite Illustrissimo.[10] If, as Emerson claimed in "Self-Reliance," an institution is the long shadow of a man, then Brook Farm evolved in the shadow of this one.[11] As Emerson himself put it, following a visit to the farm in May 1843, "G[eorge]. & S[ophia]. R[ipley]. are the only ones who have identified themselves with the community. They have married it & they are it. The others are experimenters who will stay by this if it thrives, being always ready to retire, but these have burned their ships, and are entitled to the moral consideration which this position gives."[12] Indeed, one could almost go a step further and claim that Ripley was not merely the embodiment of the Brook Farm community but the essential figure in the history of American Transcendentalism as a whole.

The movement could boast two geniuses in Emerson and Thoreau, a charismatic presence in Bronson Alcott, a quixotic gadfly in Orestes Brownson, and a thunderous social conscience in Theodore Parker. But the person who, more than anybody else, gave it coherence and

9. Ralph Waldo Emerson, "Historic Notes of Life and Letters in New England," in *Works*, 10:364.
10. See John Thomas Codman, *Brook Farm: Historic and Personal Memoirs* (Boston: Arena, 1894), 77–78, 110.
11. Ralph Waldo Emerson, "Self-Reliance," in *Essays 1*, 35.
12. Ralph Waldo Emerson, entry for May 7, 1843, in *Journals and Miscellaneous Notebooks of Ralph Waldo Emerson*, ed. William H. Gilman et al., 16 vols. (Cambridge: Belknap Press of Harvard University Press, 1960–82), 8:393. All subsequent references to this edition will be to *JMN*.

provided it with a succession of institutional manifestations was George
Ripley. He was in the thick of the fray during the first, doctrinal phase,
when he locked horns with Andrews Norton in the pages of periodicals
such as the *Christian Examiner* and (less obviously) the *Boston Daily Advertiser*. Next he became one of the leading members of the Transcendental Club as the movement moved on to a phase of philosophical
debate. The following stage involved the establishment of a larger public arena and a more literary identity, both of which were achieved
through the journal the *Dial*, of which he was a cofounder, and which
he put on a businesslike footing. Finally, the Transcendentalists developed a reforming and utopian commitment that received its biggest
and most significant manifestation in what was called, at least during its
early days, Ripley's Farm.[13]

These developments, which took place during the 1830s and 1840s,
seem to follow—at least with the benefit of hindsight—an inevitable
progression. The miracles debate, as we saw in the first chapter, was
characterized on the Transcendentalists' part by a search for a coherent and structured vision of the world and of the individual's place in
it. This search inevitably expanded from theological to philosophical
issues, and since, as an accidental by-product, the debate weakened the
authority of the Unitarian Church, an appropriately informal alternative was found within the domestic setting of Transcendental Club
members' own houses and apartments, and in the increasing camaraderie of the individuals involved.[14] Inevitably, though, there was a danger that the club could become cliquey and narrow, and the need for a
journal became apparent. It is a sequence like that envisaged in Emerson's essay on circles, with ever-larger areas being enclosed at each
successive stage, a utopian community being the next one. Ripley, trou-
bled by the social deprivation that was becoming increasingly apparent
in the neighborhood of Boston where he had his ministry, finally resigned his pulpit and established his community. The final, all-embracing stage was to come, as we shall see, with the establishment of the
Harbinger and the national reforming movement.

Despite Ripley's centrality he remains in some respects a tantalizing
and shadowy presence. Obviously he left a substantial record of his
position at the earliest stages of the Transcendentalist movement, but
for various reasons the written remains tail off. All evidence of the

13. See Henry W. Sams, ed., *Autobiography of Brook Farm* (Englewood Cliffs, N.J.: Prentice-
Hall, 1958), 1. This anthology is presented as a student reference book, but in fact
provides a handy source of primary material for all scholars of the community.
14. See Charles Crowe, *George Ripley: Transcendentalist and Utopian Socialist* (Athens: University of Georgia Press, 1967), 81–85.

club's discussions is secondhand and anecdotal. Ripley abandoned his editorship of the *Dial* as soon as it was viable, and people complained from the time of Brook Farm's founding, and for many years after it folded, about Ripley's reticence on the subject of the community. But in some ways this relative invisibility is itself evidence of his Transcendentalist bona fides, and indeed of the power of that very thought which is not receiving its full articulation. It does not need to. The deed, so to speak, is the word. If the individual's interior world is serially connected with the macrocosm, his or her thought, despite that "almostness" which can account for human restlessness, has the capacity for operating directly on the external world and thereby transforming it. A proactive ideology does not need to leave an elaborate written account of itself.

Elizabeth Palmer Peabody, as it happens, disagrees. In a letter to John Sullivan Dwight (who had not yet become a member) written a couple of months after the Brook Farm community was inaugurated, she remarks somewhat cumbersomely of Ripley that "he enjoys the 'work' so much that he does not clearly see that his plan is not in the way of being demonstrated any further than that it is being made evident."[15] In fact, in talking about evidence she actually concedes the very point that she is complaining of, thus making one suspect that she is probably trying to grapple with arguments offered by Ripley himself. She was, after all, not merely a close friend of the Ripleys but also the sister of Nathaniel Hawthorne's betrothed, Sophia Peabody, so she must have been very much in touch with the thinking behind the community. Evidence is the whole point. One recalls how, during the miracles controversy, Theodore Parker (writing as Levi Blodgett) dismissed Norton's reliance "on evidence too weak to be trusted in a trifling case that comes before a common court of law," and Ripley's own requirement of an "unerring test, by which to distinguish a miracle of religion from a new manifestation of natural powers." Peabody wants some sort of public relations exercise, whereas Ripley believes that actions speak louder than words. What we find as we review this part of his career is a series of "pulsations," each one creating change, each one generated by the one before, each one with a larger scope and a sharper focus, and reflecting a greater ambition on Ripley's part to transform the process of history.

It is testimony to the magical scope—and abruptness—of the pen-

---

15. Elizabeth Palmer Peabody to John Sullivan Dwight, June 24, 1841, reprinted in Haraszti, *Idyll of Brook Farm*, 18. The original is Boston Public Library MS E.4.1 no. 35. Peabody notes in an earlier letter to Dwight (April 26, 1841) that "Ripley still relucts [*sic*] from printing even a prospectus." Boston Public Library MS E.4.1 no. 33.

ultimate pulsation, the founding of the Brook Farm community, that
not a single member of the Transcendental Club joined Ripley in his
experiment. When Ripley broached the idea to the club in the autumn
of 1840, Alcott—who was to embark on a utopian experiment of his
own three years later—took the view that the project would be too
worldly, while Margaret Fuller doubted Ripley's powers of leadership
(wrongly, as events proved). Parker, Ripley's closest friend and ally, had
a different problem. Ripley, it must be remembered, had decided to
relinquish his ministry, partly because, like Emerson before him, he felt
his own position to be too out of phase with Unitarian orthodoxy, and
partly because he had come to believe that his church (and specifically
his congregation) had insulated itself from social injustices that were
becoming ever more apparent in the surrounding community. It is
clear that for him Brook Farm would serve as an alternative, nondoctri-
nal, socially radical ministry. Parker shared Ripley's radical views on
both religious and social matters but was determined to be an agent of
change within the church (although he was nearly thrown out on one
occasion). He therefore did not resign his ministry to take up residence at the farm, though he welcomed the proximity of his West Roxbury pulpit to the site of the community.[16]

In order to reconstruct the motives behind the founding of Brook
Farm, it is worth giving further attention to the arguments used by
Ripley in his attempt to persuade Emerson to become a member. His
main point is that the community would provide the opportunity of
solving the mind-body conflict. "Our objects, as you know," he reminds
Emerson in his letter of November 9, 1840,

> are to insure a more natural union between intellectual and manual
> labor than now exists; to combine the thinker and the worker, as far
> as possible, in the same individual; to guarantee the highest mental
> freedom, by providing all with labor, adapted to their tastes and tal-
> ents, and securing to them the fruits of their industry; to do away with
> the necessity of menial services, by opening the benefits of education
> and the profits of labor to all; and thus to prepare a society of liberal,
> intelligent and cultivated persons, whose relations with each other
> would permit a more simple and wholesome life than can be led
> amidst the pressure of our competitive institutions.

This sentence has the full rolling cadence of a considered mission
statement—not surprising if one accepts that the central doctrine of

16. See Crowe, *Ripley*, 138.

Transcendentalism is the oneness of all phenomena, and that the harmony of the totality must be based on that of the individual. The argument, in the end, is between nature and history, with nature seen as the embodiment of the laws of the universe and history as the product of human consciousness. On the individual level that divide has to be healed by reconciling the physical side of our identity with the intellectual one. Ripley's point, of course, is that this reconciliation must also occur between social classes, since they have traditionally been separated on the basis of intellectual and manual roles.

Interestingly, despite his overriding fear that to join Brook Farm would be to "hide my impotency in the thick of a crowd," Emerson feels it necessary to endorse the central objective of reconciling mental and physical work: "The principal particulars in which I wish to mend my domestic life are in acquiring habits of regular manual labor, and in ameliorating or abolishing in my house the condition of hired menial service. I should like to come one step nearer to nature than this usage permits." Emerson's step nearer nature was rapidly followed by a step back from it, as his household staff objected to being asked to sit at table with their employers.[17]

Ripley was perfectly well aware of, and at the same time exemplifies, the class tensions that could arise as a result of his proposals. In a postscript to his letter to Emerson of November 9, he talks about the desirability of accepting some members "with whom our personal sympathy is not strong," such as a washerwoman who "is certainly not a Minerva or a Venus," along with certain farmers and mechanics. As it happened, the first small group of communitarians included a genuine farmer, William Allen; a homesteader from the West, Frank Farley; and a housemaid from Maine. At the other extreme was Warren Burton, a former Unitarian minister, who was to find it difficult to cope with the outdoor life.[18] Hawthorne was the most famous member of the community in its early days—or rather would become so—and he leaves behind a comic record of how a sedentary man coped with the new demands being made on him. In his letters to Sophia Peabody we can track his journey from innocence to experience. On April 13, 1841, we find him a good-humored novice: "Mr. Ripley put a four-pronged instrument into my hands, which he gave me to understand was called a pitch-fork; and he and Mr. Farley being armed with similar weapons, we all three commenced a gallant attack upon a heap of manure." A

17. Emerson, entry for October 17, 1840, in *JMN* 7:408; Emerson, *Letters* 2:371; Ralph L. Rusk, *The Life of Ralph Waldo Emerson* (New York: Scribner's, 1949), 289.
18. Crowe, *Ripley*, 144.

week later, on April 22, he claims that "my ability increases daily" and
that he will soon become "a great, broad-shouldered, elephantine per-
sonage." Significantly, though, when he adds, "What an abominable
hand do I scribble! but I have been chopping wood, and turning a
grindstone all the forenoon; and such occupations are apt to disturb
the equilibrium of the muscles and sinews," he gives a sure indication
of problems to come, since he is already tending to put asunder what
the Brook Farmers and the Transcendentalists in general fervently believed should be united.[19]

As I have suggested, Ripley used words sparingly, in a way quite consistent with the Transcendentalist belief that a correctly arranged perspective could be carried over directly into a course of action that
would magically transform the world. The one kind of discourse such
an ideology can permit without embarrassment is contractual, a language directed explicitly at the task of turning intention into action.
Perhaps, therefore, that public statement which Elizabeth Peabody was
waiting so impatiently for Ripley to utter can in fact be seen to be
manifested in a document committed to paper within a few months of
the founding of Brook Farm: its Articles of Association, dated September 29, 1841. Here the community is given its title, one that establishes
a clear relationship between the two halves of the human conundrum:
"The Brook Farm Institute of Agriculture and Education." The document goes on to list the subscribers to the first twenty-four $500
shares in the community, ten in all, though the Ripley family—George,
Sophia, and George's sister Marianne—bought eight, a third of the
total. Moreover, to minimize the danger of a capitalist hierarchy developing, the Articles of Association established that a year's labor, defined as three hundred days (of ten hours each during the summer
months and eight hours during the winter), would not merely pay for a
member's board but also qualify him or her for a share in the annual
dividend. The administrative structure of the community was divided
into four directorates, General, Financial, Agricultural, and Educational, thus creating a structural symmetry between cash, labor, and
intellectual development.[20] George Willis Cook quotes Charles Anderson Dana as saying of the Brook Farmers that "in order to reform society, in order to regenerate the world and to realize democracy in the
social relations, they determined that their society should first pursue

19. Nathaniel Hawthorne, *The Letters, 1813–1843, Centenary Edition,* 15:528, 533.
20. Octavius Brooks Frothingham, *George Ripley* (Boston: Houghton Mifflin, 1882),
112–17. The Articles of Association are in the Brook Farm records of the Massachusetts
Historical Society.

agriculture, which would give every man plenty of outdoor labor in the free air, and at the same time the opportunity of study, of becoming familiar with everything in literature and learning."[21]

The school, which, as Emerson predicted, almost immediately became the community's most important "industry" and its main bridge to society at large, was at the forefront of Brook Farm's effort to heal the mind-body divide, as the articles make clear. But the school did not merely act as one half of the dialogue between the mind and the body: that would be to distort the integrity of the serial structure. Each stage in the system had to contain within itself that interaction which the system as a whole was devised to achieve, just as, in Emerson's words, a drop of water must contain the properties of the sea. The school had a rigorous and intellectually ambitious syllabus, covering subjects such as intellectual and natural philosophy, mathematics, belles lettres, Latin, Greek, German, music, and history. But the combination of physical work and mental improvement was a fundamental policy: the curriculum included theoretical and practical agriculture, and children were required to spend up to two hours daily in manual labor. Even the pupils of the infant school, which was run by Marianne Ripley and Abigail Morton, did light field work. At the other end of the scale, the teachers had to divide their time too. We glimpse George P. Bradford leaving his hoe to go and teach, only to find that his pupil has forgotten about the lesson and is still out hunting. Charles Anderson Dana, who joined the farm in its early days after damage to his eyesight caused by an overindulgence in Dickens while a Harvard student (a perfect example of the dangers intrinsic in one-sided development), corrected the imbalance by combining teaching with organizing a corps of waiters. Ripley himself would switch from teaching philosophy to milking cows.[22]

It is easy to mock these earnest New England intellectuals who insisted on getting their hands dirty; even members of the community occasionally felt that there was something incongruous about such behavior. Ora Gannet Sedgwick offers us an amusing glimpse of Charles Dana, in his menial role, "reading a small Greek book between courses," though she also states that his organization of the waiters

21. G. W. Cooke, "Brook Farm," *New England Magazine*, n.s. 17 (December 1897): 395.
22. The Brook Farm material is rich in anecdotes of this kind. See Nathaniel Hawthorne, *The American Notebooks, Centenary Edition*, 8; Swift, *Brook Farm*; George P. Bradford, "Reminiscences of Brook Farm, by a Member of the Community," *Century Magazine* 45 (1892): 141–48, esp. 144; Arthur Sumner, "A Boy's Recollections of Brook Farm," *New England Magazine*, n.s. 10 (May 1894): 311.

demonstrated that he "was a very orderly young man." The waiters, she says, were chosen "from among our nicest young people," suggesting, depending on how one interprets "nicest," that there was a deliberate policy to select upper-crust members for this task. Just to even things up, the "waiters in their turn were waited on by those whom they had served."[23] Arthur Sumner—like Sedgwick, reminiscing many years after the event—takes a considerably less sympathetic view, describing how "Mr. John Dwight used to come in from his toil in the hot sun at noon, to give me a lesson on the piano, and after faithfully doing that job, he would lie down on the lounge and go to sleep." Sumner's verdict: "What a piece of nonsense it was, to have a man like that hoeing corn and stiffening his eloquent fingers." Nevertheless, fair-mindedness compels him to restate the principles on which this organization of labor was based: "But the idea was (I think) that all kinds of labor must be made equally honorable, and that the poet, painter and philosopher must take their turn at the plough or in the ditch."[24]

One must be careful not to devalue both the sincerity and the radicalism that underlay these principles. In August 1841 the publicity that Elizabeth Peabody advocated was in a measure supplied by an anonymous contributor to the *Monthly Miscellany of Religion and Letters*, who provides a detailed and enthusiastic account of the farm's intentions, in the course of which he or she spells out the egalitarianism evidenced by the community from its earliest days: "How dare I sacrifice not only my own, but others' health in sequestrating myself from my share of bodily labour, or neglecting a due mental cultivation?" There is, after all, a serial connection. If harmony is achieved on an individual level, it will radiate outward through the community—and vice versa. The implications for the ordering of society are far-reaching, even if not revolutionary in the more bloodthirsty sense of the term: "It seems to me that here we see brought about, in the most peaceable manner in the world, that very rectification of things which Mr. Brownson in his article on the Labouring Classes is understood to declare will require a bloody revolution, a war such as the world has not heard of; viz., that no child shall be born richer or poorer than another, except by inward gift of God, but all shall inherit from society a good education and an independent place."[25] In 1842 a "distinguished literary lady" penned a

23. Ora Gannet Sedgwick, "A Girl of Sixteen at Brook Farm," *Atlantic Monthly* 85 (March 1900): 396.
24. Sumner, "A Boy's Recollections," 311.
25. "The Community at West Roxbury, Mass.," *Monthly Miscellany of Religion and Letters* 5

report on the farm which, together with an introduction by that self-same sanguinary individual Orestes Brownson, was published in the *Democratic Review* for November of that year. The Brook Farmers, she asserts, are not hastening, lemminglike, toward a lowest social common denominator; instead, "true democratic equality may be obtained by *levelling up*, instead of *levelling down*."[26]

It is easy to detect the snobbishness and complacency implicit in such a formulation, and indeed we have already encountered a patronizing quality in Ripley's comments about the washerwoman who wished to join the community. A similar note is struck in an undated entry in Margaret Fuller's journal. Admittedly she was not a member of the community, but she was associated with it through her visits, her friendship with the Ripleys, and the attendance of her notorious younger brother Lloyd at the school. During one of her stays at the community she describes the following scene: "All Monday morning in the woods again. Afternoon, out with the drawing party; I felt the evils of want of conventional refinement, in the impudence with which one of the girls treated me. She has since thought of it with regret, I notice; and, by every day's observation of me, will see that she ought not to have done it." Fuller seems to have had a somewhat bruising time on this visit, which may account for her icy response to the "impudence" of the poor girl in the drawing party. On the previous Saturday she had conducted one of her public conversations, on the subject of education, but had not made a hit with her audience: "The people showed a good deal of the *sans-culotte* tendency in their manners,—throwing themselves on the floor, yawning, and going out when they had heard enough."[27]

Ora Gannet Sedgwick, who was present during the first years as a boarder at the school, unconsciously reveals the patronization and tension that must have been widespread:

besides those I have mentioned others joined us, with well-trained hands, but not of such good New England blood. I recall among them two Irishwomen, one of whom, a fine cook, had lived with the Danas and others of the best families of Boston. This woman came to Brook Farm for the sake of her beautiful young daughter, an only child, who

(July 1841): 114, 116. The piece is introduced by the editor as "an extract from a letter written by a friend—not a member of the new community—to a lady in England."

26. "Brook Farm," *United States Magazine and Democratic Review*, n.s. 11 (November 1842): 491.

27. Quoted in *Memoirs of Margaret Fuller Ossoli*, 2 vols. ed. R. W. Emerson, W. H. Channing, and J. F. Clarke (London: Richard Bentley, 1852), 2:272, 270.

looked like a madonna and possessed much native delicacy. Her mother was desirous that she should be well-educated. These women were perfectly welcome to sit at the table with us all, but they preferred not to sit down until the two courses had been put upon the table, if at all.[28]

The contrast between the sentimental iconography of the noble savage tradition and the actual hierarchical pressures unconsciously communicated by the tone of Sedgwick's passage gives us an excellent vignette of the problems and dangers facing the Brook Farm enterprise. On the one hand, there is the comforting stability of traditional order, however unjust; on the other, the threat implicit in the social mobility necessary to bring about that structural equilibrium required in the Transcendental scheme of things. This tension was experienced at both ends of the social system of the farm. Ann Weston, who visited Brook Farm shortly after it was founded, complained of Sophia Ripley that "she was anxious to assure her own mind that in all she did, the canons of gentility were not infringed upon, and she was still more anxious to let all else know that fact." Two years later a certain Sophia Eastman, who was at the Brook Farm school for a time, enlarged on this issue in a jaundiced letter home: "There is an aristocracy prevailing here, although many complain of being neglected."[29] At the other end of the scale, the young housemaid from Maine left because she was accustomed to serving, and egalitarianism made her uneasy.[30]

Nevertheless, the point to be borne in mind is that the objective was one of "true democratic equality." This goal was reiterated many years later when Charles Dana addressed the University of Michigan in 1895 on the subject of the community. His words have the authority of one who was a member for virtually the whole of the farm's history, who was Ripley's right-hand man, and who was an intrinsic part of the community's fabric (he was a cousin of Sophia Ripley, and his sister was also a member). He was well qualified to pass a verdict, and his later career as an aggressive polemicist for a rather different set of social values suggests that he was hardly likely to have been tempted to exaggerate the community's reforming verve. And yet he is unequivocal in his judgment that the initial impulse for the establishment of Brook

28. Sedgwick, "A Girl of Sixteen," 396.
29. Sophia Eastman to Mehitable Eastman, July 25, 1843, in Abernathy Library of American Literature, Middlebury College, Middlebury, Vt., reprinted in Sams, *Autobiography*, 80.
30. Crowe, *Ripley*, 147, 144.

Farm—and the central purpose of the community once it was under way—was an egalitarian one. The whole enterprise was an essay in applied democracy:

> In this party of Transcendental philosophers the idea early arose—it was first stated by Mr. George Bancroft, the historian . . . that democracy, while it existed in the Constitution of the United States, while it had triumphed as a political party under Jefferson, and while it was then in possession of a majority of the governments of the States, and at times of the government of the United States, was not enough. . . . If democracy was the sublime truth which it was held up to be, it should be raised up from the sphere of politics, from the sphere of law and constitutions; it should be raised up into life and be made social.[31]

The rolling clauses of this passage, with the sense they communicate of coming into focus on particularities, are reminiscent of the rhythms of Thoreau's prose when he looks for that single abolitionist who will leaven the whole lump ("if one thousand, if one hundred, if ten men . . . if *one* . . ."). In short, Brook Farm represented a deliberate and consistent attempt to interweave democratic ideals into the very texture of social life. Yet, the trajectory involved in the process of "levelling," like the delusive gradients one sometimes encounters in hilly terrain, could sometimes seem more down than up, as Hawthorne's increasingly disillusioned testimony demonstrates. By June a certain testiness has crept into his letters to Sophia Peabody: "That abominable gold mine! Thank God, we anticipate getting rid of its treasurers, in the course of two or three days. Of all hateful places, that is the worst." On August 12 he is talking of bondage: "Even my Custom House experience was not such a thraldom and weariness; my heart and mind were freer. Oh; belovedest, labor is the curse of this world, and nobody can meddle with it, without becoming proportionably brutified. Dost thou think it a praiseworthy matter, that I have spent five golden months in providing food for cows and horses? Dearest, it is not so. Thank God, my soul is not utterly buried under a dung-heap."[32] Interestingly, even after Hawthorne returns to the farm somewhat refreshed from a sojourn in Salem, his attitude is that the Brook Farm way of life *separates*

31. Charles Dana, "Brook Farm," address given at the University of Michigan, January 21, 1895, printed as an appendix to James H. Wilson, *Life of Charles Dana* (New York: Harper, 1907), 517.
32. Hawthorne, *Letters, 1813–43*, 545, 558.

the realms of the physical and mental rather than integrating them: "My mind will not be abstracted. I must observe, and think, and feel, and content myself with catching glimpses of things which may be wrought out hereafter. Perhaps it will be quite as well that I find myself unable to set seriously about literary occupations for the present. It will be good to have a longer interval between my labor of the body and that of the mind. I shall work to better purpose, after the beginning of November," that is, after he has left the community.[33]

One man's holism is another man's split personality, particularly when the former is a Transcendentalist and the latter a skeptic. For Hawthorne the role of farmworker comes to seem a falsification of his true identity, a realization that is perhaps anticipated by his reaction earlier in his stay at the farm, when he receives a present of the appropriate garb from his betrothed: "The thin frock, which you made for me, is considered a most splendid article; and I should not wonder if it were to become the summer uniform of the community. I have a thick frock, likewise; but it is rather deficient in grace, though extremely warm and comfortable. I wear a tremendous pair of cow-hide boots, with soles two inches thick. Of course, when I come to see you, I shall wear my farmer's dress."[34] When he visits Sophia, Hawthorne will wear his farmer's "dress."

Thomas Wentworth Higginson, the Boston man of letters later to become the bemused adviser of Emily Dickinson, describes a visit to his cousin Barbara Channing by a group of young men from Brook Farm, including George and Burril Curtis, Samuel Larned, and Charles Dana, and establishes the self-consciousness of such attire even more strongly, though interestingly he associates it with a fashion among college students of the time. The delegation were "all presentable and agreeable, but the first three peculiarly costumed. . . . It was then very common for young men in college and elsewhere to wear what were called blouses,—a kind of hunter's frock made at first of brown holland belted at the waist,—these being gradually developed into garments of gay-colored chintz, sometimes, it was said, an economical transformation of their sisters' skirts or petticoats." Higginson goes on to say that Dana did not indulge in these vanities but "dressed like a well-to-do young farmer and was always handsome and manly."[35]

---

33. Ibid., 575–76.
34. Ibid., 540, letter of May 3, 1841.
35. Thomas Wentworth Higginson, *Cheerful Yesterdays* (Boston: Houghton Mifflin, 1898), 84.

Emerson talked of watching the monad "through all his masks as he performs the metempsychosis of nature," claiming that nature "hums the old well known air through innumerable variations."[36] The role-playing that is in evidence here, and the fascination it suggests with playing variations on a theme, is a central aspect of Brook Farm life. The problem in analyzing it lies with the selective nature of the evidence that pertains to the day-by-day experience of the Brook Farmers. It is one thing to explain away Ripley's initial reticence on the grounds of his commitment to action, another to shed light on the reasons for his reticence—and that of most of the central members of the community—after that action had failed the test of history.

Amelia Russell, in a two-part article "Home Life of the Brook Farm Association," written more than thirty years after the community's collapse, poses a problem noted by Hawthorne in his preface to *The Blithedale Romance* and by many other former members when the time came to pen their memoirs: "I cannot understand why no one of those who better comprehended all the machinery which kept the wheels going through many trying vicissitudes (though I suspect sometimes the operators themselves felt doubtful how it was done) has ever brought its interior life to view, since a real history of its aims and endeavors after a truer life has been asked for."[37] Some years later Arthur Sumner suggested that the cause of this lapse was that Brook Farm "never had any result except upon the individual lives of those who dwelt there." It is an explanation that certainly gives ammunition to those who wish to see the community as symptomatic of a kind of death wish, an attempt to "banish the world" (to use the phrase of a hostile commentator, Jane Maloney Johnson), particularly as Sumner goes on to say, "It was a beautiful idyllic life which we led, with plenty of work and play and transcendentalism; and it gave place to the Roxbury poorhouse."[38] The opposition he establishes between idyll and poorhouse supports commentators who want to see the experiment as an extended picnic, with the corollary that any attempt to restructure its ideology must be the equivalent of breaking a butterfly upon a

36. Ralph Waldo Emerson, "History," in *Essays 1*, 8, 9.
37. A. E. Russell, "Home Life of the Brook Farm Association," *Atlantic Monthly* 42 (October 1878):458. Hawthorne wrote in his preface: "The Author cannot close his reference to this subject, without expressing a most earnest wish that some one of the many cultivated and philosophic minds, which took an interest in that enterprise, might now give the world its history." Nathaniel Hawthorne, *The Blithedale Romance, Centenary Edition*, 3:3.
38. Sumner, "A Boy's Recollections," 313; Jane Maloney Johnson, " 'Through Change and Through Storm': A Study of Federalist-Unitarian Thought, 1800–1860" (Ph.D. diss., Radcliffe College, 1958), 277.

wheel. At least one contemporary visitor to the farm would have endorsed Sumner's point of view. Bronson Alcott and Charles Lane, who
had just embarked on their own community at Fruitlands, visited during the summer of 1843, and Lane was not impressed, describing "80
or 90 persons playing away their youth and daytime in a miserably
joyous and frivolous manner."[39]

There is, however, an alternative explanation for the retrospective
reticence, one that takes us to the opposite pole from allegations of
triviality and frivolity: that is, the almost simultaneous collapse of the
community and of the national impetus toward association must have
had a traumatic effect on those who had invested in the movement
their emotional and intellectual capital (and in Ripley's case, to a disastrous degree, his financial capital). We are surely dealing with a bitter
failure after years of high ideals, higher hopes, and strenuous effort,
and it is hardly surprising that by 1850 Ripley, Dwight, and Dana had
embarked on careers that bore little or no relation to their earlier
ideals.[40]

By an irony that seems rather appropriate in view of Brook Farm's
precarious stance between the world of fantasy and that of harsh social
realities, one of the effects of this uneasy silence on the part of the
community's leaders is that we have to rely heavily for information
about the daily life of Brook Farm on writers who lay great stress on the
fun they had there. It is small wonder that Lindsay Swift, almost echo-
ing Lane's grumpy oxymoron, should claim that "enjoyment was almost
from the first a serious pursuit of the community," when we see the
emphasis on entertainment in the reminiscences of many former members, including Ora Gannet Sedgwick, Amelia Russell, George P. Bradford, and Arthur Sumner. John Van Der Zee Sears devotes a whole
chapter to the subject (it seems a long way from the *Harbinger*'s gritty
sociology to his inauspicious opening: "Our slide down the knoll
proved very popular"), and John Thomas Codman's memoir includes a
chapter titled "Fun Alive," which deals almost exclusively with the community's addiction to punning.[41]

39. Charles Lane, letter to *New Age*, reprinted in Frank B. Sanborn and William T.
Harris, *A. Bronson Alcott, His Life and Philosophy*, 2 vols. (Boston: Roberts Bros. 1893),
2:282–83.
40. Ripley became a journalist on Horace Greeley's *New York Tribune* and, with Dana,
edited the *New American Cyclopaedia*, 16 vols. (New York: D. Appleton, 1858–63). Dana's
career as a journalist on the *New York Sun* is charted in Wilson, *Charles Dana*, and Can-
dace Stone, *Dana and the Sun* (New York: Dodd Mead, 1938). Dwight edited *Dwight's
Journal of Music* from 1853 to 1887; see G. W. Cooke, *John Sullivan Dwight* (Boston: Small
Maynard, 1898).
41. Swift, *Brook Farm*, 53; Sedgwick, "A Girl of Sixteen," 394–404, esp. 402; Russell,

The most commonly mentioned form of entertainment in the Brook Farm memoirs is masquerade, and it is surely no coincidence that this is the area of utopian high jinks covered most substantially by Hawthorne in *The Blithedale Romance*. Indeed, many of the reminiscences attempt to identify the specific masquerade that provided him with his source, which was, as *The American Notebooks* show, a party given to celebrate Frank Dana's sixth birthday.[42] The most convincing candidate is described in a letter appended to Codman's book and signed "Charles": "One of the ladies personated Diana, and any one entering her wooded precincts was liable to be shot with one of her arrows." Compare Hawthorne's "goddess Diana (known on earth as Miss Ellen Slade)" who "let fly an arrow and hit me smartly in the hand."[43] Sedgwick modestly concentrates on checking the detail: apparently Hawthorne's "one variation from the facts was making me, both there [in *The Blithedale Romance*] and in the American Note-book, the gypsy fortune-teller, whereas that part was really taken by Mrs. Ripley, and I was merely the messenger to bring persons to her." Arthur Sumner, who did not join the farm until after Hawthorne had left, remembers "a fancy dress picnic in the woods, which might have furnished Mr. Hawthorne his scene in the Blithedale Romance."[44]

There were many similar events, and they are recalled with a graphic detail that suggests the importance of the part they played in the life of the community. John Van Der Zee Sears states that "the finest pageant we ever had was arranged by the Festal Series, after the reorganization into a phalanx. It was historic in design, illustrating the Elizabethan period in England. Dr. Ripley personated Shakespeare; Miss Ripley, Queen Elizabeth, in a tissue paper ruff, which I helped to make; Mr. Dana, Sir Walter Raleigh; Mary Bullard, the most beautiful of our young women, Mary Queen of Scots, and Charles Hosmer, Sir Philip Sidney." Amelia Russell describes another one, held at Christmastime, which featured impersonations of Hamlet, the Greeks and Circassians, an Indian, Little Nell and her grandfather, and Spanish bolero dancers. Thomas Wentworth Higginson made one of his only two visits to Brook Farm to "convey my cousin Barbara to a fancy ball at 'the Community,'

"Home Life," esp. 461–62; (November 1878): 557–59. Bradford, "Reminiscences," 141–48, esp. 142; Sumner, "A Boy's Recollections," esp. 311–12; John Van Der Zee Sears, *My Friends at Brook Farm* (New York: Desmond Fitzgerald, 1912), 80; Codman, *Brook Farm*, 172–85.

42. Hawthorne, *American Notebooks*, 201–3, entry for September 28, 1841.

43. Codman, *Brook Farm*, 260, letter of October 27, 1841; Hawthorne, *American Notebooks*, 202.

44. Sedgwick, "A Girl of Sixteen," 402; Sumner, "A Boy's Recollections," 311.

as it was usually called, where she was to appear in a pretty creole dress made of madras handkerchiefs and brought by Stephen Perkins from the West Indies."[45] We also hear about other tableaux, charades, rural fetes, and a prodigious list of plays and operas performed in whole or in part by the Brook Farmers: Byron's *Corsair*, Douglas Jerrold's *Rent Day*, *A Midsummer's Night's Dream*, *The Caliph of Baghdad*, *Zampa*, *Norma*, and so on. Hawthorne himself mentions two evenings of tableaux in letters of May 3 and September 21, 1841. Other activities—music, tobogganing, dancing—are mentioned, but those requiring role-playing of one sort or another seem to have been the most popular, and the ones that had the deepest effect on the participants.[46]

Let us now explore in some detail a few relevant passages from that most contentious and problematic of all the Brook Farm texts, *The Blithedale Romance*. Hawthorne left the community after a mere six months and published this work nearly ten years later. In making use of it I am not attempting to reopen the debate about the authenticity of the book as an account of the community. Hawthorne deals with that issue definitively in his preface. He acknowledges that "many readers will probably suspect a faint and not very faithful shadowing of BROOK FARM," and concedes that he "does not wish to deny, that he had this Community in his mind, and that (having had the good fortune, for a time, to be personally connected with it) he has occasionally availed himself of his actual reminiscences, in the hope of giving a more lifelike tint to the fancy-sketch in the following pages." Nevertheless, he goes on to emphasize that "he has considered the Institution itself as not less fairly the subject of fictitious handling, than the imaginary personages whom he has introduced there."[47] One notes a characteristic ambiguity in the use of that adverbial phrase "not less fairly," which picks up an equally characteristic double entendre in the title. In establishing that his book is a fictionalization of the community, he is also suggesting that there was something intrinsically fictional about the nature of the community itself, and apparently allying himself with those who see it as a refuge from the pressures of everyday reality.

This may, broadly speaking, be the case, but Hawthorne is a past master at exploring the relativity of all judgments and at ensuring that his ambiguities are themselves ambiguous. Certainly, whatever his own

45. Sears, *My Friends*, 101; Russell, "Home Life," 462; Higginson, *Cheerful Yesterdays*, 84.
46. See, for example, Bradford, "Reminiscences," 142; Sears, *My Friends*, 80–106; Codman, *Brook Farm*, 53–68; Hawthorne, *Letters, 1813–1843*, 542, 576, letters of May 4, 1841, and September 22, 1841.
47. Hawthorne, *Blithedale*, 1.

final verdict on the community—if he ever allowed himself one—this "not very faithful shadowing" can shed some light on the communitarian impulse in general, on the motivations and behavior of the Brook Farmers in particular, and above all on the significance and the appeal of masquerade to the communitarians. Moreover, the two examples I wish briefly to explore both originate from Hawthorne's actual reminiscences of his time at the farm, as detailed in his *American Notebooks*.[48]

In the chapter titled "Leave-Takings," Coverdale, the central character of the novel, a somewhat reclusive and valetudinarian poet, reveals his decision to return from the Blithedale community to the outside world for a time. His reasons are both particular (a recent "passage-at-arms" with Hollingsworth, the dynamic and philanthropic leader of the community) and general ("an intolerable discontent and irksomeness had come over me"). He makes his intentions clear by the way he dresses: "I appeared at the dinner-table, actually dressed in a coat, instead of my customary blouse; with a satin cravat, too, a white vest, and several other things that made me seem strange and outlandish to myself." And not just to himself, in fact: his choice of dress indicates to his fellow communitarians that he has decided to leave them. As Zenobia, the community's beauty (with her own exuberant taste in clothing) complains: "You have just resumed the whole series of social conventionalisms, together with that straight-bodied coat." She clearly disapproves of Coverdale's need "to go and hold a little talk with the conservatives." Her belief is that only a dynamic and volatile temperament can cope with the instability of the world: "It needs a wild steersman when we voyage through Chaos!"[49]

Coverdale's last farewell is to the pigs. "I can in nowise explain," he confesses to the reader, "what sort of whim, prank, or perversity it was, that, after all these leave-takings, induced me to go to the pig-stye and take leave of the swine!" Certainly the pigs are about as far removed

48. Hawthorne, *American Notebooks*, 201–5, entries for September 28 and October 1, 1841.
49. Hawthorne, *Blithedale*, 138, 137, 141, 142. Charles Anderson Dana has fun with the image of a conservative in a straight-bodied coat in a satirical sketch called "Worthy Men," which he wrote at Brook Farm and enclosed in a letter to Emerson on October 31, 1843: "Your worthy man wears a suit of fine black, loosely made, with benevolent looking wrinkles intersecting the back. His waistcoat is of black silk. His pantaloons are large and comfortable. He affecteth white cravats. Straps he eschews." Later on, Dana has the worthy man giving his opinion on Transcendentalism: "I do'nt like the Movement school. We got along well enough in my time without any German nonsense, and I do'nt see why we should'nt now. Can you get money by German? I guess not." MS in Houghton Library, BMS Am 1280 (744), 1, 5.

from voyaging through Chaos as it is possible for creatures to be, and therein might indeed lie the secret of their attraction. Coverdale appears to be searching for some kind of symbolic manifestation of his need for security; that, after all, is what he is hoping to gain on his return to city life from "those respectable old blockheads, who still, in this intangibility and mistiness of affairs, kept a death-grip on one or two ideas which had not come into vogue since yesterday-morning." In short, he is looking not for a wild steersman but for a safe anchor; and the firmness of the conservatives, in holding to their principles through the "intangibility and mistiness of affairs," is balanced on a physical level by the immobility and torpor of the pigs to whom he has come to say farewell:

> There they lay, buried as deeply among the straw as they could burrow, four huge black grunters, the very symbols of slothful ease and sensual comfort. They were asleep, drawing short and heavy breaths, which heaved their big sides up and down. Unclosing their eyes, however, at my approach, they looked dimly forth at the outer world, and simultaneously uttered a gentle grunt; not putting themselves to the trouble of an additional breath for that particular purpose, but grunting with their ordinary inhalation. They were involved, and almost stifled, and buried alive, in their own corporeal substance.[50]

The pigs are as far removed as it is possible to imagine from the world of masquerade. They are themselves to the nth degree, taking the fact of simply being, as opposed to doing, as far as it can go. They can be seen as literal embodiments of nature's stasis, and it is perhaps for this reason that Coverdale admires their capacity to luxuriate in their own existence. They represent, in their own way, the sort of stability for which he is striving, and which he finds so unattainable in the complex interaction of community life. The sharp observation that irradiates the whole passage—that they grunt "with their ordinary inhalation"—is reminiscent of a line in Whitman's "Song of Myself" in which the poet celebrates "The sound of the belch'd words of my voice loos'd to the eddies of the wind."[51] Whitman's robust Anglo-Saxonism reminds us that spoken language is no more than a series of configurations of the air, eddies of the wind (in both senses of the word), and exposes our tendency to separate discourse from the world it signifies.

50. Hawthorne, *Blithedale*, 141, 143–44.
51. Walt Whitman, "Song of Myself," in *Leaves of Grass*, ed. Harold W. Blodgett and Sculley Bradley (New York: New York University Press, 1965), 29.

The porkers, like the bard, find no dichotomy between word and thing, subject and object, the world of discourse and the reality it is intended to convey. Whitman would have found nothing incongruous in the comparison ("I think I could turn and live with animals, they are so placid and self-contained, / I stand and look at them long and long. / They do not sweat and whine about their condition, / . . . . Not one is dissatisfied . . .)."[52] Hawthorne observes in *The American Notebooks* that the language of pigs "seems to be the most copious of that of any quadruped." Nevertheless, rich though it may be, it can express only nature's fixed patterning and inevitably lacks the resources of human language, and in particular the sorts of encoded meanings, double entendres, and puns generated within a community, the linguistic masquerade that reflects the other forms of role-playing that take place.[53]

John Thomas Codman devotes a whole chapter of his memoirs, as I have mentioned, to the subject of punning. The quantity, if not the quality, of this wordplay inevitably bathes the farm in an Illyrian glow. The activity of punning (however badly) involves camaraderie and cooperativeness, and the puns could be bad indeed: "'These Grahamites will never make their ends *meet*,' said one. 'You may *stake* your reputation on that,' said the other."[54] The reference here is to the Grahamite table at the farm, where strict vegetarianism was regarded as the key to a healthy cuisine, as it was at the Alcott-Lane community of Fruitlands (though nonvegetarian Brook Farmers tended to be restricted to pork and beans, and that only as a Sunday treat, with vegetables, bread pudding, and the like providing their staple also).[55]

As far as such jokes are concerned, to know all is not necessarily to forgive all. But the weaker the puns, the more they rely on accomplices—a point Codman himself makes, attacking those who pun "in toto," as he puts it. The in toto punster, he tells us, "discovers some close-mouthed, tight-fisted sort of a word or a sentence doubled up like an oyster and deliberately splits it apart, one shell on one side, one on the other and the soft thing drops out between." He does not go on to define "the soft thing," but one can take it to be the organic principle that reconciles opposites. "I could only despise the brain that would do such a deed," Codman tells us. In toto punning clearly threatens the substance of community, its utopian value and meaning, since it de-

52. Ibid., 60.
53. Hawthorne, *American Notebooks*, 205.
54. Codman, *Brook Farm*, 173.
55. Georgianna Bruce Kirby, "Reminiscences of Brook Farm," *Old and New* 5 (1872): 347–58; Sears, *Friends*, 50–52.

stroys the connective tissue necessary for creating solidarity between the different members. The sort of pun Codman admired, and which he found to be characteristic of Brook Farm, was by contrast "a part of the sunshine of words." Paradoxically, though, it achieves this warmth, whereby it imparts "a sparkle and a glow to language," by creating, albeit temporarily, an alienation effect: "It is a big pendulum that swings from torrid to frigid zone quicker than a telegram goes. If you hold on to it, you will find yourself in both places in a jiffy, and back again to the spot where you start from without being hurt, and the jog to your intellect, if you happen to have any, is only of an agreeable nature."[56]

Codman's analysis is all the more extraordinary and fascinating when one knows that he is not a man of letters, nor a linguistic theorist, but a nineteenth-century dentist. But of course he is a nineteenth-century dentist who spent much of his childhood at Brook Farm. His perceptiveness is made possible by actual experience of the operations of language within utopia. He seems here to be anticipating the sort of distinctions William Empson would make in his book *Seven Types of Ambiguity*, where the seventh type has the schismatic effect of the in toto punster—"full contradiction, marking a division in the author's mind"—whereas "in second-type ambiguities two or more alternative meanings are fully resolved into one."[57] In the case of Codman's sunshiny pun, there is not time for the "soft thing" to drop out between the extremes. The lightning journey described by Codman perhaps has something in common with those glimpses and perceptions of serial unity so hauntingly evoked by Emerson. The most memorable of them, after all, involved a journey toward (or perhaps from) the frigid zone, when, as we recall, "crossing a bare common, in snow puddles, at twilight, under a clouded sky, without having in my thoughts any occurrence of special good fortune, I have enjoyed a perfect exhilaration." When Emerson thinks specifically of human solidarity, however, he pictures the serial linkages as lying beyond the realm of discourse altogether: "I feel the same truth how often in my trivial conversation with my neighbors, that somewhat higher in each of us overlooks this byplay."[58] It might be that here one sees the difference between, on the one hand, the individualistic utopian whose mind mediates constantly between the polarities of the one and the totality, so that when he talks about communion he automatically triangulates the relationship into

56. Codman, *Brook Farm*, 176.
57. William Empson, *Seven Types of Ambiguity* (Harmondsworth: Penguin, 1961), v, vi.
58. Ralph Waldo Emerson, "The Over-Soul," in *Essays 1*, 165.

the realm of a "third party or common nature" which "is not social" but "impersonal," and, on the other, the communitarian variety, in which the interaction between people remains important.[59] Codman's punsters, far from overlooking their by-play, give it full rein, enjoying the accommodation of doubleness, the reconciliation of opposites, and the cooperation it permits.

In its own way masquerade also acts as a kind of pendulum between torrid and frigid zones. Terry Castle points out in her study of the eighteenth-century carnivalesque that "the pleasure of the masquerade attended on the experience of doubleness, the alienation of inner from outer." She is describing here the phenomenon of masquerade taking place within the status quo, not so much a structured utopia as an episode of misrule or holiday, so that it inevitably acts as a subversive or disruptive force, the effect being analogous to that of the in toto pun. In a passage that is coincidentally reminiscent of Codman's imagery of wrenched shells and jogged intellects, she claims that, "like the linguistic code, the code of dress may be subverted. Language . . . can be stripped of its referential functions; *res et verba* can be jarred apart. . . . The same might be said of the sartorial language."[60] Word and dress have a more benign and sunny function within Codman's Brook Farm, expanding their referential functions and finding new ways of matching *res et verba*.

Hawthorne's porkers are unaware of such possibilities. Lacking verbal and sartorial strategies, they represent in their uncomplicated way "the soft thing," the principle of connectivity itself: "They also grunt among themselves, apparently without any external cause, but merely to express their swinish sympathy."[61] As they are creatures of nature, one might not expect them to have anything to fear from the dialectical forces that play on human beings, but things are not as simple as that. These are *farm* animals, and as such they straddle two worlds, just as we do. They have their existence, as Coverdale points out, "betwixt dream and reality."[62] Like the "plant, quadruped, bird" of Emerson's poem "The Sphinx," they are entranced by "the Lethe of Nature." Nevertheless, because this enchantment takes place within the farm, they are also subjected to the vicissitudes of history. As Hawthorne put it in the passage in *The American Notebooks* that provided the material for

59. Ibid., 164.
60. Terry Castle, *Masquerade and Civilisation: The Carnivalesque in Eighteenth-Century English Culture and Fiction* (London: Methuen, 1986), 4, 56.
61. Hawthorne, *American Notebooks*, 205.
62. Hawthorne, *Blithedale*, 144.

Coverdale's farewell to the pigs: "I suppose it is the knowledge that these four grunters are doomed to die within two or three weeks, that gives them a sort of awfulness in my conception; it makes me contrast their present gross substance of fleshly life with the nothingness speedily to come."[63] The swing of the pendulum will be fatal: 'You must come back in season to eat part of a spare-rib,' said Silas Foster. . . . 'I shall have these fat fellows hanging up by the heels, heads downward, pretty soon, I tell you!' "[64]

If the slothful pigs provide an image of Coverdale's need when he leaves the farm, the masquerade he encounters on his return surely sums up the community as a whole and embodies exactly that instability of identity and role which he finds so difficult to cope with. As he approaches Blithedale after his comparatively short absence (he leaves in August and returns in September), Coverdale begins to suspect that everything has changed since he was last here: that some sort of disaster has overtaken the community and that the farm has been abandoned. His anxiety is not a serious one, however, but a form of self-teasing which serves to increase the shock when he discovers that the buildings are in fact deserted. His anticipation has been caused by his sense that there is something intrinsically unlikely, quasi-fictional, about the community in the first place. As with any utopia, its true locale seems to be in an if-only dimension rather than in the here-and-now:

> I indulged in a hundred odd and extravagant conjectures. Either there was no such place as Blithedale, nor ever had been, nor any brotherhood of thoughtful laborers, like what I seemed to recollect there; or else it was all changed, during my absence. It had been nothing but dream-work and enchantment. I should seek in vain for the old farm-house, and for the greensward, the potatoe-fields, the root-crops, and acres of Indian corn, and for all that configuration of the land which I had imagined. It would be another spot, and an utter strangeness.[65]

The community is still there, as it turns out, but Coverdale is right to anticipate "utter strangeness": "Stealing onward as far as I durst, without hazard of discovery, I saw a concourse of strange figures beneath the overshadowing branches; they appeared, and vanished, and came

63. Hawthorne, *American Notebooks*, 204.
64. Hawthorne, *Blithedale*, 144.
65. Ibid., 206.

again, confusedly, with the streaks of sunlight glimmering down upon them." They seem, in short, to be a trick of the light, a phenomenon of perception, teetering on the verge of Emersonian transparency (and nobody could have a more appropriately transparent eyeball—or at least a more invisible one—with which to view the scene than the secretive Miles Coverdale). The masquerade he then perceives makes an impressive catalogue, comprising the following roles: an Indian chief, the goddess Diana, a Bavarian broom-girl, a Negro, one or two foresters of the Middle Ages, a Kentucky woodsman, a Shaker elder, shepherds of Arcadia, allegorical figures from *The Faerie Queene*, Puritans, Cavaliers, Revolutionary War officers, a Gypsy, Moll Pitcher ("the renowned old witch of Lynn"), skinkers and drawers, and the "fiendish musician, erst seen by Tam O'Shanter."[66]

As a sort of yardstick to measure the extent of these transformations, and in so doing to demystify them, Hawthorne gives us the figure of Silas Foster, "who leaned against a tree near by, in his customary blue frock"—in his working garb, in short. In the *Notebooks* entry for the day before the one on which Frank Dana's masquerade is described, Hawthorne sings the praises of that same garment: "Others (like myself) had on the blue stuff frocks which they wear in the fields—the most comfortable garment that man ever invented." But as we have seen, for Hawthorne such a garment can be regarded as a form of disguise in itself; for a real farmer it is the stuff of a comforting normality, fitting the man as word should match thing. As such it "did more to disenchant the scene . . . than twenty witches and necromancers could have done."[67] At the Brook Farm masquerade which provided Hawthorne with his material, that role was performed by "our friend Orange, a thickset, sturdy figure, in his blue frock, enjoying the fun well enough, yet rather laughing with a perception of its nonsensicallness, than at all entering into the spirit of the thing."[68] The point is that Orange was not a member of the community but a helpful neighbor, and so his blue frock is not a costume but the genuine article.[69] Castle has claimed that conventional dress reinscribes "a person's sex, rank, age, occupation—all the distinctive features of the self." Orange and Foster provide a reality index to the degree of masquerade around them, a hu-

66. Ibid., 209–10.
67. Ibid., 210; Hawthorne, *American Notebooks*, 200.
68. Hawthorne, *American Notebooks*, 203.
69. See, for example, Marianne Dwight's account of his assistance in trying to save the Phalanstery when it caught fire. Marianne [Dwight] Orvis, *Letters from Brook Farm, 1844–1847*, ed. Amy L. Reed (Poughkeepsie, N.Y.: Vassar College, 1928), 146, letter dated March 4, 1846.

man equivalent of that "Realometer" Thoreau talks about, which will gauge "how deep a freshet of shams and appearances had gathered from time to time."[70]

Coverdale, too, bursts into laughter at the "oddity of surprising my grave associates in this masquerading trim." He wants to embrace the concept of a stable identity, as manifested in the porkers and Silas Foster, rather than join in the freewheeling play of the revelers, though he is less secure in his selfhood than those allies are in theirs. His laughter removes the privilege of his transparency, and he flees before the good-humored onslaught of the communitarians. There is an element of panic in his flight: "The whole fantastic rabble forthwith streamed off in pursuit of me, so that I was like a mad poet hunted by chimaeras."[71]

We can detect a number of ironies here. Emerson's description of the poet springs to mind, to start with. For him the poet is a being with the capacity of perceiving unity in diversity, of being able to make something coherent out of the variety of life's masquerade, one who "turns the world to glass and shows us all things in their right series and procession."[72] The version we are given in Coverdale's simile seems to lack the organizing perception celebrated in Emerson's definition; the series has become chaotic and the procession a predatory mob. A further irony, one that is clearly being utilized to "place" Coverdale as a character and ensure that the reader does not assume he has an objective vantage point within the romance, is that Coverdale himself is actually a poet by profession, though paradoxically the simile he has chosen denies that vocation even as it invokes its relevance, thus suggesting that he doubts his own claim to the title and establishing that the minor status he lays claim to is fair comment rather than an act of modesty.

Coverdale succeeds in making his escape, leaving "merriment and riot at a good distance in the rear. Its fainter tones assumed a kind of mournfulness, and were finally lost in the hush and solemnity of the wood." His rejection of masquerade, we note, has involved transforming merriment to mournfulness. The sunshine has gone. He immediately stumbles on a reminder of the entropy that eats away at all our attempts to impose order on the world, as he comes across a heap of firewood that had been "piled up square" many years before, since when, "by the accumulation of moss, and the leaves falling over them

70. Castle, *Masquerade*, 55; Henry David Thoreau, *Walden*, in *Writings*, 98.
71. Hawthorne, *Blithedale*, 210–11.
72. Ralph Waldo Emerson, "The Poet," in *Essays* 2, 12.

and decaying there, . . . a green mound was formed, in which the softened outline of the wood-pile was still perceptible." It is relevant to recall at this point the contrast between the spontaneous sort of Transcendentalism which lacked any a priori baggage, apart from the capacity to assimilate fresh perceptions, and the myth-sustaining kind which brought a treasury of cultural *bricolage* along with it. In the scene under discussion Coverdale fails to sustain the first stance, and is brought up short when confronted by the implications of the second. Only moments after fleeing the masquerade, Coverdale is imagining "the long-dead woodman, and his long-dead wife and children, coming out of their chill graves, and essaying to make a fire with this heap of mossy fuel!"[73]

There is a stark contrast between this ghostly vision of order struggling to maintain itself long after its occasion has passed, and the gaiety and resourcefulness of the masqueraders. In his study of Rabelais, Mikhail Bakhtin has discussed the way in which the carnivalized body "is not a closed, complete unit; it is unfinished, outgrows itself, transgresses its own limits." Terry Castle has extended this argument to the eighteenth-century masquerade in England:

From basically simple violations of the sartorial code—the conventional symbolic connections between identity and the trappings of identity—masqueraders developed scenes of vertiginous existential recombination. New bodies were superimposed over old; anarchic theatrical selves displaced supposedly essential ones; masks, or personae, obscured persons. . . . The true self remained elusive and inaccessible—illegible—within its fantastical encasements. The result was a material devaluation of unitary notions of the self.[74]

That capacity for opening his eyes with fresh sincerity which Santayana attributed to Emerson is one that ought to be particularly attuned to perceiving these new bodies superimposed over the old; but, disappointingly, Emerson seems to have spent his time at the birthday masquerade for Frank Dana deep in talk with Margaret Fuller. Nevertheless, Hawthorne himself was able to register the vertiginous effect of the existential recombinations he witnessed. To him the masqueraders seemed to be "starting out of the earth; as if the every day laws of

73. Hawthorne, *Blithedale*, 211–12.
74. Mikhail Bakhtin, *Rabelais and His World*, trans. Hélène Iswolsky (Cambridge: MIT Press, 1968), 26; Castle, *Masquerade*, 4.

Nature were suspended for this particular occasion."[75] There is an implication that if the everyday laws of nature have been suspended, what
Hawthorne was witnessing was a manifestation of deeper, permanent
laws, the sort referred to by George Ripley in a letter to Emerson later
that same year in which he claims that "so many powers are at work
with us and for us, that I cannot doubt, we are destined to succeed in
giving visible expression to some of the laws of social life that as yet
have been kept in the background."[76]

Castle goes on to claim that masquerade is a form of utopia, which is
precisely my point—and Hawthorne's, for that matter. She writes: "The
visionary anti-society the masquerade projected was at heart utopian,
for along with other oppositions, that of upper class and lower class was
temporarily abolished. Roland Barthes's maxim, 'Once the antimony is
rejected, once the paradigm is blurred, utopia begins,' has its relevance
here."[77] Ironically, the complex improvisation of masquerade has a unifying effect, destabilizing hierarchy and synthesizing dialectic. Although it is true that, for its duration, melancholy, death, the passing
of time seem suspended, this fact does not entitle us to regard masquerade as merely escapist. If it were, the conformist Coverdale would
surely be running toward it rather than away. There is, in other words,
a social agenda implicit in the occasion, one that meshes quite clearly
with the utopian ideals of Blithedale and indeed of Brook Farm: the
attempt to unite laborer and student, to enable cooks and consumers
to sit together at the table. The high jinks that Coverdale comes across
may in themselves constitute only a utopia of the impromptu moment,
but they stand for the sustained historical endeavor of the community
as a whole.

Masquerade provided a ludic paradigm of the interchangeability of
role that was part of the institutional fabric of Brook Farm from its
earliest days. What the community was trying to achieve was a holism of
the body and of the body politic, a way of accommodating that faith in
human solidarity that is intrinsic not merely to Transcendentalist ideology but to the Christian tradition generally. As John Thomas Codman
put it, the human race "was one body. It should be of one heart, one
brain, one purpose. Whenever one of its members suffered all suffered.
When there was a criminal all had part in his crime; when there was a
debauchee, all partook in his debasement; when there was one dis-

75. Hawthorne, *American Notebooks*, 202–3.
76. George Ripley to Ralph Waldo Emerson, December 17, 1841, MS Houghton, BMS
Am 1280 (2721). Ripley is trying to persuade Emerson to buy a share in the farm.
77. Castle, *Masquerade*, 78.

eased, all were affected by it; when one was poor, all bore some of the sting of his poverty. If anyone took shelter behind his possessions, wretchedness, poverty and disease found him out."[78] Because the human race can be seen as a single organism, we all play any and every role in the ongoing drama. Ironically, such protean transformations act as an affirmation of the underlying structure behind all phenomena, the serial harmony that cancels difference and distinction and enables us to perceive the monad behind the mask. We are participants in an ultimate masquerade: the criminal, sinner, impoverished wretch, Indian chief, goddess Diana, Bavarian broom-girl; the milker of cows and the teacher of philosophy. This masquerade is, so to speak, for real, not simply an extension and enlargement of the Ripleys' summer holiday, a "Transcendental picnic" that inevitably had to give way to the West Roxbury poorhouse. As Codman says, this belief in the unity underlying social roles was the "religion" of Brook Farm.

It is not a religion to which Coverdale can adhere because he sees structural integrity—the stability of porker, conservative, and woodsman—as separate from masquerade. The former lacks the flexibility to cope with history's changes; the latter lacks the consistency to be more than a rabble of chimaeras. Hawthorne himself made a more resolute attempt to deal with this problem than his fictional opposite number, but, as we have seen, his attempt also came to nothing. It is significant that in recording his experiences at Brook Farm, he should so persistently fix on his activity as a dung shoveler. As we shall see with regard to Lane and Alcott, and indeed Thoreau, manure tended to represent for the Transcendentalists the hold that the old, exhausted, compromised past maintains on the present. Hawthorne, in using the ancient conceit of dung as treasure, accidentally allies himself with Lévi-Strauss's *bricoleur*, reorganizing the cultural treasury. The problem is that this effort cannot be seen as an affirmation of lasting values because for him, lacking the credentials of the fictitious Foster or the real Orange, it is merely a disguise, and therefore associates him with the opposite camp, the masqueraders. And as the months wore on, Hawthorne began to lose his faith in disguises. On May 4 we find him describing some tableaux of the previous evening for the benefit of his betrothed: "They went off very well. I would like to see a tableaux [*sic*], arranged by my Dove." By the time he is writing the letter of September 22, in which he talks of establishing an interval between labor of the mind and the body, his attitude has undergone a radical meta-

78. Codman, *Brook Farm*, 227.

morphosis: "We had some tableaux last night. They were very stupid, (as, indeed, was the case with all I have ever seen)."[79]

Other Brook Farmers—those who, unlike Hawthorne, shared the Transcendentalist perspective—found masquerade, in the broad "religious" sense, a satisfying way of exploring life's possibilities and affirming human solidarity. Nevertheless, after a year or two they were beginning to feel the need for a more formal structure to underpin their utopian improvisations, a doorpost to write their whims upon.

79. Hawthorne, *Letters*, 543, 576.

3

Brook Farm:
The Law of Groups and Series

M
any years after the failure of Brook Farm, when George Ripley's life had taken a very different shape and his principles
and beliefs had become far more conservative, he went to bed
one night and had a vivid dream. When he awoke from it he scribbled:

Life = power of action
Cosmic life = power of cosmic action
Animal life = power of animal action
Vegetable life = power of vegetable action
Mechanical life = power of mechanical action
Chemical life = power of chemical action[1]

Many of us no doubt have had the experience of stumbling upon what
seems to be a secret of universal importance in our sleep, jotting it
down on a scrap of paper in the middle of the night, and being dis-
mayed in the cold light of morning to discover that it was either gib-
berish or banality. At first sight Ripley's formulation seems to belong to
this category of disappointments. Yet to dismiss it in this way is to misunderstand both the Transcendentalist and the Fourierist frame of
mind. Its repetitiveness is the whole point. What we have here is a late
afterglow of that vision which Emerson attributes to the poet: "all

1. Charles Crowe, *George Ripley: Transcendentalist and Utopian Socialist* (Athens: University
of Georgia Press, 1967), 260. The original (without explanation that it was a dream) is
part of a miscellaneous collection of manuscripts in the Massachusetts Historical Society
collection of George Ripley papers. From the context it clearly dates from the 1870s.

things in their right series and procession." By definition this is a vision that cannot be communicated in terms of vivid detail because it is a vision of everything. The world, to revert to Emerson's terminology again, has been turned to glass, and Ripley's formulation is like a sequence of refracted images, each manifesting the same basic outline but receiving its own coloration and dimension from its particular context.

In his autobiography the American Fourierist Albert Brisbane describes a similar moment of revelation:

> I perceived that there was unity of law with great diversity of phenomena; that the laws manifested themselves differently according to the differences of the material spheres in which they acted. Hence unity of law and variety in manifestation. The same law, for instance, which governs the distribution, co-ordination, and arrangement of the notes of music governs the distribution, co-ordination, and arrangement of the planets and the solar system. As sounds are notes in the musical harmony, so the planets are notes in a sidereal harmony. Continuing the analogy: the species in the animal or vegetable kingdom are the notes of a vast organic harmony; the bones in the human body are the notes of an osseous harmony, and these with the muscles and other parts of the human organism, are the notes of physical harmony. *Law is unchanging,* but there is infinite variety in its manifestations;—such manifestations being as rich and complex as are the varied spheres or departments of the Universe.[2]

Certain commentators have expressed surprise at Brook Farm's transition, early in 1844, from Transcendentalist community to Fourierist phalanx. Perry Miller, for example, picking up a phrase of Emerson's, claims that "nobody knows what went on in Ripley's mind as he consented, by January 18, 1844, to change Brook Farm from a Transcendental picnic into a regimented phalanx." He goes on to quote Lindsay Swift to the effect that Ripley must have come "to lay more stress on the method by which individual freedom was to become assured, than on the fact of personal liberty in itself."[3] This verdict can receive some

2. *Albert Brisbane, A Mental Biography,* ed. Redelia Brisbane (Boston: Arena, 1893), 258. Despite its title, this is an autobiography, dictated by Albert Brisbane to his secretary, and posthumously supervised through publication by his widow, Redelia Brisbane.

3. Perry Miller, *The Transcendentalists* (Cambridge: Harvard University Press, 1950), 469. In "Historic Notes" Emerson describes Brook Farm as "a perpetual picnic, a French Revolution in small, an Age of Reason in a pattypan" (*Works,* 10:364). The reference to Lindsay Swift is to his *Brook Farm: Its Members, Scholars, and Visitors* (New York: Macmillan, 1900), 135.

support from the testimony of the Brook Farmers themselves. Amelia Russell, for example, writing many years after the event, describes how the changeover affected her. She had been living in the Cottage, "which was in itself a beautiful little home, and I had become attached to it." With the reorganization, however, it was decreed that this building should be used as a school for the younger pupils: "As it was decidedly the prettiest house on the place, it was thought the youthful mind would be impressed by it and lessons become easier; and it was held that every means should be employed to make the hours of school discipline pleasant, so that the pupils should forget it was not an agreeable recreation." One gathers by the way she expresses herself here that she was not exactly convinced by this reasoning, and indeed she goes on to provide evidence to back up her case. She has seen the state of the desks in the present schoolroom, she tells us, and that of the other fixtures. Their sorry condition recalls the plight of the furnishings in the "academy for both sexes" that she attended in her own youth. The implication, of course, is that good facilities are wasted on the young. Nevertheless, she has no choice but to move to the Pilgrim House, which "was placed in a very barren spot, with no trees near it." She concludes her account of this upheaval: "The new Fourierite system began to be organized, and the poetry of our lives vanished in what we hoped would prove more substantially advantageous."[4]

Charles Crowe, in his excellent biography of George Ripley, places his emphasis slightly differently. He points to the spiritual and intellectual struggles that the community's founding fathers underwent during the years that preceded its establishment, and, for that matter, during the years that followed. He takes it for granted that Ripley and his colleagues were sincere in their desire to place the whole of society on a new basis. But to the extent that they were, or developed into, programmatic thinkers, they lost the authentic Transcendentalist afflatus. "If they embraced Fourierism completely," he asks, "what became of the much-vaunted Transcendental individualism?"[5] His answer is, very little. In effect, he tracks what amounts to a process of action and reaction operating through time. The Fourieristic Brook Farmers step back into history and attempt to reconstruct the social order which, as Transcendentalist Brook Farmers, they had originally opted out of. Such narrow linearity seems incompatible with the complex interweaving of oppositions that we have already seen in Transcendentalist thinking, and it is not surprising to find Crowe claiming, in a previous article,

4. Amelia Russell, "Home Life of the Brook Farm Association," *Atlantic Monthly* 42 (November 1878): 562.
5. Crowe, *Ripley*, 173.

that the "ideology of the Brook Farm leaders was from the beginning closer to Fourierism than to Transcendentalism."[6] In short, from one point of view Transcendentalism is too frivolous and self-centered to coexist with Fourierism; from the other Fourierism is an alien imposition draining the vitality from Transcendentalism. Miller describes the Brook Farm phalanx as sitting "foreign and forlorn in West Roxbury."[7] Crowe and Miller agree that Transcendentalism and Fourierism do not mix, a view that conveniently builds in the structural tension necessary to account for the demise of the community in 1847.

The basis for this sort of analysis is the belief that Transcendentalism is synonymous with individualism. Certainly it is true in the case of the major literary figures the movement produced, Emerson and Thoreau, and I shall in due course be exploring the individualistic dimension of Transcendentalist utopian thinking. Nevertheless, Carl J. Guarneri, whose book *The Utopian Alternative: Fourierism in Nineteenth-Century America* is the definitive treatment of its subject, has provided a more balanced viewpoint: "It is not so much that early Brook Farm was closer to Fourierism than to Transcendentalism (one can only say this by equating Transcendentalism with Emerson) but rather that Ripley's 'fraternal' or social version of Transcendentalism meshed remarkably well with Fourierist ideas." He adds, however, that "where Fourierism differed most clearly from early Brook Farm was in its systematic character and the very explicitness of its blueprint." It is my contention that Fourierism's "elaborate taxonomy of human nature" is in fact perfectly compatible with the Transcendentalists' fundamental beliefs.[8] The point I made in my first chapter—indeed, the argument that I wish to pursue throughout this book—is that the essential feature of Transcendental-

6. Charles Crowe, "Fourierism and the Founding of Brook Farm," *Boston Public Library Quarterly* 12 (April 1960): 87. Morris Hillquit makes the same point in his *History of Socialism in the United States* (New York: Funk & Wagnalls, 1903), 103. Anne C. Rose, in *Transcendentalism as a Social Movement, 1830–1850* (New Haven: Yale University Press, 1981), also takes this basic position. She sees a development from individualism to a "social vision" as basically an inevitable next stage in Transcendentalist attempts to "apply religious principles more effectively in modern society" (144).

7. Miller, *Transcendentalists*, 464. Rose, having mentioned the Brook Farmers' appetite for enjoyment, goes on to say rather intriguingly: "This drive to live as fully as possible is the simplest reason why Brook Farm changed in the course of its six-year history . . . beginning as an experiment in practical Christianity and becoming a center of reform activity to promote the social science of Charles Fourier" (*Transcendentalism*, 131). She is, however, simply testifying to the reserves of energy and enthusiasm of the Brook Farmers, not attempting to establish a structural connection between the two classes of activity.

8. Carl J. Guarneri, *The Utopian Alternative: Fourierism in Nineteenth-Century America* (Ithaca: Cornell University Press, 1991), 52.

ism is not individualism but a belief in the all-embracing principle of
seriality, the doctrine of the law of series. Tony Tanner once made a
memorable complaint about the movement in these terms: "There is
the leaf—and there are the hidden laws of the universe; and nothing
in between. Certainly not society, the notable omission in Emerson."[9]
The point is that what connects the leaf with society is the very existence of those hidden laws of the universe that rank and order the
whole substance of things, ensuring a series of intermediate stages between the unit and the totality, each one of which is structured in a way
that parallels and fits in with all the others: "unity of law with great
diversity of phenomena." As John Sullivan Dwight was to put it in a
lecture to the New England Fourier Society he delivered in February
1844, one month after the switch to Fourierism:

> Was not the law of my individual being appointed with perfect knowl-
> edge of all the laws of the whole universe of things, and with full
> regard to the laws of all other individual natures like myself, so that I
> in my true self-development must harmonize with others, and not
> clash? . . . We are harmonies, born each into our preëstablished place
> in an infinite system of harmonies; every man is a microcosm, or world
> in miniature, reflecting all the laws of all things; and each mortal
> child is as indispensable to the balance and completeness of the world
> into which he comes so small an atom, as is each planet in the system
> of our sun, or each sun in the celestial sphere, or each note in the
> great music of God.[10]

In short, what Fourierism had to offer was not the replacement of
poetry with substantiality, as Amelia Russell claimed, but a substantial
rendering of the poetic vision that was at the heart of Transcendentalism from its early days. It turns a mystical intuition of a patterned world
into a practical program. In his *Dial* article on Fourier Emerson says,
perhaps with tongue in cheek, that "mechanics were pushed so far as
fairly to meet spiritualism."[11] As George Ripley put it in a lecture on
Fourier, "Experience has shown, that it is among those whose souls are
most exquisitely susceptible to the sublime harmonies of sound, his

9. Tony Tanner, *The Reign of Wonder* (Cambridge: Cambridge University Press, 1965),
37–38.
10. John Sullivan Dwight, *Association in Its Connection with Education* (Boston: Benjamin
H. Greene, 1844), 4 (delivered Boston, February 29, 1844).
11. Ralph Waldo Emerson, "Fourierism and the Socialists," *Dial* 3 (July 1842): 87.

vast system of the Harmonies of the Universe, has found its most enlightened and earnest adherents."[12]

There is a paradox involved in achieving a picture of Fourier's structure in its pure form. To revert to Jakobson's terminology, the language must inevitably approach the condition of "blab," since it must be a language that expresses "only the framework, the connecting links of communication."[13] Nevertheless, we can catch a glimpse of that framework in Fourier's *Traité de l'association domestique-agricole*:[14]

$$
\begin{array}{cc}
\textit{Præ.} & \textit{Post.} \\
\text{Citra.} & \text{Ultra.} \\
\text{Cis.} & \text{Trans.} \\
& \text{Intra.}
\end{array}
\left.\begin{array}{l} \\ \\ \\ \\ \end{array}\right\}
\begin{array}{l}
\text{Série simple de bas degré} \\
\text{à trois termes et leurs} \\
\text{transitions.}
\end{array}
$$

What we have here is simply a shape, the words no more than indicators of position, in terms of both their content (or lack of it) and their placing on the page. And in looking at the shape, one might well recall Thoreau's talk of lobes and lapsing and, above all, of leaves. In fact, this is the structure of a Fourierist serie (Brisbane, Fourier's most important translator, found it helpful to adopt the French distinction between singular and plural forms of the word *series*). The structure does not, of course, have to be presented this way up. At the blab-level—where, as Jakobson puts it, concrete terms have dissolved into abstract anaphoric substitutes—the serie floats as freely as an astronaut in space. Here it is in *La fausse industrie*,[15] swelling like a low hill:

Inter
Citer . . Ulter
Anter . . . . . . Poster
Avant pr : . . . . Final.

12. "George Ripley's Unpublished Lecture on Charles Fourier," ed. David Zonderman, in *Studies in the American Renaissance, 1982*, (Boston: Twayne, 1982), 190.
13. Roman Jakobson, "Two Aspects of Language and Two Types of Aphasic Disturbance," in *Selected Writings*, 8 vols. (The Hague: Mouton, 1962–88), 2:245–46.
14. Charles Fourier, *Théorie de l'unité universelle*, in *Oeuvres complètes de Charles Fourier*, 12 vols. (Paris: Editions Anthropos, 1966–68), 2:55.
15. Charles Fourier, *La fausse industrie*, in *Oeuvres complètes*, 8:393vv (pagination is chaotic, with letters, then double letters, supplementing page numbers).

More characteristically we find the serie on its side. Let us move from this abstract level to a concrete one, from the unity of law to an explicit manifestation of the diversity of phenomena. Pears, for example, range from the hard cooking sort at one extreme of the species to the soft mealy variety at the other, with the ripe juicy type in between. The serie, therefore, ranks them accordingly:

> Quinces and hard hybrids
> Hard cooking pears
> Crisp pears
> Dessert pears
> Compact pears
> Mealy pears
> Medlars and soft hybrids

There is what Fourier calls an ascending wing from the hardest variety to the intermediate point, and a descending wing from the intermediate point to the softest. It does not take a Thoreau to detect something rather pear-shaped about that structure as a whole. And, sure enough, when Fourier comes to depict the phalansterian arrangements for pear husbandry,[16] the form becomes apparent:

SÉRIE DE LA CULTURE DES POIRIERS,

Composée de 32 groupes.

Divisions.	Progression numérique.	Genres de culture.
1° Avant-poste.	2 groupes.	Coings et sortes bâtardes dures.
2° Aileron ascendant.	4 groupes.	Poires dures à cuire.
3° Aile ascendante.	6 groupes.	Poires cassantes.
4° Centre de Série.	8 groupes.	Poires fondantes.
5° Aile descendante.	6 groupes.	Poires compactes.
6° Aileron descendant.	4 groupes.	Poires farineuses.
7° Arrière-poste.	2 groupes.	Nèfles et sortes bâtardes molles.

Series are racked not merely horizontally in space but also vertically in time. Needless to say, Fourier's "Formula of the Movement of a Serie"[17] is itself a serie:

16. Charles Fourier, *Théorie des quatres mouvements et des destinées générales,* in *Oeuvres complètes,* 1:294.
17. Translated in Albert Brisbane, *Social Destiny of Man; or, Association and Reorganization of Industry* (Philadelphia: C. F. Stollmeyer, 1840), 228.

Simple Formula of the Movement of a Serie.

Ascending Transition	or	Birth.
First Phasis	or	INFANCY.
Second Phasis	or	YOUTH.
Apogee	or	MATURITY.
Third Phasis	or	DECLINE.
Fourth Phasis	or	DECRIPITUDE.
Descending Transition	or	Death.

Brisbane's fellow Fourierist Parke Godwin has some interesting things to say about this particular formula in his book *A Popular View of the Doctrines of Charles Fourier*. He points out that the right-hand column is "not arranged by caprice; the swelling of the white intermediate surface, appropriately represents to the eye the nature of that regular development which it characterises."[18] It is hardly surprising, given the shape of that white intermediate surface, that Fourier gives us the phases of the moon in the form of a lunar crescent:[19]

Neu-croissant................	1 3/4....	jours.
1. Præquartier.............	5	
2. Cis-quartier.	7	
Foyer { hyper-plein..........	1 1/4	
{ hypo-plein.	1	
3. Trans quartier.	8	
4. Post-quartier...........	4	
Vieux croissant..............	1 1/4	

One recalls Brisbane's words, describing his moment of revelation: "As sounds are notes in the musical harmony, so the planets are notes in a sidereal harmony." Or Emerson picturing "spine on spine, to the end of the world."[20] Vertebrae, after all, partake of this serial form. As Brisbane puts it: "The bones in the human body are the notes of an osseous harmony."

I hope this whirlwind tour of the Fourierist serie is sufficient to establish an essential compatibility between the Transcendentalist picture of universal architecture and that generated by the French utopian thinker. What we now have to explore is how these two visions of the world came together. The most important linking figure is undoubt-

18. Parke Godwin, *A Popular View of the Doctrines of Charles Fourier* (New York: J. S. Redfield, 1844), 34.
19. Charles Fourier, *Manuscrits*, in *Oeuvres complètes*, 10:69.
20. Brisbane, *Mental Biography*, 258; Ralph Waldo Emerson, "Swedenborg, or the Mystic," in *RM*, 61.

edly Albert Brisbane. Indeed, he was the agent by means of which Fourierism penetrated the United States in the first place. In fact, one can go a step further and claim that Brisbane was one of the main factors in the upsurge of interest in Fourier's doctrines in the years following the philosopher's death in 1837.

Brisbane was born in 1809 into a well-to-do mercantile household in Batavia, New York. He traveled widely in his youth, attending lectures by Cousin in Paris and Hegel in Berlin. Under the influence of the set of Berlin intellectuals who attended the salon of Mme. Varnhagen von Ense, he became interested in utopian socialism, and in due course served as a propagandist for the Saint-Simonians. When the movement split under the rival leadership of Enfantin and Bazard, he began to seek out another system of belief to subscribe to, and soon after (in 1832) was lent a copy of Fourier's *Association domestique-agricole.* In his *Mental Biography* he describes his conversion in rather moving terms: "Now for the first time I had come across an idea which I had never met before—the idea of *dignifying* and *rendering attractive* the manual labor of mankind; labor hitherto regarded as a divine punishment inflicted on man. To introduce attraction into this sphere of commonplace, degrading toil—the dreary lot of the masses—which seemed to overwhelm man with its prosaic, benumbing, deadening influence; to elevate such labors, and invest them with dignity, was indeed a mighty revolution!"[21]

François Marie Charles Fourier is one of the strangest figures in French (and, owing to Brisbane's efforts, American) intellectual history. Like his disciple he was born into a wealthy merchant family, at Besançon in 1772. He inherited a fortune from his father but lost it all in the Revolution. Nevertheless, a small annuity from his mother, together with odd jobs and commercial transactions, enabled him to eke out a meager living while concentrating on his life's work. In 1808 he published his first book, *Théorie des quatres mouvements et des destinées générales; prospectus et annonce de la découverte.* That last word is significant. Fourier lays strong emphasis on the fact that his system is a discovery. In the "avant-propos" of a book published at the other end of his career, *Le nouveau monde industriel et sociétaire* (1829), he says that "il est plus pressant de faire connaître au lecteur le sujet dont on va l'occuper, l'échelle des sociétés supérieures à la civilisation, et dont le mécanisme est enfin découvert" (it is more urgent to let the reader know the subject which is going to occupy him, the ladder of societies

21. Brisbane, *Mental Biography,* 172.

superior to civilization, the mechanism of which has at last been discovered). Brisbane comments: "It is interesting to remark how emphatically he [Fourier] condemns every semblance of speculation. In a hundred places in his works he asserts that he gives no theory of his own. 'It is not by speculation and theorizing,' he says, 'that men are to discover the normal organization of society: it is by going back to the eternal laws of nature.' "[22]

Perhaps the nearest equivalent in our age to this combination of revelation and intricacy is the Mandelbrot set. The paradoxical nature of the very phrase "chaos theory" brings to mind the Transcendentalist concern with a serial law that can advance "on Chaos and the Dark." And this endlessly repetitive form also materialized with sudden completeness on Benoit Mandelbrot's computer screen. "Like Mount Everest," as Roger Penrose has put it, "the Mandelbrot set is just *there!*" Penrose goes on to emphasize that the set was not invented by Mandelbrot but was discovered by him, even though it can be located only in the abstract world of mathematics, just as Fourier's serial structure can be identified only by extrapolating from physical reality to its abstract formal principles—by turning the world to glass, as Emerson's poet does. "It is a feeling not uncommon among artists," Penrose goes on to claim, "that in their greatest works they are revealing truths that have some kind of prior etherial existence," and he quotes Borges to the effect that "a famous poet is less of an inventor than a discoverer."[23]

In an unpublished manuscript Fourier actually gets around to classifying the process of invention itself with his usual precision: "1. The cultivated genre, the genius of invention. 2. The rough genre, the instinct of invention. 3. The fortuitous genre, invention by chance." Fourier places himself in the second category, which he regards as the most "prolific in discoveries" because it is not inhibited by any preexisting structure of false doctrine. The point is that discoveries "fall to the lot of instinct as much as to that of genius; one finds mechanics by instinct who would be able to construct a clock without ever having looked inside one."[24] Here is another example of the intrinsic compatibility of Fourierism and Transcendentalism, exactly the sort of distinction I have been pursuing between the revelatory perspective that in-

22. Charles Fourier, *Le nouveau monde industriel et sociétaire* (1829; rpt. Paris: Flammarion, 1973), 28; Brisbane, *Mental Biography*, 184.

23. Roger Penrose, *The Emperor's New Mind: Concerning Computers, Minds, and the Laws of Physics* (Oxford: Oxford University Press, 1989), 125, 127.

24. Charles Fourier, unpublished MSS, Archives nationales, Paris, cahier 10/9, 132, quoted and trans. Nicholas V. Riasanovsky, *The Teaching of Charles Fourier* (Berkeley: University of California Press, 1969), 106 n. 113.

spects the universe afresh each morning and the mythic one, which confines itself to manipulating the cultural treasury (or adjusting the cogwheels of a clock). Fourier's allegiance to the concept of spontaneous apprehension, combined with his distaste for the cult of personality (which is, after all, a mythic construct, persisting through time), went so far as to lead him to announce in his later years that he was not himself a Fourierist but a theorist of the laws of attraction like Newton.[25]

After the *Théorie des quatres mouvements,* Fourier beavered away at his philosophical system. One cannot exactly say that he developed it because that is to misunderstand the totalizing nature of his original claim. He repeated himself (but, after all, so does nature); he explored the endlessly intricate ramifications of the doctrine. Having discovered the blueprint for utopia, he was famously uninterested in trying to put it into practice, believing that a partial attempt would challenge the integrity of the structure, and expecting that when the time was ripe, the phalansterian series would somehow come into existence at a stroke. He spent much of his later years waiting for a millionaire to knock on the door of his Paris apartment and present him with the wherewithal to conduct a full-fledged experiment.[26] Albert Brisbane knocked instead, and paid $5 an hour for twelve lessons on Fourier's system.[27]

A few years later, in 1837, Fourier died, without having seen the social arrangements to which he had devoted his life come to fruition. This gnomic assertion was carved on his tombstone in the Montmartre cemetery: "The Series distribute the harmonies. The Attractions stand in relation to the destinies." The meaning of these claims will become clearer as we go on, but for the present it is worth noticing their symmetry, the first sentence describing the macrocosmic order, with its picture of the general ("the harmonies") becoming specific, while the second focuses on the microcosm, asserting that human energies, like the other forces of nature, are directed at teleological fulfillment.

Meanwhile, Brisbane had returned to America and begun to proselytize. The important breakthrough occurred with the publication of his exposition of Fourierist doctrine, the *Social Destiny of Man,* in 1840. More than half the book consisted of direct translations of Fourier's texts, the rest taking the form of summaries, explications, and connecting links. It was read by most of the leading Transcendentalists, includ-

25. See Jonathan Beecher, *Charles Fourier: The Visionary and His World* (Berkeley: University of California Press, 1986), 487.
26. See ibid., 355–71, for a full exploration of Fourier's search for a benefactor.
27. Brisbane, *Mental Biography,* 187.

ing Ripley. By 1842 Brisbane had won over the influential journalist Horace Greeley and had begun to attract national attention. His articles in Greeley's *Tribune*, his four *Democratic Review* pieces, titled "Association and Attractive Industry," which came out in 1842, and his *Concise Exposition of the Doctrines of Association*, published in 1843, laid the basis for America's Fourierist project.[28] Experiments began to spring up in the early 1840s, including the North American Phalanx at Albany, New York, which was established in 1843 with a constitution written by a team that included Brisbane, Greeley, and George Ripley, the last not yet an enrolled member of the movement, though close enough to involve himself in this way. Ripley came out, so to speak, at the convention of the Friends of Social Reform, held in Boston in December 1843, where he was made a vice president of the organization, with Charles Dana elected secretary.[29] A month later, on January 3, 1844, Dana was sent to a meeting of the Friends of Association to describe the "present condition of the Brook Farm association," and on January 18 Brook Farm amended its original constitution in accordance with Fourierist principles.[30]

The "Introductory Statement" to the amended constitution, signed by Ripley, Minot Pratt, and Dana, emphasizes continuity rather than change. The new constitution is "the same as that under which we have hitherto acted, with such alterations as on a careful revision seemed needful." The difference, they claim, lies in the audience they are addressing, or rather in the fact that they are consciously addressing an audience. In its early stage the community bore "the character of a private experiment"; almost as if still reacting to Peabody's complaint, the signatories explain that "until the present time . . . [it] seemed fittest to those engaged in this enterprise to publish no statements of

28. Brisbane, *Social Destiny*; idem, "On Association and Attractive Industry," *U.S. Magazine and Democratic Review*, n.s. 10, no. 43 (January 1842): 30–45; no. 44 (February 1842): 167–82; no. 46 (April 1842): 321–36; no. 48 (June 1842): 560–81; idem, *A Concise Exposition of the Doctrine of Association or Plan for the Reorganization of Society* (New York: J. S. Redfield, 1843); idem, *Mental Biography*. The following chapters of *Social Destiny* are translations of Fourier's French: 1, 3, 4, 5, 6, 11, part of 12, 13, 14, 26, 28, 29, 30, 31, 32, 33, 34, 35.
29. John Humphrey Noyes, *History of American Socialisms* (1870; rpt. New York: Dover Publications, 1966), 512–15, esp. 514.
30. "Constitution and Minutes of the Brook Farm Association, 1842–1847," MS, 97–98, 129–36, in the collection of the Brook Farm records, Massachusetts Historical Society. This amended constitution was published in October 1844 as *Constitution of the Brook Farm Association for Industry and Education, West Roxbury, Mass., with an Introductory Statement*, 2d ed. [with the by-laws of the association] (Boston: Brook Farm Association, 1844).

their purposes or methods, to make no promises or declarations, but quietly and sincerely to realise . . . the great ideas which gave the central impulse to their movement." That time has passed, however, and the beginning of public interest in association makes it imperative that the Brook Farmers should share the "results of their studies and experience." One cannot help but feel there is something a little disingenuous in their failure to mention the fact of their conversion. They contrive to imply they have been Fourierists from the beginning and that the issue at stake is simply the present need to let the public know where they stand. And where they stand is that "while on the one hand we yield an unqualified assent to that doctrine of Universal unity which Fourier teaches, so on the other, our whole observation has shown us the truth of the practical arrangements which he deduces therefrom." These practical arrangements boil down to "the law of groups and series," which "is, as we are convinced, the law of human nature, and when men are in true social relations their industrial organization will necessarily achieve these forms."[31]

We have already had a glimpse of the way this law of groups and series is composed. It is now time to explore its ramifications a little further. (Incidentally, to avoid confusion it should be pointed out that a group is nothing but a lowest common denominator serie: by the very nature of this system, organizational differences can be only of scale, not of nature. Like Emerson's Swedenborg, Fourier possessed "the fine secret that little explains large and large little.")[32] In the Fourierist model each individual has a certain number of drives or "passions"; each of these directs him or her toward a certain objective, which has only to be achieved and he or she will be perfectly happy. These passions can be analyzed and tabulated. They consist of: five sensitive passions, one arising out of each of the senses, which have as their object "Elegance, Riches and Material Harmonies"; four affective passions: friendship, love, ambition, and paternity, which tend toward "Groups and Passional Harmonies"; and, more obscurely, three "Distributive and Directing Passions," the "Emulative," "Alternating," and "Composite." These are, respectively, the desire for intrigue and rivalry, for variety of occupation, and for the double enjoyment of intellectual and emotional satisfaction; all together they lead to "Series and Concert of

31. *Constitution of the Brook Farm Association*, 6–7.
32. Emerson, "Swedenborg," *RM*, 106. In his article "Fourierism and the Socialists," Emerson claims: "One could not but be struck with strange coincidences betwixt Fourier and Swedenborg" (*Dial* 3 [July 1842]: 87).

Masses." This whole nexus of desires can find fulfillment if only work is arranged according to Fourier's blueprint.[33]

All workers are to be divided into groups and series of groups. A group is the basic unit of labor and "should be composed of at least seven persons." These "form three divisions or three sub-groups, the centre one of which should be stronger than the two wings or extremes. A group of seven persons will furnish the three following divisions: 2-3-2 (two persons at each wing and three in the centre). Each division would be engaged with some department of the work with which the Group was occupied." A series is made up of groups in the same way that a group is composed of individuals. It "must contain at least three Groups—a Centre and two wings: twenty-four persons is the least number with which a Series can be formed. The central Group should be stronger than the Groups of the wings." This structure enables one's emulative passion to be fully engaged. "The ascending wing will be occupied with the heaviest branch of a work, if the Series be engaged in manufactures, and with the largest variety, if engaged in the cultivation of grains, fruits, vegetables or flowers; the centre will be occupied with the most elegant and attractive branch or variety; and the descending wing with the lightest and smallest."[34] The idea is that the two wings will unite to excel the center; they will have numbers on their side, while the center will have the satisfaction of producing the highest quality of article. (We noticed earlier that even in respect of inventing Fourierism itself, the *middle* category of invention was the one that did the trick.) The careful discrimination of function avoids the danger of easily resolved and therefore ineffective competition.

This organization of labor caters not merely to emulation but to all the other passions as well. One will never spend more than an hour or two on any particular activity, thus satisfying alternation; the industrial system will be so highly specialized that each person will be able to do exactly the work he or she wants to do, and will do it in the company of those who are also happy in their jobs, thus providing the composite pleasure of interesting employment and good company. Friendship, love, and paternity are fulfilled because the workers' mobility enables them to choose their company: husbands and wives can work side by side if they want to, and for as long as they want to. Ambition is allowed for by the possibility of rivalry, and because the individual is making maximum use of his or her abilities. The five sensitive passions—sight,

33. Brisbane, *Social Destiny*, 157–80.
34. Brisbane, *Concise Exposition*, 44. The work distribution within the group is exactly the same.

hearing, smell, taste, and touch—can play on the beautiful environment that is the result of living in a community and thereby breaking down the distinction between home and work, and of the joint-stock system by which everyone receives a share in the whole and therefore possesses both the worker's needs and the proprietor's powers.[35]

Fourier's system claims, then, that the deepest wishes of individuals can be identified and provided for. We go about our business as if participating in a masquerade, donning the appropriate costume for any occupation that takes our fancy (in Brisbane's words, "unity of law with great diversity of phenomena"). But in this context at least masquerade is synonymous with utopia because our whims prove to be structured, our frolics architectural. It is masquerade with a blueprint. As John Codman explains, God has made exactly the number and variety of "empty places" in the order of things for the number and variety of talents in the world. He goes on to point out that although the structure looks formal on paper, it does not in fact "intrude itself, any more than the rules of arithmetic do when we are buying a few apples."[36] The concept of an exact number of "empty places" is the ultimate logical counterpart of Emerson's claim in "Self-Reliance" that "no law can be sacred to me but that of my nature."[37]

Moreover, we are capable of accomplishing all the tasks that we want to perform; or, to put it another way, the tasks we want to perform always happen to be tasks that we can accomplish. A preemptive strike is made against the skeptics who might find such virtuosity unbelievable:

> It will be objected that if an individual takes part in so many branches of Industry, he will become perfect in none; this difficulty will be entirely obviated by the minute *division of labor*, which will take place, and by assigning to each individual of a Group the performance of a detail of the work with which it is engaged. In a Group of fruit-growers, for example, a person will attend to the grafting; now an intelligent person can learn to graft as well in a few days as in a lifetime, and his knowledge in this branch will enable him to belong to several Series of horticulturists. Thus, while changes of scene and company would prevent monotony and apathy, the same detail of a work could be performed. A skilful turner could belong to Groups of

35. Brisbane, *Social Destiny*, 119–27.
36. John Thomas Codman, *Brook Farm: Historic and Personal Memoirs* (Boston: Arena, 1894), 87–88.
37. Ralph Waldo Emerson, "Self-Reliance," in *Essays 1*, 30.

chairmakers, without varying materially the nature of his work; a person skilled in working leather could belong to the Series of saddlers, glove-makers, and shoe-makers, and the part in which he excelled might be performed in each of the branches of Industry.[38]

The "division of labor" referred to here (technically speaking "parcelled exercise") is very minute indeed. One wants to work not just with, say, a flower, but with a specific part of a tulip, and one's taste will exactly complement that of one's colleagues: "For among twelve persons with a love for the tulip, none of the twelve will have a love for the twelve functions connected with its cultivation; therefore unless they make a parcelled division of their work and distribute functions according to tastes, disagreements and discord will break out."[39] It is entirely characteristic of Fourierism's ambivalent response to the industrial revolution that this anticipation of the conveyor-belt philosophy should be so irrepressibly floral. Interestingly, one of Fourier's sources must be the opening of *The Wealth of Nations*, written half a century before his *Nouveau monde industriel*, where we find Adam Smith also waxing lyrical about "the division of labour." The example Smith chooses, however, is the manufacture of pins ("One man draws out the wire, another straights it, a third cuts it, a fourth points it, a fifth grinds it at the top for receiving the head," and so on). Fourier's brave new world, by contrast, is as arcadian as Marie Antoinette's old one.[40]

After focusing on one's work with such microscopic intensity, one would expect to feel something of a jolt in switching occupations at the rate that is suggested:

> A Man, for example, may be
> At five o'clock in the morning in a Group of Shepherds;
> At seven o'clock in a Group of gardeners;
> At nine o'clock in a Group of fishermen.[41]

One might anticipate a Coverdale-style vertigo at the rapidity of this role-changing. Nonetheless, Fourier is confident that the individual will fit exactly into each of the costumes that have been made available for him or her (and again it is worth noting that they are charmingly preindustrial). He asserts that "THERE IS NOTHING ARBITRARY IN THE SYS-

38. Brisbane, *Social Destiny*, 47.
39. Ibid., 149.
40. Adam Smith, *An Inquiry into the Nature and Causes of the Wealth of Nations*, ed. R. H. Campbell, A. S. Skinner, and W. B. Todd (Oxford: Clarendon Press, 1976), 14–15.
41. Brisbane, *Social Destiny*, 184.

TEM WE PROPOSE, we resort to no laws or regulations of human invention; we make use of three of the twelve passions to direct the other nine with the freest and most economical of systems, that of Serie of Groups, which system is a universal desire of the human heart, as well as the distribution followed in the whole order of known Nature."[42]

Again, the contrast with Adam Smith is significant. According to *The Wealth of Nations*, "It is impossible to pass very quickly from one kind of work to another, that is carried on in a different place, and with quite different tools. . . . A man commonly saunters a little in turning his hand from one sort of employment to another. When he first begins the new work he is seldom very keen and hearty; his mind, as they say, does not go to it, and for some time he rather trifles than applies to good purpose."[43] With Fourierism no such seepage of momentum occurs; there is not room in this system for sauntering and trifling. The point is that the configuration of the individual's passions actually corresponds, on its own small scale, with the intricate topography of the natural order. We saw in the "Serie de la culture des poiriers" that the working groups and the pear varieties both followed the exact curve of the serial structure. The individual, too, locks into place in a work scheme that resembles a jigsaw puzzle, or at least would do so within a phalanx. Sadly, in civilization that puzzle has become disarranged so that, in Emerson's terms, the world of Rome became detached from that of rat and lizard, "the whole order of known Nature." When the phalanx is established, the human pieces will be fitted together again in a way that provides an exact image of the structure of nature itself. The masquerade will become a stable social machine.

The phalanx is a self-sufficient community, able to cope with all of life's needs. As Emerson sarcastically expressed it: "It takes 1680 men to make one Man, complete in all the faculties; that is, to be sure that you have got a good joiner, a good cook, a barber, a poet, a judge, an umbrella-maker, a mayor and alderman, and so on. Your community should consist of 2000 persons, to prevent accidents of omission."[44] Despite Emerson's sneer, the premise on which the phalanx is based has its points of resemblance to that underlying the individualistic variety of Transcendentalism. In this connection it is worth looking at an extract from a letter to John Sullivan Dwight from George William Curtis, an ex–Brook Farmer who disapproved of Fourierism:

42. Ibid., 189.
43. Smith, *An Inquiry*, 18–19.
44. Emerson, "Fourierism and the Socialists," 87.

Raphael could have sung as Shakespeare, and Milton have hewn as many forms as Angelo. Yet a divine economy rules these upper spiritual regions, as sure and steadfast as the order of the stars. Raphael must paint and Homer sing, yet the same soul gilds the picture and sweetens the song. So Venus and Mars shine yellow and red, but the same central fire is the light of each. In the capacity of doing all things well lies the willingness to serve one good. The Jack of all trades is sure to be good at none, for who is good at all is Jack of one only. It seemed a bitter thing to me, formerly, that painters must only paint and sculptors carve; but I see now the wisdom. In one thing well done lies the secret of doing all.[45]

The letter is dated November 25, 1843, shortly after Curtis left the community, and shortly before what he (as a Transcendentalist of the picnicking type) would term the "earlier, golden age of the colony" gave way to the Fourierist period.[46]

Curtis has come to accept—at first unwillingly—that in order to achieve anything, one must confine oneself strictly within a single discipline. This idea is at the opposite pole from Fourier's scheme, where the capacity to undertake a variety of occupations is perceived to be one of the fundamental human attributes. Such Fourieristic versatility, however, is not the same as being a jack-of-all-trades. There is a quality of approximation and improvisation about what Lévi-Strauss called the *bricoleur* which would be alien in the phalanx and disruptive to the smooth operation of its well-oiled machinery. Lévi-Strauss points out that the old verb *bricoler* applied to ball games and billiards, to hunting, shooting, and riding, but that it was "always used in reference to some extraneous movement: a ball rebounding, a dog straying or a horse swerving from its direct course to avoid an obstacle."[47] An adaptive technique derived from a tradition of swerving is entirely incompatible with Fourier's discovery, since it compromises the ideal structure of utopia with a messy intrusion from the contingent: it lets in the sauntering and trifling that Adam Smith talked about.

Variety of occupation for Fourier depends not on a capacity to make do but on an intricate and repetitive structure of specialization that enables an individual to undertake one of the twelve functions con-

45. George William Curtis, *Early Letters of George Wm. Curtis to John S. Dwight*, ed. G. W. Cooke (New York: Harper, 1898), 127–28.
46. Cooke quotes this phrase from an "Easy-Chair" essay in his introduction, ibid., 9.
47. Claude Lévi-Strauss, *The Savage Mind* (London: Weidenfeld and Nicholson, 1972), 16.

nected with the cultivation of tulips and then to go away and undertake something equally intricate somewhere else. Swerving is something that happens in civilization; in the phalanx it is a matter of hitting the bull's-eye—or at least the pistil or stamen—each time. Fourier, in short, lays as much stress as Curtis on the task well done, rather than an improvised job. The distinction between Curtis's master of one thing and Fourier's alternating worker does not parallel Lévi-Strauss's distinction between the engineer and the *bricoleur* because Fourier and Curtis both emphasize a nonentropic interaction between the unit and the totality. The only difference between them has to do with the size of the unit.

Curtis has an atomic view of the structure of the universe. Things are inextricably connected in such a way that even though each of us deals with only a single point in the overall pattern, the reverberations of our actions run right through the whole framework, so that "in one thing well done lies the secret of doing all." Fourier believes that the basic unit of the human universe is an organized system which is composed of almost two thousand people and which can be reproduced in the form of the phalanx. Both, however, assume that once you have mastered the part, you have access to the whole; that the universe has a consistent and repetitive order; that it is designed in accordance with the law of series. The two men are simply disagreeing over the scale and complexity of the basic component.

Curtis's description is the one we have come to associate with Transcendentalism: it is the Emersonian position. "One man is stronger than a city," Emerson wrote in his journal when Ripley suggested he join in the Brook Farm venture; or, from the other point of view, to join would be "to hide my impotency in the thick of a crowd."[48] What disturbed him about the enterprise was not the utopian agenda but simply the intermediate scale of the community. "Perhaps it is folly this scheming to bring the good & like minded together into families, into a colony," Emerson suggested in his journal for September 26, 1840, going on to use that metaphor for abrupt transformation, both magical and natural, that Frederic Henry Hedge had chosen earlier, and Thoreau would use after him: "Better that they should disperse and so leaven the whole lump of society."[49]

Nevertheless, the Fourierist structure, with its assertion of a form of collective identity, provided certain solutions and rewards that individ-

48. Emerson, *JMN*, 7: 408, entry for October 17, 1840.
49. Ibid., 7:401.

ualism could not achieve. Emerson himself gives negative evidence of its appeal when he claims in his "American Scholar" address:

> There is One Man,—present to all particular men only partially, or through one faculty; and . . . you must take the whole society to find the whole man. Man is not a farmer, or a professor, or an engineer, but he is all. Man is priest, and scholar, and statesman, and producer, and soldier. In the *divided* or social state, these functions are parcelled out to individuals, each of whom aims to do his stint of the joint work, whilst each other performs his. The fable implies that the individual to possess himself, must sometimes return from his own labor to embrace all the other laborers. But unfortunately, this original unit, this fountain of power, has been so distributed to multitudes, has been so minutely subdivided and peddled out, that it is spilled into drops, and cannot be gathered. The state of society is one in which the members have suffered amputation from the trunk, and strut about so many walking monsters,—a good finger, a neck, a stomach, an elbow, but never a man. Man is thus metamorphosed into a thing, into many things.[50]

There is a fusion here of the mythology of the noble savage, of the severed limbs of Dionysus, and of the Fall. Emerson is harking back to a prelapsarian golden age in which the adaptability of the *bricoleur* was not compromised by any tendency to swerve or approximate. This unified Man was not a manipulator of the cultural treasury because there wasn't one: he was an "original unit." He would therefore also have possessed the "autonomous, undismayed, calmly revolutionary" characteristics Santayana talks of, the ability to address the universe.[51] Then, like Humpty-Dumpty, Man takes a tumble and his original integrity is shattered into fragments. Not all the king's horses nor all the king's men are able to put him back together again. But, one might argue, Fourier can—at least to a degree.

Fourier's phalanx admirably accommodates fragmented man. It provides a place where the individual can "return from his own labor to embrace all the other laborers." Indeed, in an 1848 issue of the *Harbinger,* John Sullivan Dwight neatly translates Emerson's doctrine into Fourierese:

50. Ralph Waldo Emerson, "The American Scholar," in *NAL*, 53.
51. George Santayana, "The Genteel Tradition in American Philosophy," in *Winds of Change* (New York: Scribner's 1913), 196.

The human body is organized, its multitudinous members are united in an organic series of series of parts [*sic*], as the only means of securing the identity and unity of the person, of making the whole physical man at once subject to his one will, his force of character. In the same manner, we are members one of another, each in himself one distinct, complex organ of the Grand Man, which is Humanity. And Humanity as a whole can not fulfil its destiny, nor can each separate individual thereof *be himself*, except they enter into unitary and organic relations with each other and co-operate towards the general destiny, in which alone each individual destiny is found.[52]

It is worth noting, incidentally, that Emerson is a little vague on the subject of the identity of his original Man—the Grand Man, as Dwight was to call him. Emerson's notion of returning and embracing the other laborers suggests that he is actually picturing a small-scale community, a tribal one, perhaps, in which one could achieve a sense of collective endeavor and of a composite human identity running through the community. From this point of view the phalanx can be seen as the reestablishment and formalization of just such a community. But it does more than offer embracing space (though it offers *that* with more literalness than the Brook Farmers could ever acknowledge). It heals the wounds and reestablishes the integrity of the "original unit": it puts Humpty-Dumpty together again. The variety of occupations available provides the individual with the opportunity to fulfill so many different functions that he is no longer a mere member—in both senses of the word—but a complete person, or more nearly one than in civilization. Fourierism has an answer to Emerson's metaphor of dismemberment. Many kinds of work, we are told in *Social Destiny of Man*, lead to physical illnesses—to hernias, obesity, and so on—but this danger will be avoided by the short-term occupations of phalansterian life. We are then informed, almost in answer to Emerson's complaint, that the "health of man is promoted by this perpetual variety of functions, which exercising successively all faculties of the mind, maintains activity and equilibrium."[53] This argument is, of course, exactly the same one put forward by the Brook Farmers from the beginning of the community in their advocacy of a combination of mental and physical labor.

It is clear, then, that there is no contradiction between festival and

52. John Sullivan Dwight, "The Idea of a Divine Social Order," *Harbinger*, April 1, 1848, 170.
53. Brisbane, *Social Destiny*, 154.

industry, picnic and phalanx. The attraction of role-playing for the
Brook Farmers—whether in the form of masquerade or of manual labor—is obvious. A simple accumulation of diverse activity frees the individual from a fixed and arbitrary social function and enables him or
her to become more nearly a whole person. Moreover, the phalanx
integrates its members into a new unity, helps them to become what
Emerson so much wanted everyone to be: "One Man." After all, the
phalanx is a limited manifestation of that collective mind, a kind of
finite over-soul.

Perhaps from this point of view the Brook Farmers were not being
deceptive when they failed to acknowledge the fact of their conversion.
What Fourierism did was to give a formal basis to the assumptions on
which they had been working all along. We can see this process hap-
pening in a document from the early days of the new regime, a letter
written by Marianne Dwight, John Sullivan Dwight's sister, to another
brother, Frank:

> Now my business is as follows (but perhaps liable to frequent change):
> I wait on the breakfast table ($\frac{1}{4}$ hour), help M. A. Ripley clear away
> breakfast things, etc. ($1\frac{1}{2}$ hours), go into the dormitory group until
> eleven o'clock,—dress for dinner—then over to the Eyrie and sew till
> dinner time,—half past twelve. Then from half past one or two
> o'clock until $\frac{1}{4}$ past five, I teach drawing at Pilgrim Hall and sew in the
> Eyrie. At $\frac{1}{4}$ past five go down to the Hive, to help set the tea table, and
> afterwards I wash teacups, etc., till about $\frac{1}{2}$ past seven. Thus I make a
> long day of it, but alternation of work and pleasant company and
> chats make it pleasant. I am about entering a flower garden group
> and assisting Miss Russell in doing up muslins.[54]

The occupations described are the routine chores of housework, but
the precision of the times, the references to "groups," and above all the
praise of "alternation of work" identify the Fourierist structure that
gives meaning to Marianne Dwight's working day.

Fourierism had not been in operation long, and Marianne Dwight
herself was a very recent arrival at the community, so the fact that she
was assigned the conventional roles for her gender was hardly surprising. During the next three months she thought a great deal about "the

---

54. Marianne [Dwight] Orvis, *Letters from Brook Farm, 1844–1847*, ed. Amy L. Reed
(Poughkeepsie, N.Y.: Vassar College, 1928), 9, letter of April 14, 1844. Similar accounts
can be found in the letters of Elizabeth Curson, who was head of the dormitory group.
See "Elizabeth Curson's Letters from Brook Farm," ed. Stephen Garrison and Joel Myerson, *Resources for American Literary Study* 12 (Spring 1982): 1–28.

elevation of woman to independence, and an acknowledged equality with men," and began to foresee the opportunity of breaking free from the domestic round:

> Women must become producers of marketable articles; women must make money and earn their support independently of man. So we, with a little borrowed capital (say twenty-five or thirty dollars; by we, I mean a large part of the women here), have purchased materials, and made up in one week about forty-five dollars worth of elegant and tasteful caps, capes, collars, undersleeves, etc., etc.,—which we have sent in to Hutchinson and Holmes, who have agreed to take all we can make. . . . Of course, if we succeed (and we are determined we will), it will be very desirable for other ladies to come here on purpose to take a part in our fancy work; then our domestic work which now presses too heavily, will get more divided, and we shall each have less housework and more fancy work. By and by, when funds accumulate (!) we may start other branches of business, so that all our proceeds must be applied to the elevation of woman forever.[55]

Again, she does not move out of the traditional domain of women's work, except perhaps in her vision of "by and by," but the autonomy of the fancy work group and the significance she attaches to the division of labor, point to the secure framework for fulfillment that Fourierism has provided.[56]

We have seen how in the early days of the Farm Charles Anderson Dana contrived to combine the study of Greek with waiting on table. Fourierism gives a structural and economic basis to such quick changes of masquerade. The Brook Farm account book for May 1844 to April 1845 shows us that Dana's typical working month was divided up as follows: 10 days (of 10 hours each) 3 hours, agricultural; 1 day 7 hours, domestic; 6 days 9 hours, educational; 1 day 6¼ hours, miscellaneous; 2

---

55. Orvis, *Letters*, 32–33, letter of August 30, 1844.

56. Rebecca Codman records that the charm of work at Brook Farm "is accounted for partly upon the ground that in a great number of the occupations women were associated with men, in performing the labor." Slightly contradictorily, though, she claims a little later that "as a rule, the labors were divided between the Sexes much as is usual in ordinary Society." Her central point, however, is that the easier social relations between the sexes were a valuable feature of Brook Farm life: "At Brook Farm opportunities for knowing each other *thoroughly* were constantly afforded and the result was satisfactory in the highest degree." Moreover, she goes on to claim that Brook Farm during the Fourierist period achieved a "full recognition of the Equality of the Sexes," pointing out that a council of arbiters was established for dealing with complaints: "This Council was to consist of *Seven Persons, a majority of whom shall be women.*" "Rebecca Codman Butterfield's Reminiscences of Brook Farm," ed. Joel Myerson, *New England Quarterly* 65 (December 1992): 615, 607, 626.

days 8¾ hours, functional.[57] It is through such intricate bookkeeping that those spilled drops Emerson talked about are to be gathered again.

Codman explains that it was the responsibility of the heads of the groups to record the hours individuals spent in each occupation. The groups themselves were arranged in three series: agricultural, domestic, and mechanical. Despite Fourier's tendency to think in terms of the husbandry of flowers and fruit, there is no doubt that Brook Farm's conversion was partly motivated by a desire to encourage the development of the mechanical arts. In the Fourierist constitution the name of the association was changed from "The Brook Farm Institute of Agriculture and Education" to "The Brook-Farm Association for Industry and Education."[58]

Of course, given that the numbers involved were usually not much more than a sixteenth of the complement of a full-scale phalanx (120 members being about the maximum the farm ever comprised at one time), a certain amount of overlapping and improvising—of swerving—was necessary.[59] The farming serie, for example, was divided into the cattle, milking, ploughing, nursery, and planting groups. Milking, however, was separate from cattle only in times of abundance; the planting group mutated into a hoeing, weeding, or haying group according to season. The mechanical serie, meanwhile, consisted of groups of shoemakers, carpenters, sashmakers, and blindmakers, and the membership of these skilled teams stayed relatively fixed, though occasionally some of the teams would go off to work in the agricultural serie for a time. There were several freestanding groups, which had no serie to attach themselves to. According to Codman, these were the teachers' group, the miscellaneous group, the commercial agents, who bought and sold goods for the association, and the Sacred Legion.[60]

This last group has great significance in terms of the central Fourierist doctrine that attractions are proportional to destinies. Fourier was aware that his whole theoretical edifice could founder on one simple

---

57. Brook Farm Account Book, Houghton Library MsAm931f. Marianne Dwight's schedule for the same month was: 4 days 2 hours, mechanical; 19 days 3¾ hours, domestic; 4 days 3 hours, educational.

58. When the constitution was again revised in the spring of 1845, both its Fourierist allegiances and its need for a hard-nosed approach were further emphasized, as the community renamed itself "the Brook Farm Phalanx for the organization and pursuit of Industry, Commerce, and Education." "Constitution of the Brook Farm Phalanx," May 1, 1845, Massachusetts Historical Society.

59. Swift, *Brook Farm*, 118.

60. Codman, *Brook Farm*, 85–86.

conundrum: Who on earth is likely to be attracted to the task of disposing of sewage? This issue became a symbolically important one for Hawthorne, as he struggled with the fecal treasury of Brook Farm's barn. The answer Fourier came up with demonstrates the strange combination of shrewdness and naïveté that seems to run through so much of his thinking. Children were the one category of human being who were naturally drawn to filth and excrement. He calculated that two thirds of boys and one third of girls between nine and fifteen felt this attraction, and in addition tended to use filthy language and generally misbehave. These unfortunate tendencies could be directed toward a positive contribution to the well-being of the phalanx. Thus, he was able to coordinate a wasteful phase of human development with the waste products of the community and triumphantly vindicate the total economy of his theory—in Codman's words, match inclinations with "empty places." Fourier's name for these children was the Little Hordes, and he envisages their departure for work in the morning in terms that are frenzied to the point of being Bacchic: "The charge of the Little Hordes is sounded by a din of alarm bells, carillons, drums, trumpets, barking dogs, and mooing cows. Then the Hordes, led by their Khans and their Druids, rush forth with great cries, passing before the patriarchs, who sprinkle them with Holy Water. They gallop frenetically to labor."[61]

The sway of pragmatism over theory at Brook Farm dictated that the Sacred Legion was in fact composed of adults, with a higher wage than the common standard as compensation for doing unpleasant work.[62] Something of the mass enthusiasm that Fourier advocated is evident, however, in Marianne Dwight's account of the return from their labors of some of Brook Farm's young people: "Hearing a great hurrah, I have just been to the window, and lo! Martin and a group of boys returning from their work,—little Fourierites, with banners flying. I believe if they have been idle, the banners are not permitted to wave. The boys are really getting to enjoy their work, and these banners are a grand excitement." The structural ramifications of the Fourierist outlook are nicely revealed by her next thought: "Probably the fancy group will have to work them a very handsome one."[63]

The Brook Farmers were from the beginning concerned to reconcile bodily and mental labor, and we have seen how they attempted to chal-

---

61. Fourier, *Théorie de l'unité universelle*, 5:149, trans. in Beecher, *Charles Fourier*, 287.
62. See G. W. Cooke, *John Sullivan Dwight* (Boston: Small, Maynard, 1898), 125.
63. Orvis, *Letters*, 42, letter of September 19, 1844.

lenge class barriers by means of a process of "levelling up" at the least. As Terry Castle has pointed out, masquerade eliminated the distinction between upper and lower classes. But Fourier's law of groups and series provided a much more decisive challenge to social hierarchy because it followed the principle of seriality through to its logical extreme, where large and small explain each other and all phenomena can be broken down to the same basic shape. On a more mundane level, Fourierism brought to the community an increased engagement with the outside world, which took the form of attendance at conventions and lectures and, from 1845, the publication of the Fourierist newspaper the *Harbinger* at Brook Farm.

Internally there was a new emphasis on the practicalities of sound labor organization and a concentration on industrial productivity; both associated with an influx of artisans and their families. During 1844 sixty-seven new members joined the community, many more than had joined in any previous year, and most of them were manual and craft workers.[64] The signatories of the amended Fourierist constitution of 1844 were required to record their previous work. Of the forty-nine occupations listed, there were two clergymen, three teachers, one student (Charles Dana), one attorney-at-law, one clerk, and one broker. All the remaining previously employed members had been tradespeople, artisans, and laborers.[65] This social shift was obviously intended to increase the community's industrial productivity, and for a time it did

---

64. See Guarneri, *Utopian Alternative*, 58.

65. The material, in the possession of the Massachusetts Historical Society, is situated very confusingly in the bound MS of the Brook Farm records ("Constitution and Minutes of the Brook Farm Association, 1842–1847"), since it immediately follows the minutes of the discussion of the *next* edition of the constitution, which was to be formally incorporated during the course of 1845. These discussions began on December 22, 1844, when a committee was set up to draft the new constitution, and continued until March 6, 1845, when the amendments to the draft were approved. This covers pp. 123–28 of the MS book. The amended constitution of 1844 then immediately follows (129–34), and this is in turn followed by the signatures of those who signed up to that edition of the constitution (135–36). The signatures are dated from February 11, 1844 (these include the Ripleys and other stalwarts), through April 23, 1845. After this ten pages are blank, and then details are given of the 1845 constitution (145–55). The 1845 constitution was legally finalized in May 1845. It was more rigorously Fourieristic than its predecessor (the 1844 constitution refers to "the Brook Farm Association for Industry and Education" whereas the 1845 one calls it "the Brook Farm Phalanx"), and it had gone through the formal incorporation procedures of the Commonwealth of Massachusetts. The amended constitution of 1844 was signed by seventy-three members in all, forty-seven males and twenty-six females. Only six of the declared previous occupations were women's: all three teachers, plus two dressmakers and a tailoress. The most popular male occupations were shoemaker (8), farmer (5), carpenter (4, plus 2 cabinet makers), and printer (4).

indeed have that effect (Brook Farm made its first annual profit in 1844.)[66] The stress on artisanship had begun as early as 1843, with the arrival at the farm of Lewis Ryckman, a New York Fourierist who was a cordwainer by trade. He organized a shoemaking workshop, and after the conversion of the community, a sash and blind group was set up on similar lines, in addition to the fancy group described by Marianne Dwight, which itself subdivided in March 1845 to produce a separate group for painting fans and lampshades.[67] An influx of carpenters was given the task of erecting the community's new residential building, its own Phalanstery.

Fourier's plan for a phalanstery inevitably conforms to the serial structure that was discussed earlier in this chapter:[68]

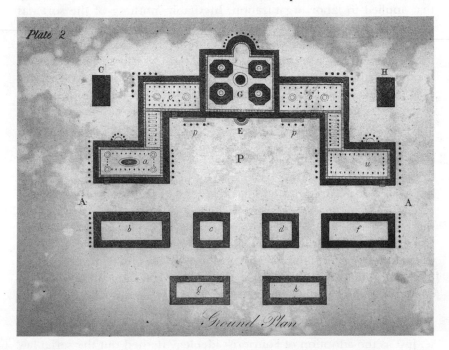

The Brook Farmers' willingness to compromise and improvise meant that this design was to be erected in stages, the initial phase being the construction of an oblong wooden building, though the intention was to add the two wings when it became financially possible to do so. The

66. Guarneri, *Utopian Alternative*, 58.
67. Rose, *Transcendentalism*, 169; Orvis, *Letters*, 32, 33, 71, 94, 102, 105, 168.
68. Brisbane, *Social Destiny*, plate 2, reproduced by permission of the John Rylands Manchester University Library.

building was to include "houses" that were distinct from one another, except that they were connected by corridors and were all under the same roof, and apartments which would be available for single people. In addition, there were to be communal rooms: parlors, a reading room, reception rooms, and a dining room, with adjoining kitchen and bakery. The idea was that there would no longer be separate buildings for different families and separate arrangements for families and single people. Instead, both variety and unity, those two Transcendental and Fourierist desiderata, would be available under one roof. "Thus," says Codman, "could privacy be maintained, and sociability increased."[69]

Fourier, of course, advocated sexual encounters on lines that conformed to the same principles of attraction, alternation, and variety that applied to labor organization. Inevitably, nothing of the sort was permitted at Brook Farm, though relations between young men and women were certainly more informal and less tense that in the outside world, as one can see from Marianne Dwight's letters. Carl Guarneri appositely sums up the prevailing atmosphere as depicted in Dwight's accounts of sentimental attachments, flirting, picnics, and parties: "Such casual contacts gave Brook Farm a coed campus atmosphere otherwise unavailable in America of the 1840s."[70] Nevertheless, despite the maintenance of a basic decorum, the notion that the days of the nuclear family were numbered may have been implicit in the very design of the Phalanstery. Certainly it is interesting to note that Charles Dana had to resort to a secret wedding with fellow community member Eunice Macdaniel, an event that caused some considerable resentment at the farm.[71] The only wedding that actually took place there—that of Marianne Dwight and John Orvis—happened at the end of 1846, by which time the community was obviously in terminal decline.[72] Certainly the building of the Phalanstery represented a commitment to communal living, which in turn—though there was to be qualitative and quantitative variation in the accommodation offered—embodied a desire for social solidarity and reconciliation, if not egalitarianism per se. Just as the adoption of Fourierist ideology fleshed out the serial law

69. Codman, *Brook Farm*, 114.
70. Guarneri, *Utopian Alternative*, 198; see 197–99 for an excellent general discussion of this issue.
71. See the letter from George Ripley to John Sullivan Dwight of March 19, 1846, in Zoltan Haraszti, *The Idyll of Brook Farm* (Boston: Boston Public Library, 1937), 38. The original is Boston Public Library MS E.4.1 no. 61. Dana's own explanation is given in a letter to Dwight of March 1, 1846, Boston Public Library MS E.4.1 no. 57.
72. Orvis, *Letters*, 195. Swift, *Brook Farm*, claims that fourteen marriages were ultimately traceable to friendships begun at Brook Farm (117).

that underlay Transcendentalism, and the influx of artisans contributed a productive momentum to Brook Farm's output, so the supple-
mentation of the scattered and improvised living arrangements by the
erection of the Phalanstery was intended to give an architectural endorsement to the principles of communal living.[73] All these developments had the effect of giving focus and substance to the principles
(and the poetry) underlying the community.

It is difficult to reconstruct the degree of tension that accompanied
the changes. Certainly there was some. The school provides an obvious
example. A couple of months after the conversion to Fourierism, on
April 4, 1844, Charles Dana stated the principles of the school in his
address to the General Convention of the Friends of Association in the
United States. He makes it quite clear that he is describing not a new
program but a policy that has been well established in the community,
and that therefore unites its two phases. Nevertheless, there is an evangelical edge to his utterance which is clearly intended to make a public
challenge. He affirms that every child, irrespective of social and financial background, is entitled to a complete education at Brook Farm.
Moreover, "it is not doled out to him as though he were a pupil of
orphan assylums [*sic*] and almshouses—not as the cold benefice and
bounty of the world—but as his right—a right conferred upon him by
the very fact that he is born into this world a human being—and here
we think we have made great advances."[74]

One can test the way such a stance might have gone down with a
more cautious Fourierist by looking at some interesting comments by
James Kay of Philadelphia, one of the farm's most important support-
ers and Ripley's business adviser. In a letter to J. S. Dwight written just
over a month after Dana's speech, on May 10, 1844, he offers some
proposals to aid the community in its fight for survival. He urges the
school to dismiss (among others) "those three or four" pupils who are
receiving board and education at half price.[75] The numbers may seem
insignificant, but it must be remembered that the older children could
work in exchange for their education anyway (and their contribution
probably represented a higher value in principle than in hard cash).

In point of fact, despite a note of panic in Kay's letter, this policy

---

73. The "large unitary edifice," as Ripley describes it, afforded "accommodations and
conveniences in the Combined Order." George Ripley, "Fire at Brook Farm," *Harbinger*,
March 14, 1846, 220, 221.
74. Charles Anderson Dana, "Address to the General Convention," *Phalanx*, April 20,
1844, 114.
75. James Kay to J. S. Dwight, May 10, 1846, in "Three Letters by James Kay Dealing with
Brook Farm," ed. Clarence Ghodes, *Philological Quarterly* 17 (October 1938): 383.

had been in operation, on a limited scale, since the early days of the community. In Chapter 2 I quoted the complaint of a certain Sophia Eastman regarding the aristocratic tendencies of a sector of the farm's population. It is clear from the tone of her letter that she does not fit in with the prevailing atmosphere of the community, and it comes as no surprise, four months later, in November 1843, to find Ripley writing to her father, Phinehas Eastman, recommending that she be withdrawn from the school. Ripley points out that "she is not the kind of person contemplated in our plan of admitting a few pupils to defray their expenses by their services."[76] But as important as the evidence this interchange provides of social unease is the fact that it establishes that such an arrangement was part of pre-Fourierist policy at the farm. By the following year the "plan" is now part of a public platform. Kay sees the assistance provided as blind defiance of the rules of success ("No business in civilization could stand such a drain"). His real concern becomes evident, however, when he turns to a rather different question:

> I have one more remark to make, & that is, respecting the presence of impure children. My views, I know, are well understood; but I must claim the privilege of friendship to insist on them—if you will, "in season & out of season." Little importance as you attach to them, I am a true prophet when I say, that indifference or contumacy in this matter will break you down, if all other conditions were excellent. You cannot know how much harm has been done to you from this cause already; nor do you seem to be aware that the public are perhaps overwell informed on the subject in Massachusetts; and strange as it may seem, more than a few here are better informed than they are willing to say. I know not where or from whom they procured their knowledge nor whether it is of truth; but the story is here. I say that this enormous evil ought to be abated.[77]

The tone here is that of someone with an axe to grind—a couple of axes, in point of fact. Kay combines the alarm of a man whose son is being allowed to hobnob with undesirables and the testiness of one whose previous advice has been ignored. But even taking these two provocations into account, his expression still seems unduly violent,

76. Letter of November 24, 1843, Abernathy Library, Middlebury College, Middlebury, Vt., quoted in Henry W. Sams, ed., *Autobiography of Brook Farm* (Englewood Cliffs, N.J.: Prentice-Hall, 1958), 85.
77. Kay, "Three Letters," 383.

and testifies to the amount of popular hostility, in this and other respects, that the community must have been facing. His mention of im-
purity, of "enormous evil," his setting himself up as a "true prophet,"
implies that much more than economic efficiency, mere success, is at
stake. His language is that of someone unable to cope with the prospect of radical social change, who views association from a certain aesthetic distance. In an earlier letter he expresses his admiration of the
new Fourierist constitution, "the beautiful structure which you have
erected." He goes on to claim, with a revealing choice of words, that "if
it were simply a literary exercise, it would win universal applause for its
author."[78] We get the picture of a dilettante at bay. Ironically, given that
the pre-Fourierist phase of the community is sometimes seen as a period of undoctrinaire joie de vivre, what Kay sounds like is a picnicking
Fourierist. But Kay was a valetudinarian publisher residing in Philadelphia. He visited regularly but was not one of the members of the
community, who were made of sterner stuff, as Dana's robust assertion
reveals. Amelia Russell, also writing of the school, suggests the amount
of opprobrium that the community had to put up with: "People were
shy of us; we were supposed to nourish some very fantastic views which
encroached much on the decencies of society. I will not enumerate all
the absurd stories which were circulated with regard to us." Obviously
unacquainted with Kay's correspondence, she goes on to claim that
"our outside friends, who still continued to feel an interest in us, paid
no heed to these ridiculous inventions"; nevertheless, "there were thou-
sands who looked upon us as little less than heathens who had returned to a state of semi-barbarism."[79] The conjunction of a more mili-
tant approach and the kind of rumor that Fourier's sexual theories
inevitably gave rise to undoubtedly brought about an uneasy atmosphere in the school.

And the influx of mechanics brought about other, related difficulties. If the memory of Arthur Sumner, who was about sixteen at the
time, is to be trusted, the internecine social conflict that resulted rose
to a fairly serious level for a while. "Soon after this Fourierist agitation

---

78. Ibid., 379, letter of March 14, 1845.
79. Russell, "Home Life," 464. It is clear that the Brook Farmers had to endure a considerable amount of hostility as a result of their adoption of a Fourierist constitution. John
Van Der Zee Sears claims that "there was bitter feeling against us among the old Puritans
of Roxbury. They hated us and took occasion to annoy us and injure us in many mean
ways" (*My Friends at Brook Farm*, 169 [New York: Desmond Fitzgerald, 1912]). Codman
mentions the press campaigns that were conducted against the community, usually on
the grounds that Fourierism threatened the sanctity of marriage, which indeed it did,
though not at Brook Farm (*Brook Farm*, 204).

began," he recalls, "some very unpleasant people appeared on the scene. They seemed to us boys to be discontented mechanics. They soon fell into a group by themselves. After dinner, they would collect together in the great barn, and grumble; and when the others passed through, the malcontents eyed them with suspicion, and muttered 'Aristocrats!' All because they knew themselves to be less cultivated and well-bred." As in the case of Ora Gannet Sedgwick describing the Madonna-like cook, Sumner has a knack for demonstrating the very assumptions and perspectives that underlie the problem he is describing. He adds innocently, "Yet there was the kindest feeling of brotherhood among the members; and it did not need that a man should be a scholar and a gentleman to be received and absorbed."[80]

An equally elitist but slightly more generous perspective is apparent in a letter by Marianne Dwight to her friend Anna Q. T. Parsons. She is describing the wife of the man at the center of the community's social unrest, the carpenter W. H. Cheswell, and Dwight's verdict on Mrs. Cheswell, who was pregnant at the time, gives one the sense that considerable water has flowed under the bridge: "We have noble spirits here at Brook Farm. I have been much affected lately, by the noble devotedness of our good Mrs. Cheswell. This coarse woman, as I once thought her, and as she was, is really becoming very charming—a most zealous and untiring worker, full of nobleness and enthusiasm in a good cause, sweet and cheerful too, so that it does one good to look upon her. In her, we see what Association is going to do for the uneducated and rude."[81] What we have here is in fact an attempt to reverse Rousseau's doctrine of the noble savage. The picture is of someone coming to the community in a state of nature, "uneducated and rude," but with coarseness as the attendant characteristic. Mrs. Cheswell has had to go through a process of refinement until nobility (mentioned three times in as many sentences) can finally be achieved. Inescapably, the attitude remains one of paternalistic manipulation in the service of bourgeois ideals.

Fourierism was not a magic wand. Some of the conflicts that followed the transition were class-based, and there is evidence that the doctrine of leveling *up* continued to hold sway. Nevertheless, it is also true that Fourierism provided a structure that could cut across traditional hierarchies. The carpenters List and Reynolds, like Cheswell, were involved in a dispute with their work team and "were unanimously

80. Arthur Sumner, "A Boy's Recollections of Brook Farm," *New England Magazine*, n.s. 10 (May 1894): 310.
81. Orvis, *Letters*, 104, letter of "Summer 1845."

dispelled from the carpenters' group in consequence of being discordant elements,—so they went to the general direction requesting to be furnished with work, and that body have set them to work upon the frame of the Phalanstery,—so they are working right in the midst of the group, but not of the group, doing just what they are told to do,— a sort of solitary labor and imprisonment."[82] Here we have not a vertical stratification between classes but lateral banishment: and implicit within that the possibility and goal of a lateral structure of harmony, a way of binding people together through what they do, what they are, and above all what they want to be—a form of human solidarity that, however tainted by the remnants of class structure, represents both the Transcendentalist and Fourierist vision of the world as it should be.

82. Ibid., 40–41, letter of September 19, 1844.

4

Brook Farm as Sacrifice

I t is not difficult to see how Fourier's law of groups and series could be superimposed on the serial perspective of the Transcendentalists. As masquerade was supplemented by phalanx, the effect would have been no more extreme or contradictory than a swift sharpening of focus. Nevertheless, this process has to be retrospectively reconstructed because, during the transitional period, the leading thinkers of the Brook Farm community showed no more desire than before to shed light on their developing mental processes. Just as they had failed to issue resonant manifestos when they founded the community, and left no nostalgic apologias in later life, Ripley and the other leading members were disappointingly reticent in midcareer as well. Despite the claim in the introduction to their new constitution that it was time they shared the "results of their studies and experience" with the public at large, the Brook Farmers reveal little about how Fourierism accommodated itself to their worldview or how it affected the daily life of the community. Of the hundreds of articles that appeared in the *Harbinger*, the Fourierist journal published by the community every week from June 1845 to June 1847, only two give a direct account of Brook Farm itself, and they concern the calamitous destruction by fire of the newly completed Phalanstery in 1846.[1]

1. George Ripley, "Fire at Brook Farm," *Harbinger*, March 14, 1846, 220–22; idem, "To Our Friends," *Harbinger*, March 21, 1846, 237–38. In the first of these articles Ripley seems apologetic for broaching the matter in the first place: "We shall be pardoned for entering into these almost personal details, for we know that the numerous friends of Association, in every part of our land, will feel our misfortune, as if it were a private grief of their own" (221).

This policy of omission is a deliberate one, however, and testifies not to any halfheartedness but, on the contrary, to the depth of the institution's commitment to Fourierism and to the cause of association generally. The journal is devoted to all the "socialisms" then prevalent, its articles and reviews covering the whole gamut of social wrongs and reforming possibilities.[2] In the first volume alone there are articles on capital punishment, the abandonment of children in Boston, prisons and the rehabilitation of criminals, the influence of machinery, the encroachment of capital on labor, the superiority of justice to charity, living conditions in Lowell, the advantages of a short workday, slavery, the Working Men's Association, wrongs against women, and many other causes. Ripley explains the editorial position in the third issue: "We trust that our brothers of the different Associations in the United States will not regard the Harbinger as the exclusive organ of the Brook Farm Phalanx. Although issued from its press, it is intended that it should represent, as far as possible, the interests of the general movement which is now spreading with such encouraging progress throughout the land."[3]

Roland Barthes has offered some illuminating remarks on the subject of utopian reticence—or rather of utopian reticence in conjunction with utopian garrulity—in his discussion of the writings of Fourier. He proposes the term "counter-paralapse" to describe the avoidance of subject in the vast acreage of the philosopher's works. Paralapse is a rhetorical strategy that involves spelling out what it is one is not going to spell out: as Barthes succinctly puts it, *"I shall not speak of . . .* followed by three pages." Its opposite, "Fourier's counter-march," "obviously translates the neurotic fear of failure," demonstrating "the vacuum of language: caught in the toils of the meta-book, his book is *without subject*: its signified is dilatory, incessantly withdrawn further away: only the signifier remains, stretching out of sight, *in the book's future.*"[4]

Certainly this analysis meshes with what we know of Fourier's testiness with his followers and his unwillingness to allow experiments in his social arrangements to be undertaken in his lifetime. But, on the face of it, the argument would not seem to apply to the leaders of Brook Farm. How can they be accused of counter-paralapse when they are actually running a community? And yet, the *Harbinger* material re-

2. The plural form of "socialism" is used in the title of John Humphrey Noyes's important *History of American Socialisms* (Philadelphia: J. B. Lippincott, 1870). Virtually the only light relief for readers of the *Harbinger* was a translation of George Sand's *Consuelo*, running as an almost interminable serial.

3. "To Our Friends in Association," *Harbinger*, June 28, 1845, 47.

4. Roland Barthes, *Sade/Fourier/Loyola*, trans. Richard Miller (New York: Hill and Wang, 1976), 90.

Brook Farm as pictured in John Codman's *Memoirs* (1894).

Photograph of the Fruitlands farmhouse in Clara Endicott Sears, *Bronson Alcott's Fruitlands* (1915).

Sophia Thoreau's drawing of her brother's hut, used on the title page of *Walden*.

mains as a meta-book in Barthes's sense, a book about a book, stretching away both geographically, into other regions and activities, and temporally, into a better future. It skirts its true text, which is the community itself. In his article "The Commencement of Association," Ripley describes Fourier's refusal to conduct a partial experiment and then goes on to say that, by contrast, "without waiting for this gradual preparation, a chosen band of men and women have commenced the work of Association in different parts of the United States." The explanation he gives is significant: "They have entered this field of labor, under the influence of an impulse, which was sacred to them as the voice of God." The notion of a sacred impulse catches exactly the paradoxical combination of spontaneity and pattern that is intrinsic to utopian development. But Ripley makes a sharp distinction between the ultimate utopian destination and these efforts to reach it: "No doubt rests on their prospect of ultimate success. . . . But they are engaged in a work which all cannot share. They are not living in Association, but preparing a true and happy life for those who shall come after them. . . . They are laboring, with toil surely, and often perhaps, in tears, amid the dust, and confusion, and discomfort of a new structure; but others will rejoice in the free and spacious halls, whose glittering pinnacles will hereafter salute the skies."[5]

Perhaps this problem always exists with utopia: semantically speaking, it simply cannot be here and now. One recalls Emerson's comment in "Circles" about the "Unattainable, the flying Perfect." Every circle is enclosed by a bigger one, and at every point in the system we are aware of the "series and procession" that takes us onward and out of sight. For Ripley as member of the Transcendental Club, Brook Farm itself was the book; for Ripley as Brook Farmer, the book became the American Fourierist movement as a whole. After the burning down of the Phalanstery, Ripley made some revealing remarks in the *Harbinger* in his introduction to a letter expressing sympathy for the Brook Farmers:

> We do not altogether agree with the writer, in the importance which he attaches to the special movement at Brook Farm. . . . We have never attempted anything more than to prepare the way for Association, by demonstrating some of the leading ideas on which the theory is founded; in this we have had the most gratifying success, but we have always regarded ourselves only as humble pioneers in a work, which would be carried on by others to its magnificent consummation, and we have been content to wait and toil, for the development of the cause and the completion of our hope.[6]

If that magnificent consummation had been achieved, the next book would no doubt have been a mystical one, concerning itself with those celestial harmonies described in the passages from Brisbane and Dwight quoted in the preceding chapter. The nearest Ripley came to writing *that* book was in the scribbled account he left of his dream.

In effect, then, this tendency to avoid the issue, so to speak, by writing a different book from the one we, as members of a later generation, would most like to read provides a negative connection between

5. George Ripley, "The Commencement of Association," *Harbinger*, August 16, 1845, 159–60.
6. George Ripley in *Harbinger*, March 21, 1846, 237–38.

Transcendentalism and Fourierism to add to the positive ones I have been discussing. There are other negative connections arising out of the gulf between nature and history. The first of these is the problem of wasted time. If nature is a patterned and harmonious structure, and if the law on which it is based runs through the universe, why has human history been so erratic, and human society so often lurched into barbarism and futility? On the one hand, we have "plant, qua-druped, bird, / By one music enchanted," while on the other man "crouches and blushes, / Absconds and conceals." Hawthorne, con-sciously or unconsciously, made himself into a living metaphor of the problem when he described himself so repeatedly in the *Notebooks* shov-eling manure in those early days of the Brook Farm utopia. How can the brave, clean lines of a new order emerge from the excremental treasury of the past? How can one talk, as Fourier and Brisbane do, of "the normal organization of society," based on "the eternal laws of na-ture," when this normalization has never actually been achieved?[7]

At the outset of his book *Millennium and Utopia*, Ernest Lee Tuveson discusses the need all utopians feel for a detectable pattern in history. Indeed, he makes the point that the word *history* itself has come to include the notion of progress. He quotes John B. Bury's claim that only "when facts and events cease to be unconnected, when they ap-pear to us to be linked together according to some design or purpose, leading us back to some originating cause or forward to some destined end, can we speak of history in the sense which the word has acquired in modern language." Tuveson continues: "Every event in human his-tory . . . has had its 'place' in a series of ascending 'epochs,' extending from barbarism to a future utopian state of harmony and happiness which, though dimly seen, may not be far off. Even if the advancement has not been entirely unbroken—even if progress is 'spiral'—there is still a forward drift in history which eventually carries temporary obsta-cles before it."[8]

As I have noted, Frederic Henry Hedge points to a solution to this problem with his notion of pulsations. In fact, both Transcendentalism and Fourierism are prepared to take a more complex view of the mat-ter of historical progress than Tuveson himself does at this point. Tuveson concedes the possibility of periods of stasis, when the evolu-tionary climb goes into a spiral until (and it is his own implicit meta-phor that switches) pressure is built up, like a river in spate, and the

7. Charles Fourier, *Le nouveau monde industriel at societaire* (1829; rpt. Paris: Flammarion, 1973), 28; *Albert Brisbane, A Mental Biography*, ed. Redelia Brisbane (Boston: Arena, 1893), 184.
8. Ernest Lee Tuveson, *Millennium and Utopia: A Study in the Background of the Idea of Progress* (Gloucester, Mass.: Peter Smith, 1972), 2.

impeding detritus is forced forward. Meanwhile, the Transcendentalists and the Fourierists—and the Transcendental Fourierists—incorporate collapse or regress into the very fabric of their models.

We have seen that Fourier's series operate in time as well as in space. This structure, and its specific historiographic consequences, establish Fourier as just the sort of "philosophic historian" that Hedge, in John the Baptist mood, awaited: one who was able to "trace and exhibit" the process's "successive impulses" and thereby "furnish a systematic history of Man." Human history has consisted of four of these temporal series so far: the savage, patriarchal, barbarian, and civilized. The movement of the fourth, civilization, can be tabulated thus:[9]

TABLE OF THE MOVEMENT OF CIVILIZATION, WITH ITS FOUR AGES OR PHASES.

FIRST AGE. *Infancy.*
Exclusive marriage or Monogamy.
Feudality of the Nobles.

ASCENDING MOVEMENT.

PIVOT: CIVIL RIGHTS OF THE WIFE.
Federation of the Great Barons.
Illusions in chivalry.

SECOND AGE. *Growth.*
Privileges of free Towns and Cities.
Cultivation of the Arts and Sciences.

PIVOT: ENFRANCHISEMENT OF THE SERFS OR LABORING CLASSES.
Representative System.
Illusions in Liberty or Democratic Agitations.

MATURITY: { EXPERIMENTAL CHEMISTRY: ART OF NAVIGATION.
NATIONAL LOANS: CLEARING OF FORESTS WITHOUT EXCESSES.

THIRD AGE. *Decline.*
Commercial and Fiscal spirit.
Stock companies.

DESCENDING MOVEMENT.

PIVOT: MARATIME MONOPOLY.
Anarchical Commerce.
Financial Illusions.

FOURTH AGE. *Decrepitude.*
Agricultural Loaning Companies.
Associated Farms; discipline system of cultivation.

PIVOT: COMMERCIAL AND INDUSTRIAL FEUDALITY.
Contractors of Feudal Monopoly: Oligarchy of Capital.
Illusions in Association.

9. Albert Brisbane, *Social Destiny of Man; or, Association and Reorganization of Industry* (Philadelphia: C. F. Stollmeyer, 1840), 284.

This scheme may be a prime example of history as the interconnectedness of "facts and events," but it is not, confusingly, a blueprint for "progress," at least not in the usual meaning of the term. Indeed, Fourierism is scathing about the whole concept. A little earlier in *Social Destiny of Man*, reference is made to

> the numerous philosophical theories which have appeared in support of the principle of *continued progress* in history; theories which endeavor to prove that the troubled career of mankind has been one of necessity, and even of wisdom; that all the great events which have taken place were subservient to this law of progress, that they could not have happened at any other epoch, nor in any other manner; that the sufferings and wars of the human race, the rises and downfalls of nations, have contributed to this progressive movement, and that they are links in a Serie through which man must pass to attain to his Destiny.

But the theories are not true: "We cannot consider the history of the past a regular and necessary progress, marked out by Providence, without attributing to the Deity the errors of the human race." By contrast, Brisbane tells us, Fourier "followed an entirely different rout [*sic*]; he laid down the principle of absolute doubt of pre-existing theories, and proceeded on the ground of a systematic deviation from civilized and other social systems."[10] The question that immediately arises is how to reconcile a principle of "systematic deviation" with Fourierism's penchant for historical charting, for making maps of time, for insistent and detailed teleology.

The solution can be found in the specific structure of the serial unit. The temporal serie has the same ascending-descending configuration as any other serie. This gives it what we might term organic form, a beginning, a middle, and an end: serie follows serie as generation follows generation. Thus, history is not a simple success story, a matter of the (cultural) survival of the (spiritually) fittest. Instead, new stages of human development arise like the phoenix out of the collapse of the old. Fourierism's fabric is based on discrete but repetitively composed units, and as a result it can have successiveness without continuity, amelioration without progress: to use Fourier's phrase, systematic deviation. The structure of the serie is admirably suited to recording the successive "pulsations" of the human mind, that "Eterne alternation" celebrated by the poet in Emerson's "The Sphinx," while at the same time providing a satisfactory explanation of the present state of society.

10. Ibid., 199–201.

What we have is an essentially Neoplatonic model, whereby interstices appear within the historical continuum which allow the normal—that is to say, the ideal—laws of human society to make their staged (or serial) appearances. To revert to Santayana's analysis of the opposing perspectives implicit in Transcendentalism, it is as though most of the time the human race looks at its institutions as structures that persist within the medium of history, but at intervals is persuaded to look through this fabric into an ahistorical world where institutions are ordered according to the law of nature. Once again, Emerson is able to evoke this process beautifully and memorably: "The landscapes, the figures, Boston, London, are facts as fugitive as any institution past, or any whiff of mist or smoke, and so is society, and so is the world. The soul looketh steadily forwards, creating a world before her, leaving worlds behind her."[11] Karl Mannheim invokes the concept of *kairos* to define further this kind of transforming episode: "In Greek mythology Kairos is the God of Opportunity—the genius of the decisive moment." He goes on to quote Paul Tillich's definition of the Christianized version of the concept: "Kairos is fulfilled time, the moment of time which is invaded by eternity. But Kairos is not perfection or completion in time."[12] We are, as it happens, in a period of decline; but for that very reason we are able to look forward to a more glorious future.[13] And Fourier provides a means whereby the eternal truths of nature and the temporal development of society can be reconciled.

So though it is true that Fourier's scheme is not progressive in the usual sense of the word, it does share with Hedge's punctuationism and the spiraling evolutionism described by Tuveson an overall purposiveness, despite the waste that history generates. There is a pattern that will finally become evident, a great plan that will ultimately be fulfilled. And this brings us to the second negative connection between Transcendentalism and Fourierism, the problem of determinism. As Tuveson goes on to say: "The great plan which works itself out through the historical process, and not through the will and reason of individ-

11. Ralph Waldo Emerson, "The Over-Soul," in *Essays 1*, 163.

12. Karl Mannheim, *Ideology and Utopia* (London: Routledge and Kegan Paul, 1936), 198, quoting Paul Tillich, *The Religious Situation*, trans. H. R. Niebuhr (New York: H. Holt, 1932), 138–39.

13. Although by the same token we can look even further ahead to ultimate chaos. In his "Tableau du cours de mouvement social," Fourier follows the whole Order of Creations from "Enfance ou incohérence ascendante" through the "Apogée du bonheur," which lasts eight thousand years, into the "Vibration descendante," which culminates in the "Fin du monde animal et végétal, après une durée approximative de . . . 80,000 ans." Charles Fourier, *Théorie des quatres mouvements*, in *Oeuvres complètes de Charles Fourier*, 12 vols. (Paris: Editions Anthropos, 1966–68), 1: facing 32.

ual men, is the explanation for events; individual human beings merely play their parts in the great plot."[14]

The determinism implicit in a patterned and teleological version of the meta-historical process (that is, the process that includes both historical development and the serial input of natural law) could not have been easy for Transcendentalists to swallow, brought up as they typically were on a Unitarianism which, however dry and inconsistent it may have been, represented a reaction against Calvinism and embodied certain Enlightenment values. It taught a respect for the powers of the human mind, for the ability to choose between good and evil and the right to select one's own destiny. The Transcendentalists had in fact emphasized these very features, diminishing the power of authority in favor of a doctrine of personal responsibility. And yet it is very difficult to combine a belief in the possibility of moral choice with a doctrine of the approaching social millennium. Since the human race is proceeding inevitably, if not necessarily on a direct route, toward a heaven on earth, then surely by taking one's own contribution seriously one is participating in the youthful error of Holgrave in Hawthorne's *House of the Seven Gables* "in fancying that it mattered anything to the great end in view, whether he himself should contend for it or against it."[15] What is the point of taking to heart Theodore Parker's passionate injunctions to live a divine life? Surely we humans are simply tools in the hands of Providence, without free will of our own?

As usual, Emerson is a good representative of Transcendentalist ambivalence on this subject. "The Over-Soul" provides an example of the paradoxical nature of the individual's status. Here we find that human beings possess enough independence of will to be able to "forsake their native nobleness" in "habitual and mean service to the world." At the same time, however, we are told that the facts of human nature, intractable though they may appear, will finally give way before our true destiny. We can be optimistic because "the argument which is always forthcoming to silence those who conceive extraordinary hopes of man, namely the appeal to experience, is for ever invalid and vain. We give up the past to the objector, and yet we hope." Despite everything—ourselves included—we have access to a higher life, the over-soul: "By virtue of this inevitable nature, private will is overpowered, and maugre our efforts or our imperfections, your genius will speak from you, and mine from me. That which we are, we shall teach, not

14. Tuveson, *Millennium and Utopia*, 2.
15. Nathaniel Hawthorne, *The House of the Seven Gables*, in *Centenary Edition*, 10:180.

voluntarily but involuntarily. Thoughts came into our minds by avenues which we never left open, and thoughts go out of our minds through avenues which we never voluntarily opened."[16] Emerson offers a sort of inverted fatalism: we are all part of the "eternal ONE" whether we like it or not.

Fourierism, of course, shares this belief in the irresistibleness of good. According to the "Table of the Movement of Civilization" we are now in the third age, rapidly approaching the fourth. The new age will dawn because the businessmen and speculators, unphilanthropic though they may be, will begin to find that association is the most profitable social form. After a period of misguided experimentation (Robert Owen's work at New Harmony, if not the more successful attempt at New Lanark, suggests an example), they will introduce the new order. But the question that then arises is: What of Fourier's own position in this process? What is the point of being the discoverer or inventor of the utopian pattern if that pattern has an objective existence within reality and will come into being as an inevitable result, or at least as an inevitable by-product, of historical developments?

It is intriguing to watch Fourier himself explore this issue, in a document Brisbane did not translate, and which was not published in France until 1848, when it appeared in *La Phalange*, a publication dedicated to printing Fourier's uncollected manuscripts. The piece, which internal evidence suggests was written in the 1820s, is called "Le sphinx sans Oedipe, ou l'énigme des *Quatre mouvements*." What is uncanny about this document is the way in which the myth of Oedipus and the Sphinx, along with the figure of Harlequin, relate to the imagery used by Emerson and Hawthorne, which I have already discussed.[17]

The occasion for the piece is Fourier's indignation at the public's failure to respond appreciatively to the appearance in 1808 of his *Théorie des quatres mouvements et des destinées générales; prospectus et annonce de la découverte*.[18] The French, he tells us, though skilled at unraveling the riddles of children and at interpreting charades and solving anagrams, were stumped by the strangeness of that particular work (which he calls "un livre bizarre"—in accordance with his picture of himself as

16. Emerson, "The Over-Soul," 278, 267, 286.
17. Charles Fourier, "Le sphinx sans Oedipe, ou l'énigme des *Quatres mouvements*," *Phalange* 9 (1849): 193–206. This piece receives a brief but characteristically perceptive (and amusing) discussion in Frank E. Manuel, *The Prophets of Paris* (Cambridge: Harvard University Press, 1962), 244–45.
18. Charles Fourier, *Théorie des quatres mouvements et des destinées générales; prospectus et annonce de la découvert* (Leipzig, 1808). The place of publication was actually Lyons, but was given as Leipzig to avoid censorship.

the discoverer of the theory rather than its deviser, he uses the indefinite article, as though he just happened to come across the book). In point of fact, though, Fourier knew all along that his work would be scorned, and took appropriate action from the start:

> I kitted myself out in fancy-dress to test the lie of the land. I chose the best-known disguise, that of Harlequin. I made a book out of patchwork: bizarre, a medley of colors and tones. Some people said to me, on the subject of this book, "You have passages of great power, then all of a sudden you fall to the depths." Yes, according to the material with which I was dealing; when I dared to speak frankly, I was very grave, very formal. When the discussion became tricky, on the subject of marriage, for example, I fell away on purpose, I hid myself under a mask of lewdness, of affected paradoxes, in short I imitated Harlequin's costume which changes all of a sudden from red to gray, from yellow to blue.[19]

Already we can see a distinction between formality and patchwork, a curious counterpoint between the universality of truth and the particularity of disguise, the monad and its masks. True, Fourier's argument at this point appears to be a purely pragmatic one: he has put on Harlequin's costume because its capacity for abrupt changes will allow him to slip from the clutches of a disapproving and uncomprehending reader. But this procedure is not just strategic: it reflects the actual nature of genius. It calls to mind the abrupt shifts of labor allowed for in phalansterian life; and, perhaps even more significantly, it brings to mind Codman's pun-pendulum that "swings from torrid to frigid zone quicker than a telegram goes."[20] We find on the next page of Fourier's piece that masquerade, far from being simply the cloak of discovery, is intrinsic to the procedure by which discovery is made: "One knows that bizarre and original spirits have the ability to discover what wise men have missed and that where discoveries are concerned there are more resources and means in a bizarre head than in those of twenty academics who have become fossilized in their method, and who can only follow familiar paths without ever conceiving a bold and felicitous idea. It was therefore a matter of complete indifference to me that my pros-

---

19. Fourier, "Le sphinx," 194. All translations from "Le sphinx" are my own.
20. John Thomas Codman, *Brook Farm: Historic and Personal Memoirs* (Boston: Arena, 1894), 176.

pectus lacked method, since one sees by that the unmistakable signs [*indices péremptoires*] of a great discovery."[21]

Fourier's twenty fossilized academics no doubt have something in common with Hawthorne's "respectable old blockheads, who still, in this intangibility and mistiness of affairs, kept a death-grip on one or two ideas which had not come into vogue since yesterday-morning," and who therefore provide Coverdale with a holiday from the whirligig of utopian masquerade. By contrast, Fourier's phrase "indices péremptoires," which cannot be effectively translated, beautifully conveys that immediate vision of deep structure, that combination of the frolic and the architectural, which Emerson described in "The Snow-Storm."

Fourier's Sphinx, again like Emerson's, is not the equivocal and equivocating beast of Greek tradition but the principle of unity itself. Fourier is at pains to emphasize the structural integrity of the system he has discovered; but he also informs us over and over again, with a peculiar combination of sneering and self-pity, that only fragmentary glimpses are available to the onlooker. This insistence, coupled with his persecution complex, leads him close to paradox. On the one hand, his system of unity must itself have unity or it is nullified. To be asked to mutilate it in order to accommodate the petty-mindedness of his contemporaries would be like asking Praxiteles to mutilate his Venus: "Take up your chisel and with great blows knock off a leg, break off an arm, poke out an eye, cut off an ear, to make it suitable for the intelligentsia." This, Fourier claims, is what it would amount to if he heeded the behest of his century, which has asked him to break up his theory of attraction, deleting love and tacking on marriage and lies instead. On the other hand, though, his presentation of that theory apparently involves just such manipulation and subterfuge. His truth, he tells us, is like a pearl embedded in the mud. His strategy, he gloats, resembles a trick of the confessional: slipping a big sin in among a lot of little ones to escort it through.[22]

In short, because he will not fragment his discovery, he presents it in fragments. There is a valid strategic distinction here between bowdlerizing a text and publishing it piecemeal. But the dangerous proximity of Fourier's alternatives makes one wonder if at bottom Harlequin simply finds it irresistible to niggle away at the strange doubleness of unity in multiplicity. One can afford to be diverse and patchwork if one has absolute confidence in the unity that underlies variety. Emerson's

21. Fourier, "Le sphinx," 195.
22. Fourier, "Le sphinx," 200, 202.

Oedipus and his Sphinx became one, uniting the multiplicity of perception with a deep harmony. This union is achieved because the Oedipus of the poem happens to be a poet himself, one of those who can turn "the world to glass" and show us "all things in their right series and procession"—and is, therefore, ultimately able to perceive the Sphinx's monad(nock)-like unity beneath her masks.

Fourier's Oedipus, too, is a mediator, a visionary—is, in short, Fourier himself. But in this case he has dressed up as Harlequin in order to keep an unappreciative world at a distance from the Sphinx. In Barthes's terms, out of fear of failure he has adopted the technique of counter-paralapse, as the consequence of which his book's signified is "incessantly drawn further away" and "only the signifier remains, stretching out of sight, *in the book's future.*" It is Fourier as Harlequin who writes that book, explicitly out of a perception that his text will thus accommodate itself to the dilatoriness of civilization, but perhaps also out of an instinctive sense that the written word may thereby more adequately mime the procedures of nature. In this respect his book itself becomes a masquerade, and Fourier, the self-appointed master of ceremonies, only too aptly fulfills Zenobia's requirement of a steersman conforming to the configurations of Chaos. Unity and diversity, pattern and process, the absolute and the contingent are all simultaneously available in his text, achieving what Foucault calls an "empirico-transcendental doublet."[23] The text establishes unity of law together with great diversity of phenomena; a universal dame being mediated thorough a thousand voices; the spontaneous discovery of a frolic architecture and its slow mimicry, "stone by stone, / Built in an age." "Le sphinx sans Oedipe," in short, establishes the integrity of serial law in the subjective domain of Fourier's consciousness and its painful unfolding in the objective world of history. The bitterness and hysteria everywhere evident in the text testify to the appalling difficulties that attached to the task of establishing a bridge between the world of nature and of natural law, visualized as eternal and Edenic, and that of history, perceived as dynamic and inconclusive.

Ironically, the Brook Farmers were spared some of the existential anguish experienced by Fourier in this short work. Although, as Transcendentalists, they faced parallel problems, in the second half of their community's history they acquired one advantage that Fourier lacked: Fourier himself. They did not have to face the painful task of reconciling revelation and myth because their revelation was at secondhand—

23. Michel Foucault, *The Order of Things* (London: Tavistock, 1970), 318.

was, in effect, the revelation of a revelation. When Perry Miller describes the Brook Farm phalanx as sitting "foreign and forlorn in West
Roxbury," he is perhaps missing the whole point. Just as Brisbane was
able to achieve immediate revelatory access to a lifetime of Fourier's
work—to his history, or myth—so Ripley and others were able to
achieve revelatory access to the doctrine by purchasing and reading
Brisbane's translations and explications. Fourierism represented a pattern already completed, a complete myth, a legacy, having been written
in the past across the sea in another language. But its totality became
manifest, in effect, in an instant. It had been translated into English; it
was there to be read and acted on. In the same way, the ideas of the
English philosopher James Pierrepoint Greaves traveled across the Atlantic to provide the basis of the Fruitlands community, as we shall see
in the chapters that follow. The process is a two-for-the-price-of-one
phenomenon, providing the immediate gratification of that "decisive
moment" described by Mannheim plus a solution, worked out through
time, to the problems posed by time. Nature and history come in a
package, already reconciled (at least in theory). In their own small way
these incursions by Fourier and Greaves represent an example of that
eastern frontier that would shortly be explored by the ex–Brook
Farmer Hawthorne, and later by Henry James, and later still by Lost
Generation writers such as Hemingway and Fitzgerald, where the quest
for the embodiment of freedom and spontaneity in a great good place
undergoes a geographic reversal, and Europe is where we find the
American soul "creating a world before her, leaving worlds behind
her," an environment where spontaneity and revelation capture the
imagination all the more forcibly because they arise out of a culture
that has an established historical and mythic identity.[24]

Nevertheless, though the Brook Farmers did not have to share Fourier's dilemma of being the particular individual entrusted with the serial key to the universe, they still faced the task of achieving a balance
between the spiritual independence of the individual and the teleological determinism of the Fourierist structure. Their willingness to mud-
dle through, with inadequate numbers and occupations and only a
vague approximation of Fourier's model, testifies to a continuing faith
in the role of the individual in the broad historical effort, and to their
belief that one can exert leverage on the course of events by the power
of one's will. Fourier's escapades as Harlequin were a psychological
strategy for dealing with disappointment and were designed to conceal

24. Emerson, "The Over-Soul," 163.

the complete utopian structure from a public unworthy to perceive it (and therefore, within the terms of that design, unready for the privilege of participating in it). By contrast, the Transcendentalists had a touch of Yankee practicality and pragmatism in their makeup, in addition to that emphasis on individual responsibility that runs right through American puritanism, American enlightenment, and American romanticism. The problem for the Brook Farmers stems from an excess of optimism, which leads simultaneously to confidence in a benevolent providence and to an increased respect for the individual's powers. But, as it turns out, the incompatibility of these two perspectives opens the door to a tragic sense of destiny and, ironically, to a solution to the dilemma by means of a Christian concept of self-sacrifice.

The key figure in this respect is William Henry Channing, a Fourierist who played an important part in the later history of Brook Farm, though he was prevented by circumstances from becoming a full-fledged member of the community. As his biographer O. B. Frothingham tells it, he "resigned his ministry in New York in order to throw himself unburdened into this enterprise; he traced out a line of exposition; he meditated a permanent settlement in the pulpit of Theodore Parker, at West Roxbury. But his ill-health, domestic anxieties, a multitude of engagements, prevented him doing what he would." Nevertheless, for much of the Fourierist period he was, in effect, Brook Farm's chaplain, spending most of his time at the community in the last months of 1845 and then acting as minister at the West Roxbury church for a good part of the following year, and taking every opportunity to preach to and guide the Brook Farmers. Frothingham says that during Channing's stay at West Roxbury, he was at the farm "constantly, talking in private, preaching in public, in full sympathy with the highest aims of the community, stimulating those aims to the utmost extent of his power, and eulogizing Fourier as the discoverer of the method of organization."[25] Marianne Dwight describes him officiating at a Sunday meeting in the community in late August 1845: "'A new day,' yes, that was well said. Channing gave us a pictorial sermon, a sketch of a temple of worship to be raised here on Brook Farm, as he saw it in his mind's eye. The picture was real to us, so glowingly was it described."[26]

25. O. B. Frothingham, *Memoir of William Henry Channing* (Boston: Houghton Mifflin, 1886), 211, 209.
26. Marianne [Dwight] Orvis, *Letters from Brook Farm, 1844–1847*, ed. Amy L. Reed (Poughkeepsie, N.Y.: Vassar College, 1928), 115–16, letter of August 31, 1845.

Perhaps the best picture of Channing in action is provided by John Codman:

> One Sabbath afternoon we were invited to meet with him in the nearby beautiful pine woods, for religious services; and like the Pilgrims and reformers of old, we there raised our voices in hymns of praise, and listened to a sermon of hopefulness from his eloquent lips. Would we had a picture of that marked company as they were seated around on the pine leaves that covered the ground, following their "attractions" by joining in groups with those they most admired or most sympathized with—young and old, bright and cheerful, as they mostly were . . . ; hearts and eyes illuminated with great thoughts; hands and faces browned with working for great, world-wide ideas. . . .
>
> After the music and an inspiring address under the trees, and the arches of Nature's temple, looking heavenwards, he said, "Let us all join hands and make a circle, the symbol of universal unity, and of the *at-one-ment* of all men and women, and here form the Church of Humanity that shall cover the men and women of every nation and every clime."[27]

Codman, with his interest in the pun-pendulum, not surprisingly latches on to the double meaning of "atonement," and indeed it is a significant one, suggesting at the same time suffering and solidarity, the problem of evil and the prospect of utopia, a historical process and the vision of a permanent truth.

Other members of the community seem to have been similarly impressed by Channing. According to Amelia Russell he "sanctified" the place, while George Ripley produced a characteristically measured testimonial: "[Channing's] presence with us . . . has been a source of unmingled satisfaction and benefit."[28] Marianne Dwight was less inhibited: asked to stay in her room for a day as a precaution during the smallpox outbreak that hit the farm in November 1845, she raged against the consequence of confinement: "So I have not seen our glorious Channing. I believe I am a *consummate fool* to have lost this. Oh! I said worse and harder things still to Mr. Ripley."[29] Elizabeth Curson, who confessed to being uninterested in theological and Fourieristic discussion, nevertheless carefully monitored Channing's comings and

27. Codman, *Brook Farm*, 72.
28. Russell's remarks occur in the book which was an amplification of her article: A. E. Russell, *Home Life of the Brook Farm Association* (Boston: Little, Brown, 1900), 110; Orvis, *Letters*, 127; Ripley, "Fire at Brook Farm," *Harbinger*, 221.
29. Orvis, *Letters*, 127, letter of November 9, 1845.

goings in her letters home, which provide a delightful account of the Brook Farmers' efforts to ascertain whether he had managed to attend the meeting of the New England Fourier Society held in Boston on January 27, 1846 (the "talkee talkee," as she disrespectfully calls it): "Mr Kleinstrop sent a carrier pigeon to bring back word whether Mr Channing was there—the pigeon was not full grown, and had not been out but two or three times, so he did not find his way home till to day when he came with his note. It is supposed the Boston pigeons are very hospitable & kept him to tea and to spend the night."[30]

Certainly Channing was well qualified to act as a sort of guru to the community during the second phase of its development. He was the domestic corresponding secretary of the American Union of Associationists (he gives his address as Brook Farm in the notice of its constitution), and through his journal the *Present*, his articles in the *Harbinger*, (of which he was an editor), and his presence on the rostrum at all the major Fourierist conventions, he became an agitator for the cause second only in importance to Albert Brisbane.[31] But unlike Brisbane—and this surely was the source of his influence on the Brook Farmers—he was no mere ideologue but was able to identify Fourier's shortcomings in a fashion that rang many bells for the Transcendental communitarians. He pointed out that Fourierism gave the individual no real control over his or her own destiny and that of society; that it recognized no moral distinctions but advocated instead the pursuit of pleasure; and that it was thoroughly contemptuous of religion. Having analyzed the problems, Channing proposed solutions. His contribution to the doctrine—probably the only truly original one in the whole American movement—was to alter its stance on all these issues.[32] What he achieved was to effect a reconciliation between Fourierism and Christianity.

On June 9, 1842, Channing wrote a letter to Theodore Parker, thanking him for a copy of his *Discourse of Matters Pertaining to Religion* and offering some comments on it. He complains that Parker has not done justice to "one conviction, which I presume you to hold, of course." The belief is "one of my deepest convictions, and is indeed the

30. "Elizabeth Curson's Letters from Brook Farm," ed. Stephen Garrison and Joel Myerson, *Resources for American Literary Study* 12 (Spring 1982): 12.
31. See Frothingham, *Channing*, for a general account of his reforming activities, esp. 171–252, and the journals *Present* and *Harbinger*, passim.
32. Other American modifications to the doctrine tended to be more a matter of omission (particularly as far as Fourier's sexual theories were concerned) than addition. See Carl J. Guarneri, *The Utopian Alternative: Fourierism in Nineteenth-Century America* (Ithaca: Cornell University Press, 1991), 93–120.

ground of my Christian faith—and my reconciliation with the church. It is this: 'That the Race is inspired as well as the Individual; that Humanity is a growth from a Divine Life as well as Man, and indeed that the true advancement of the individual is dependent upon the advancement of a generation, and that the law of this is providential, the direct act of the Being of beings.'" He goes on to say, rather more tentatively:

> It is my theory—though it is granted that a mere enunciation of it does not demonstrate its truth—that not only all races, but all the myriads of men who have ever lived, and are living, or yet to live, are needed to express God's idea of man. Hence the shading which separates characters, and the formation which wide popular common sense, and yet more the direction which the impulsive enthusiasm of whole nations and ages, give to opinions and conduct, are sacred to me. The past justifies itself and explains itself in the present, and a perfected race alone will give adequate utterance to the "Word of God."

The theory deals with the whole temporal scope, past, present, and future. That triadic division is followed by another: the "shading which separates characters," the "formation" contributed by "wide popular common sense," and the "direction" provided by the "impulsive enthusiasm of whole nations and ages."[33]

The symmetry is suggestive, giving a progressive implication to the second set of categories. The first stage, in the past, is one of differentiation, and is characterized by means of a metaphor of surface qualities, "shading"; the second, in the present, involves the coalescing of difference into a cultural consensus and attracts a structural metaphor, "formation"; and the third, which is prospective, implies emotional and ideological unity with its metaphor, "direction," suggesting a composite organic form moving along in its own right. What we have, in short, is a series of pulsations. Overall, the letter asserts that individuation has a collective function: not to provide a lonely or heroic set of destinies but to ensure a contribution to the total good by the full spectrum of human possibilities. Every individual has a foreordained part to play, and in fulfilling it contributes to a cultural, and indeed racial, identity.

Now comes the volte-face. Channing next suggests that Parker join him in speeding up this process by means of "a little moral galvanism."

33. W. H. Channing to Theodore Parker, June 9, 1842, in Frothingham, *Channing,* 174–75.

It is a proposal that puts the two of them outside the order of history, outside the racial identity of mankind. It is as illegitimate, and indeed as impossible, to galvanize as it is to obstruct this kind of utopian process, and Channing lacks Fourier's somewhat shaky justification of being in a personally privileged position: he is not a unique discoverer, only a tentative theorist. It is clear that at this point in his thinking he had not yet realized how enervating a doctrine of comprehensive and inevitable evolutionary growth must be. Caught in the toils of teleology, gesturing in the direction of free will, he does at least have the self-awareness to admit in a postscript that he may have been "too enthusiastic."[34]

By the following year the confusion is even more apparent. In his *Statement of the Principles of the Christian Union* Channing manages to perpetrate a nonsequitur:

> The laws of Providence are living realities. They cannot be changed by our imaginations, nor made inert by our neglects. Man cannot fabricate a machine of society. Its germ of life, its organizing principles, its growth, is from God. Again, there is danger that the strong intellectual bias of our day towards tolerance and universality, sifting all systems, examining all science, as it does, may end in a vanity of knowledge, and a pride in powers of thought, more barren of results than untaught instinct, or even bigotry. The tree of knowledge, of good and evil, may again fill our minds with seeds of death.[35]

Here Channing is contrasting mechanical and organic imagery to emphasize the impossibility of our refuting the laws of Providence (which are implicitly related to those governing the natural world) and determining our own future. Although, in terms of grammar, he seems to be developing this point through the adverb "again," he proceeds to say exactly the opposite, claiming that the intellectual hubris that underlies current eclecticism may lead to humankind's downfall. Our synoptic and synthesizing capabilities may prevail after all. What he clearly feels as the danger here is the loss of a specific moral vision, though ironically, as he indicates by the introduction of the image of the tree of knowledge, a tendentious variant on the more generalized growth imagery earlier in the passage, cultural relativism itself offends against, and thereby affirms the existence of, a fundamental moral imperative.

34. Ibid., 176.
35. William Henry Channing, *A Statement of the Principles of the Christian Union* (New York: Hunt's Merchants' Magazine, 1843), 8–9.

Indeed, it provides a reenactment of the oldest transgression of them all. In short, Channing appears to expect us to discard the apple and eat it too.

This confusion is temporary. By 1844 Channing had succeeded in making room within Fourierism to accommodate moral concepts and the free will on which they depend. His is a two-pronged achievement, accounting for the evils of the past and allowing for evil in the future. On the one hand, he explains why the long and painful development of society, with all its wasteful history of conflict, brutality, and war, is actually necessary: why, in fact, God has allowed us to suffer evil in the first place. On the other, he shows that even when society has reached its final and perfect form, we will not live the life of moral automata, never having to make a choice between good and evil, never exercising our individual will. On the contrary, the price of participation in the phalanx will be a conscious act of goodness.

Fourierism is contemptuous of the doctrine of original sin, and resolutely opposes the moralists who offer it as an explanation of life on earth. In the second of his *Democratic Review* articles titled "On Association and Attractive Industry," Brisbane puts the Fourierist case:

> It will be said, perhaps, that the passions were created good, but that when man fell, they became depraved. In answer I will state, that the creator does not give man control over his organic nature; he does not allow the finite being, by acts or will of his own to vitiate the passions and attractions which he has given him. Man may perfect or degrade God's work, but he cannot change it organically. When he fell, his passions became deranged in their action, and took a false development; but he can regain his original condition, and restore the harmonies which were dissolved.[36]

The complexities of this argument bring to mind the paradoxes of the covenantal theology of Calvinist New England, with its strivings after a kind of reverse or retrospective causality by means of justification. A classic example occurs in Thomas Shepard's explanation of the operation of grace in his preface to Peter Bulkeley's volume of sermons, *The Gospel-Covenant; or the Covenant of Grace Opened* (1651). Shepard vividly evokes the tendency to sin: "The soul of man rusheth most violently and strongly against God when it breaks through all the light of the mind and purposes of the will that stand in his way to keep him from

36. Albert Brisbane, "On Association and Attractive Industry," *U.S. Magazine and Democratic Review*, n.s. 10 (February 1842): 179.

sin," enquiring rhetorically, "And is this not done by breach of Covenant?" That case having been established, he hotfoots it to the other one, like one of those virtuosi who keep a number of plates spinning simultaneously on the top of canes: "It is true, the Covenant effectually made can never be really broke." Then back to the first sagging plate again: "Yet externally it may."[37] The same sort of agility is apparent in Fourierist reasoning, when Brisbane claims at one and the same time that "man may perfect or degrade God's work" and that "the creator does not give man control over his organic nature." The similarity is not as remarkable as it seems, since in both cases the apologist has to reconcile a predetermined agenda with the actual record that history dictates.

The Fourierist position on the passions is that they are binary, switchable. They are governed, in fact, by the law of "duality of movement." Any passion can move in one of two directions: to benign fulfillment if society is correctly organized, or to perversion and evil if it is not. In short, the misdirection of a passion reflects more on outer circumstance than on inner motivation. It is an "accidental and deranged development"—terms that bring to mind Aristotle's concept of *hamartia*, whereby misfortune occurs "not by vice and depravity but by some error of judgement"—which has no implications for the ultimate viability of utopia.[38] For example, we cannot conclude, just because we see a drunkard, that there is a "destiny proportional" to this particular "passional perversion." "The love of intoxication," Brisbane tells us, "is the perversion or false development of a true passion, which is called the *composite*, or passion of enthusiasm." We need to make an "intelligent discrimination," therefore, between the alcoholic who is in front of us and the "true and universal attraction" which he negatively implies, and which is the real pointer to our racial destiny.[39]

Fourierism succeeds in providing a method of reconciling individual behavior, however unsavory, with a utopian destiny, just as it provides a method of reconciling human history, however disastrous, with teleological fulfillment. In both cases there is a safety valve, an area of negative space, for the countercurrent to wash into. Just as collapse and regress were built into the historical blueprint, so perversion and derangement are built into the psychological one. This parallelism is inevitable since, of course, the inner and outer realms of behavior are

37. Reprinted in Perry Miller, ed., *The American Puritans: Their Prose and Poetry* (New York: Doubleday, 1956), 147.
38. Aristotle, *On the Art of Poetry*, trans. Ingram Bywater (Oxford: Clarendon Press, 1920), 50.
39. Brisbane, "On Association and Attractive Industry," 180.

connected, as Brisbane makes clear in another example: "The noble passion, Ambition, impels man—if it acts according to its true nature—to the performance of high deeds, . . . and to the fulfilment of numerous important social functions. But this passion is terrible in its false development; if perverted it leads to hatred, envy, revenge and other outrages, and if misdirected in the minds of rulers, it leads to tyranny, injustice, war and devastation." An understanding of the law of duality of movement therefore ensures both that immediate evil can be perceived to have no implications for ultimate good, and that individual examples of perversion do not disqualify human beings from fitness to participate in a phalansterian destiny: "This great law will render an important service to the cause of the social elevation of the human race, as it will inspire the world with that faith which it requires most—FAITH IN MAN. It relieves human nature from the responsibility of those odious and fiendlike characteristics which result from perversion of the passions, and places it where it should rest—upon our false systems of society."[40]

Once the passions are operating correctly, they will move us inexorably toward social harmony in accordance with the "Analytical and Synthetical Table of the Passional System," which appears in the twelfth chapter of *Social Destiny of Man.*[41]

ANALYTICAL AND SYNTHETICAL TABLE OF THE PASSIONAL SYSTEM.

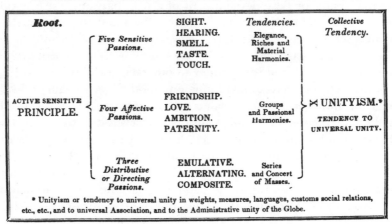

* Unityism or tendency to universal unity in weights, measures, languages, customs social relations, etc., etc., and to universal Association, and to the Administrative unity of the Globe.

40. Ibid., 172–73.
41. Brisbane, *Social Destiny*, 160.

As we can see, ambition contributes toward "Groups and Passional Harmonies" when, by means of the law of duality of movement, its favorable qualities are permitted to come into operation, whereas the composite passion, which is what the drunkard's habit is transmuted into by the same process, tends toward the larger conglomerations of "Series and Concert of Masses." The two fuse together, along with the other passions, in a "Collective Tendency to Universal Unity."

This account achieves its verdict of not guilty by refusing to pursue the implications of the existence of "false systems of society." Given that we have, on the one hand, an essentially innocent human nature, and on the other a law that will ultimately, and despite appearances, enable harmony to prevail in society, the question that then arises is: How on earth are we to explain what went wrong in the first place? How did this "accidental derangement" ever occur? Why didn't the dawn of association, which is, after all, the social manifestation of the principles underlying the very structure of the universe, coincide with the dawn of human life on earth?

In "Heaven upon Earth," an important two-part article published in the *Present* in March and April 1844, Channing provides an answer to that question. His project is to "reconcile the necessary evil of the Finite with the necessary good of the Infinite." In doing so he provides historical evolution with a purpose as well as a pattern. First of all he reminds us that harmony is not the same thing as unanimity. It is composed of different but interlocking parts: "What is an organization but an alliance,—a friendly grouping, a society of many forces conspiring to one common end?" This assertion is straightforward enough, corresponding to the Fourierist emphasis on fine discrimination of function in the organization of work. But Channing goes on to point out that this specialization, this productive discrimination between one unit and another, is the same as individualism, and we naturally expect individualism to go hand in hand with discord. Ergo, discord has its part to play in the procedure that ultimately leads to that fine-tuning required by phalansterian life. He describes the process by means of a series of rhetorical questions:

> Must every spirit be separate from good, before it can be united to it; must it feel its finiteness, before it seeks full exercise of power in co-operation with other limited existences, and perfect freedom, by obedience to him whose law of love is liberty; must it commence in disorder, ere it can learn how order binds all creatures, by mutual dependance [*sic*], into one living organization, and so through ignorance

grow up to intelligent justice, and through destructive lawlessness, to power of creative beauty? . . . He [God] would make us angels from the first, if he could do so. But the spirits, who come to blend their selfish discords in unison with him, must commence their journey far away in the chaos of extreme individualism. We must be men, before we can be angels.[42]

The table provided in Brisbane's *Social Destiny of Man* almost achieves this perspective, with that specifying and listing which is such a Fourier- ist compulsion, followed, as one's eyes move to the right of the page, by a converging development towards coordination and integration. In- deed, the title "Analytical and Synthetical Table of the Passional Sys- tem" suggests the twofold process of individuation (the analytical phase) as a prelude to harmony (the synthetical one). Channing's con- tribution is, in effect, to add the *perverted* side of the passions, the other face of the duality, to the table, and place it on the far left of the system so that we can see a large-scale evolution taking place over the whole span of spiritual life. The passions, in short, begin as chaotic and become orderly. The apparent wastefulness of history has served a pur- pose after all, for "existing limitations are the means of growing unions. Accords are the blending of discords."[43] Individualism is neces- sary to create a sufficient variety within the race to enable people to complement one another's qualities and render cooperation both meaningful and necessary.

We find, from this perspective, that Channing has inserted a sense of dynamic purposiveness into the past. He is able to direct deviation, waste, and suffering back into the ongoing system as a form of nutri- ment. This does not merely achieve the values of economy and pur- posiveness, but also serves to establish a visualizable interaction be- tween the one and the many. Part of the appeal of the theory of pulsations lies in its organicism. Yet we have seen in Emerson's essay "History" how paradoxical and unhelpful such a doctrine can become when pursued to its logical limits. His attempt to demonstrate to his reader—and to himself—that phylogeny somehow acts out ontogeny, that there is a racial "Man" who moves through history in a way that parallels the individual's movement through life, has the awkward cor- ollary, for a utopian, that the racial variety will eventually grow old and die. But the particular kind of purposiveness Channing injects into his model means that individual humans are self-consciously engaged in

42. William Henry Channing, "Heaven upon Earth," *Present*, March 1, 1844, 298–99.
43. Ibid., 299.

creating a collective variety which, far from being merely the sum of its parts, transcends the very people who have brought it into existence.

The other, opposite, problem with Emerson's equation of the totality and the individual is that it is *too* utopian. It implies utopia willy-nilly, here and now. The individual, by encapsulating and representing the race as a whole, must be a sort of walking phalanx. Emerson posits this individual in the future. "He shall walk," we are told, "as the poets have described that goddess, in a robe painted all over with wonderful events and experiences." But at some level or other he must already be—he must always have been—wearing that historical robe. The racial unity toward which we aspire has been implicit from the beginning, though only intermittently evident. Emerson gives us no sense that the outcome has to be *earned*. Since, however, we manifestly do not live in a utopia at present, his hero is destroyed by the pragmatic blows of history itself, that very process which he emblematizes. His problem is that he is history rendered ahistorical, and as a result cannot cope with time. Small wonder that Emerson instantly rejects what he himself has written.[44] Channing, meanwhile, by maintaining a distinction between individual effort and prospective accomplishment, between humans and angels, has accommodated his racial organism to the sequential world in which it has its origin.

It could be argued, though, that in doing so he merely defers the problem, projects it forward into the future. It may be better to travel than to arrive, but in a utopian scheme one cannot eradicate the destination altogether. The problem with the historical past, as usually perceived, is that it is too catastrophic. The organic nature of the Fourierist serie, allowing as it does for decline and death, coupled with Channing's stress on purposiveness and amelioration, deals with that difficulty. The problem with the utopian future, by contrast, is that it is unacceptably bland. Brisbane does not devote much space to describing utopian fulfillment, except in terms of negatives, as a relief from the endlessly catalogued drawbacks of life as it is lived in civilization. His failure to do so may be in part because he intuited something of the philosophical paradox involved, which has been elegantly summarized by Barthes. Utopia, says Barthes, is a place where "Desire" is perpetually fulfilled; but "*perpetually* . . . [means] simultaneously *always* and *never* fulfilled." Brisbane, too, may have been aware that that "Desire" ought not to be spelled out too fully, in view of American sensibilities. But perhaps the most significant problem is that the erotic

44. Ralph Waldo Emerson, "History," in *Essays 1*, 22.

(and culinary) gratifications Fourier envisages in "Harmony" are available instantly, without effort. As Barthes again points out, within Fourier's discourse the fantasy is "that every love demand *at once* find a subject-object to be *at its disposal.*" In other words, what we face is the end of process, which for most of us must feel like reaching the end of life. This realization, perhaps, is what Emerson is getting at when he states that "Fourier has skipped no fact but one, namely Life."[45] Channing's most important contribution to Fourierist ideology is to endow even phalansterian man with a sense of purpose.

In order to demonstrate the relevance of his argument, it is worth preceding an exploration of it with a look at Elizabeth Peabody's critique of Fourierism. Her analysis is more sympathetic and more perceptive than Emerson's, and indeed is probably the most intelligent response to the movement by an outsider. In an article titled "Fourierism" in the *Dial* of April 1844, she complains, in Emersonian fashion, that "Fourierism stops short, and, in so doing, proves itself to be, not a life, a soul, but only a body." Although it is admirable to create a perfectly functioning organization, she argues that to do so is not enough: "The question is, whether the Phalanx acknowledges its own limitations of nature, in being an organization, or opens up any avenue into the source of life that shall keep it sweet, enabling it to assimilate to itself contrary elements, and consume its own waste; so that Phoenix-like, it may renew itself forever in great and finer forms."[46] The trick for the Fourierists (as for other Transcendental utopians), is to develop an excremental economy, a means of avoiding polluting the environment with the waste associated with history. A little later she reverts to one of her earlier contributions to the *Dial*—"A Glimpse of Christ's Idea of Society"[47]—in order to revise her conclusions about the place of institutional Christianity in modern society, and in doing so she sheds further light on her objection to Fourierism:

> In a former article, we suggested the idea, that the Christian churches planted by the Apostles, were only initiatory institutions, to be lost, like the morning star, in the deeper glory of a kingdom of heaven upon earth, which we then fancied Socialism would bring about.
>
> Since then, by the study of ancient nationalities, and also of Nean-

45. Barthes, *Sade/Fourier/Loyola*, 114; Ralph Waldo Emerson, "Fourierism and the Socialists," *Dial* 3 (July 1842): 88.
46. Elizabeth Peabody, "Fourierism," *Dial* 4 (April 1844): 481–82.
47. Elizabeth Peabody, "A Glimpse of Christ's Idea of Society," *Dial* 1 (October 1841): 214–28.

der's History of the Churches of Christ up to the time of Constantine, together with observations on the attempt at West Roxbury [i.e., Brook Farm], we have come to see that initiatory churches will have an office as long as men are born children; and that a tremendous tyranny is necessarily involved by constituting society itself the VISIBLE church of Christ. Those who have ideas, and who, individually, and free from human constraining, have pledged themselves to live by them alone, or die, must be a select body, in the midst of the instinctive life that is perpetually arriving on the shores of Being, and which it is not fair or wise to catch up and *christen* before it can understand its position, and give its consent. We must be men before we are Christians, else we shall never be either Christians or men.[48]

At first sight one might almost imagine that she is writing in the late seventeenth century, arguing against theocracy and in favor of the Halfway Covenant in order to cope with the increasing separation of church and township. At least that seems to be the gist of her conclusion: that it is unfair and unwise to make the assumption that by dint of being members of a community, individuals should also be considered members of a church. She is arguing for the existence of churches, not because their absence would establish society as godless, but because without them religion would be diffused throughout its whole range. Society and Christianity would be coextensive, even synonymous. Such religious saturation, she suggests, gives the individual no room for maneuver; his or her religious identity therefore would involve no specific act of commitment. In the profoundest spiritual and psychological sense, it would not allow for the existence of identity at all.

In the *Present* of the same month, April 1844, Channing makes an almost identical point. "From his relations with nature comes the enforced mode of man's existence," he tells us. "But the Divine in the Soul contrasts dimly at first, but with ever increasing clearness, the eternal with the transient, principles with facts, the absolute with the accidental . . . and in this two-fold consciousness of an inner world and an outer world, *the Man* awakes, awakes to the mysterious and awful knowledge of Self, of Individual Power, of existence as a Spirit." Every person, even in association, has to become aware of his own uniqueness.

48. Peabody, "Fourierism," 482–83. Peabody had anticipated this argument in a rather gnomic comment she made at one of Margaret Fuller's "Conversations," held March 22, 1841: "Miss P replied:—'Life is division from one's principle of life in order to a conscious reorganization. We are cut up by time and circumstance, in order to feel our reproduction of the eternal law." *Memoirs of Margaret Fuller Ossoli*, 2 vols, ed. R. W. Emerson et al. (London: Richard Bentley, 1852), 1:346.

Only when he has done so can he offer it as a sacrifice to the community, for the good of his fellows: "His destiny is first to know himself, as
one of many in a Universe, and then to give himself away in ever en-
larging communion with all creatures and with God, and so become
immortal."[49]

Fourier would have been horrified at the suggestion that a tension
exists, and even worse that a tension *should* exist, between the individual and association. Yet by insisting on it, Channing is superimposing a
moral law on the social structure. Fourierism claimed that the law of
the duality of movement of the passions restored faith in humanity
because it "relieves human nature from the responsibility of those
odious and fiendlike characteristics which result from perversion of the
passions, and places it where it should rest—upon our false systems of
society."[50] But this deterministic explanation deprives human nature of
the dignity of choice. If we do not have to accept responsibility for our
odiousness and our fiendlike behavior, we cannot lay claim to virtue
and self-abnegation either. Despite Brisbane's capitals, "FAITH IN MAN"
in this analysis turns out to be a distinctly lower-case affair. That problem is removed by Channing.

Humankind's "peculiar endowment," Channing tells us, "is the intermediate one of a spiritual nature."[51] By this he means a nature situated
halfway between the celestial and the terrestrial, rather on those lines
laid out as long ago as 1642 by Sir Thomas Browne: "We are only that
amphibious piece between a corporal and spiritual essence; that middle frame that links those two together, and makes good the method of
God and nature, that jumps not from extremes but unites the incompatible distances by some middle and participating natures."[52] The
"special function" of this intermediateness, as far as Channing is con-

49. William Henry Channing, "Heaven upon Earth," *Present*, April 1, 1844, 417–18.
50. Brisbane, "On Association and Attractive Industry," 172–73. Guarneri emphasizes
the deterministic implications of Brisbane's position, and indeed of orthodox Fourierism
generally, in *The Utopian Alternative*, 118–19. In his necessarily brief but lucid survey of
the interaction of Fourierism and Christianity, Guarneri cannot confront the impact of
these moral issues on motivation and psychology. But he does make the point that Channing tried to separate environmental causality from individual responsibility: "In their
own response, Godwin, Channing, and the Brook Farmers tried to stake out a compromise position between Brisbane's utilitarian dogma and the moralism of traditional
Christianity. Insisting upon social reorganization as the most important reform tool, they
nevertheless qualified Brisbane's utopian environmentalism by acknowledging that personal wrongdoing contributed to social ills" (119).
51. Channing, "Heaven upon Earth," 418.
52. Sir Thomas Browne, *Religio Medici* (1642), ed. James Winny (Cambridge: Cambridge
University Press, 1963), 42.

cerned, is "rational liberty": "By affections from within, and sensations from without, by ideas from the absolute and impressions from transient phenomena, by spontaneous impulse and enforced activity, [man] . . . becomes an image at once of the Creator and Universe." The world "within" is characterized by "ideas" and "impulses"; it is "absolute" and "spontaneous" at the same time. By contrast, the world "without" manifests itself in the form of sense impressions, which in turn lead to "enforced activity." The universe of forms meets contingent reality; nature confronts history ("transient phenomena"); Law is face to face with law. As human beings we represent the transitional point between these two domains. For Channing this means that instinct, "the enforced mode of man's existence," gives way to the possibility of conscious self-sacrifice. Each individual is able to add a moral, and religious, dimension to his or her experience, and "as with individuals now the process is from instinct into wilfulness, and through sad experiences up to willing co-operation with all creatures and joyful devotedness to the Good; so was it with the Human Race."[53]

The implication and tendency of Channing's thinking here can be clarified by reference to some of his writings in the *Spirit of the Age* a few years later, when his Fourierist theology had had time to crystallize in his mind (Channing edited this magazine on a weekly basis from July 7, 1849, to April 27, 1850). He develops his ideas interestingly in a series called "Criticism Criticized," which takes the form of a dialogue between himself and Parke Godwin on the subject of an earlier contribution by Channing which had pointed out limitations in Fourier's philosophy. Here we find him expounding at considerable length on the subject of Fourier's pantheism. In Fourier's scheme, Channing tells us, the Divine Being is composed of the twelve basic passions of the universe (as we have seen in the "Analytical and Synthetical Table of the Passional System"):

> By putting various passages side by side and interpreting them in the light of his method, the Theology of his system appears to be—that the Divine Being is complex—composed of twelve primordial passions, (v. Nouv. Monde p. 445)—subject to a dual mode of development, Univ. Unit. 1. p. 82—the original Unity and composite Unity of all Nature; and that the material World constitutes his SENSITIVE existence, which is *passive*, Spirits Human, Planetary, Universal, Biniversal,

53. Channing, "Heaven upon Earth," 421.

&c. his AFFECTIONAL existence which is *active,* while the Order of
Movement, intermingling in endless variety and harmony all modes of
existence constitutes his DISTRIBUTIVE existence, which is *neutral.*

The irony of a staccato style and patched-together sources, all at the
service of a claim of original and composite unity, is a familiar one to
readers of "Le sphinx sans Oedipe," as is the Harlequinesque elusive-
ness of its progenitor, which causes Channing to introduce his conclusion by means of some rather defensive maneuvering: "If this was Fourier's view,—and whether he was conscious of it or not it seems
impossible to make anything else consistently of his analogy between
man and the divinity,—then one is constrained to say, that no writer in
any land or age, has produced Pantheism in a more pure, perfect,
uncompromising a [*sic*] form."[54]

In short, the Deity is impossible to distinguish from his world. This
doctrine should not be hard for a Transcendentalist to swallow, given
the Emersonian tendency to regard man, God, and nature as synonymous. And yet, for Channing it was unacceptable. His tone is accu-
satory: he is "constrained" to come to his conclusion, which itself is
expressed with a forensic resonance that sends his grammar slightly out
of control. Even more significantly, he has already established, in an
article published in the edition of *Spirit of the Age* for the previous week,
exactly how pantheism lines up with the three basic religious options.

In the present historical situation, he tells us, we have to choose one
of the following doctrines: "CATHOLICISM, PANTHEISM, and DIVINE HU-
MANITY," which have as their respective destinations "divine order,"
"harmonious joy," and "uniting in heavenly communion the perfected
races of all globes." The account of Catholicism is conventional
enough, a matter of "super-human influence, hierarchically transmit-
ted and diffused," and "sanctified obedience." Pantheism, meanwhile,
"instinct with Natural impulse, amidst the ever-varying sphere of hourly
circumstances, longs for unchecked freedom to realize the harmonious
joy of earthly existence, in consummate art." This description sounds a
bit tentative, a matter of aspiration rather than achievement, and the
final phrase inevitably strikes one as an anticlimax, however much al-
lowance one might make for the nineteenth century's capacity to aes-
theticize piety. Our suspicions are confirmed by the third definition:
"Divine Humanity, conscious of the everlasting series of descending
mediations, whereby the One Absolute Good progressively fulfils his

54. William Henry Channing, "Criticism Criticized," *Spirit of the Age,* December 8, 1849,
360.

infinitely benignant purpose of uniting in heavenly communion the
perfected races of all globes, stands willing to do the exact work allotted to mankind, upon this globe, to day, assured of exhaustless growing
good, and aspiring to the end of religious Unity and Art made one by
perfect Love."[55]

The references to series, to a structure of "descending mediations,"
the particularity of the alignment of the worker and the task ("the
exact work allotted to mankind"), all these elements in the passage
make it clear that Channing is talking about the phalansterian system.
It is also obvious that he finds this doctrine superior to the others: it
unites Catholic "Unity" and pantheistic "Art," "by perfect Love." Yet, a
week later, he was to label Fourier a *pantheist.*

The criticism implied by this categorization is confirmed by some of
Channing's remarks in a subsequent contribution to the series. He
poses the question: "Is spontaneous, individual impulse or Passional
Attraction, the infallible indication of Divine Order?" He cannot accept
Fourier's idea that a community can be kept running efficiently by
allowing the passions to operate freely. The main ground of his argument is that the consciousness is bound to impose its control eventually:

> In action and reaction, each impulse encounters circumstances which
> it moulds, or is moulded by, and from all combined experience of
> pleasure and pain is formed a reflected image of the harmonious con-
> ditions of Integral existence. Finally, impulse, judgment, experience
> converge, intermingle, blend in a Character or Personality, which is
> inwardly conscious of being Manly, and felt by all men to be so, in
> proportion to its Unity. A man is loved by his fellows, as at once hu-
> mane, natural, and divine, in degree as in deed, thought, feeling he
> progressively realizes unity in variety, and becomes a beautiful whole.
> And in the process of this development he ascends from a merely
> instinctive passionate existence, through consciously governed exis-
> tence, to free co-operative existence.[56]

We have, in the first part of the passage, the sketch of a solution to
the problem posed by the law of the duality of movement. We shape
the world; the world shapes us. The process involved takes us back to
Hedge, for surely these "impulses" are the equivalent of the latter's
"pulsations," sporadic raids on the substance of life. To an extent this

55. Ibid., December 1, 1849, 344.
56. Ibid., December 15, 1849, 377.

shaping is harmonious and feeds into the ultimate unity; to an extent it is aberrant. The successful shaping gives us pleasure and enables us to glimpse the deep pattern that exists in the structures on which we labor; the unsuccessful variety causes us pain and indicates where we went wrong as a result.

Channing has given a dynamic to the structure of Fourierism. He has accommodated Elizabeth Peabody's point that Fourierism needs to "assimilate to itself contrary elements, and consume its own waste; so that Phoenix-like, it may renew itself forever in great and finer forms," and has also charted the same sort of evolution from, as she put it, "the instinctive life that is perpetually arriving on the shores of Being" to the maturity of deliberate choice. In the last sentence of the quoted passage Channing becomes tautological—"process," "development," "ascends"—in order to ensure that we properly envisage the metamorphosis involved.

Obviously in the course of this process something is lost. The adjective "free," coming as it does at the final stage of a development from instinctive, through consciously governed, to cooperative existence, suggests free will rather than the free gratification of desires that is envisaged in Fourierism. There is a hint here of loss, of tragic possibility, that Fourier's relentless optimism could never countenance. Channing goes on to stress the element of sacrifice:

> Not only is it true, then, that an individual man is approximately conformed to Divine Order in proportion as all his Passional Attractions are regulated by the Law of Right Reason, enacted and executed by a Unitary, Personal Will, fitly experienced, enlightened and sanctified; but yet more is it true, that a man fulfils the Divine Idea, just in degree as with loyal love he yields up his own personal inclination, judgment, interest, to the guidance of the Law of Right Reason in the Society of which he is a living member. The correlative of this is the complementary truth, that a Society can best attain to a knowledge of the Ideal Law of Justice, by duly respecting the highest conscience of each of its members. And both these truths are involved in a third, that the various Societies of the Human Race, with all their constituent members, approach to an infallible science of Divine Wisdom, according to the entireness of their conformity to the Reason of Humanity, wherein the Word of God, hierarchically distributed through the whole Spiritual Universe, manifests Himself to Man.[57]

57. Ibid.

Without doing anything to alter the workings of Fourier's machinery, Channing has managed to provide it with a new direction—perhaps one need only say, with a direction. We have a kind of social contract: the individual must respect the "Right Reason" of his or her society; society must respect the conscience of its members; and the cumulative experience resulting from this interchange becomes synonymous with "Divine Wisdom." Channing is basically repeating the commandment "Love thy neighbor," which retains its point in a world where, it turns out, we cannot do just as we please without hurting someone else. This is a long way from the structural gratification of orthodox Fourierism, splendidly parodied by Roland Barthes, with his fantasy of mutually sustaining rivalries between lovers and haters of rancid couscous. If Fourier's democratic appeal is that no sensual pleasure is too humble or bizarre, whether arguing over the merits of sweet cream and small pies or having one's buttocks gently patted by a soubrette, Channing's moral order fulfills another, more acute and more American need: "The desire truly is to give up lust and vanity, self-confidence and sloth, to feel habitually that affection and thought and power are ever fresh gifts from heaven, to break out of restraining fears into glad obedience, and so become the willing instrument of the ever living Father."[58] In this context it is impossible not to remember his appeal for "at-one-ment," that double-edged word, diligently recorded by Codman, that takes us from the torrid zone of human solidarity to the frigid one of sacrifice and remorse and back again in a twinkling.

During the autumn of 1845 Channing began his task of establishing a Christian institution within the framework of the Brook Farm phalanx. In a letter of October 5 Marianne Dwight describes a meeting held at the farm to discuss "our church." Channing wanted a place set aside for worship, although there was naturally a problem in finding a form that would satisfy everyone. The letter continues: "Of course, the whole of life should be worship,—all labor, consecration, and not desecration,—and so all life should be poetry, should be music. But as we have a particular expression of poetry and music, but adapted to these sentiments, why may we not have a form of worship peculiarly adapted to the religious sentiment?"[59]

The wording here would seem obscure indeed if one were not familiar with the ideological context. The notion of a "particular expression" of poetry which is adapted to the "sentiment" of poetry is hard

---

58. Barthes, *Sade/Fourier/Loyola*, 77–78; William Henry Channing, "Call of the Present, No. 3—Oneness of God and Man," *Present*, December 15, 1843, 154.
59. Orvis, *Letters*, 121.

enough to swallow; the proposal of a form of worship "peculiarly adapted to the religious sentiment" seems at first sight a puzzling form of tautology. But what Dwight is getting at is the coming into focus of religious commitment from a background of vague pantheism. The law of series is a holistic mechanism, and endows all one's activities with harmony and spirituality. But Channing's contribution establishes the necessity for a sacramental and sacrificial heart to maintain the vitality and health of the Fourieristic body—or, to go back to Peabody's imagery, a kind of Transcendental kidney that would allow the organism to consume its own waste and thereby renew itself.

Dwight goes on to suggest that a perfect phalanx would have a worshiping series, in which one group would provide "the spirit of prayer," a second, "song and thanksgiving," another "silent worship," and a fourth, preaching. This proposal almost certainly originated with Channing. It resembles his New York plan for a Christian union, when the idea was to have three different kinds of meeting: the first under the guidance of a leader, the second of a wholly spontaneous character, and the third for "the frankest interchange of thought in conversation."[60]

At a meeting two weeks later it was decided to consecrate one of the rooms in the Phalanstery (then under construction) as a place of worship. The services were to begin and end with music and to utilize books such as "Mr. Clarke's and the Swedenborgian ritual or book of worship." A committee of seven was appointed to make the arrangements, and it was decided, according to Marianne Dwight, that "Mr. C. will not be considered as a priest—we do not want a priest." Instead, "the exercises will be left to the person who may conduct them for the day."[61] Appropriately enough, in view of Elizabeth Peabody's remarks on "a select body" and Channing's emphasis on a deliberate sacrifice of the self, the proposals caused a division at the farm, and only about twenty people attended the first meeting. These included some of the most important members of the community, however, since John Sullivan Dwight and Mrs. Ripley were among those appointed to the committee, and Ripley, Allen, Orvis, and others were added to it a fortnight later.[62] The machinery of the phalanx was now powered by volatile spiritual fuel, and an opportunity had been provided for the testing of

60. Ibid.; Channing, *Statement of the Principles of the Christian Union,* 11–12.
61. Orvis, *Letters,* 123–24, letter of October 19, 1845.
62. Ibid., 123, 125.

Peabody's theory that "Christian churches in the midst of a Phalanx, might be the Dorian cities of another Greece."[63]

As it happened, however, the Christian church was never to be consecrated. For a while, Fourieristic Christianity looked as if it was on the way to establishing itself. On March 1, 1846, Marianne Dwight tells of a "holy solemn afternoon" in which Channing made much of his theme of self-sacrifice: "He compared our work with others that have demanded sacrifice; that of the crusaders, that of the religious brotherhoods and sisterhoods. As the crusaders sacrificed so much to restore the tomb of the buried Lord, how much more ought we to sacrifice, whose work it is to restore the whole earth, so that it may become the dwelling place of the living Lord!"[64] Two days later the Phalanstery, containing as it did the new church, burned to the ground. Another blow came when Channing lost his position at the West Roxbury church. His appointment was, according to Frothingham, "terminated by the active agency of a few."[65] Soon afterwards Brook Farm itself broke up.

The reasons for the community's collapse are clear enough, though one can argue about how they should be ranked. The destruction of the Phalanstery perhaps marked the point of no return. The structure had obvious symbolic significance, in that it would have been a tangible embodiment of the Fourierist ideology that the community had adopted, the first stage of the construction of a concrete serial unit. Moreover, it was designed to accommodate the influx of working people necessary to enable the phalanx to begin to approximate the dimensions of Fourier's model, and to establish on the Brook Farm site the kind of varied industrial base that alone could make the community viable in the long term, given the poor farming conditions. The fire destroyed overnight an existing investment and the basis for future income. At the same time, the school, the farm's most profitable "industry," was beginning to contract as rumors circulated about the sexual license advocated by Fourier, and as a result of the smallpox scare.

On an ideological level one could suggest that although Fourierism, as I hope I have shown, could be grafted admirably onto the stem of New England Transcendentalism, the resulting hybrid could not survive for long. I have previously mentioned how at each stage in the development of George Ripley's ideas his perspective became wider. In

63. Peabody, "Fourierism," 482.
64. Orvis, *Letters*, 144.
65. Frothingham, *Channing*, 193.

the imagery of Emerson's "Circles," Fourierism insisted on enclosing the whole world. Although this was the natural destination of the serial structure that underlay Transcendentalism, it also took the participants away from their local sustenance, that tightly knit and highly focused cultural scene that provided them with so much of their energy and idealism. On June 6, 1846, Channing, as domestic corresponding secretary of the American Union of Associationists, issued an announcement "to the Associationists of the United States." He gave his address as Brook Farm, but his program was for his country as a totality:

> We have a solemn and glorious work before us,—
>   1. To indoctrinate the whole People of the United States, with the Principles of Associative Unity;
>   2. To prepare for the time, when the Nation like one man, shall reorganize its townships upon the basis of perfect Justice.[66]

Even though the comparison of the nation with one man suggests serial continuity, there is no sense here that a phalanx provides the midpoint in the chain. Rather, the task ahead, once the American people have been indoctrinated, is for the nation as a whole to sort out its intermediate social units ("reorganize its townships"). Perhaps this reversal of cause and effect is an inevitable consequence of Channing's notion of sacrifice. In providing a spiritual dimension to the individual's contribution, he had also let in the notion that the totality was more than the sum of its parts, and that, after all, was why it was worth sacrificing oneself for. But this analysis ultimately, and paradoxically, leads to a devaluing of the individual's contribution to the development of utopia.

In an article in the *Harbinger* from the previous October, John Sullivan Dwight provides the rationale for this switch of priority: "We are prepared to take the ground that there is not and never can be Individuality, so long as there is not Association. Without true union no part can be true. The members were made for the body; if the whole body be incoherent, every member of it will be developed falsely, will become shrunken or overgrown, distorted and weakened, since it will have either more or less than its share, both of duty and sustenance."[67] On the face of it this use of the metaphor of "members" of the body

66. William Henry Channing, "To the Associationists of the United States," *Harbinger*, June 13, 1846, 14.
67. John Sullivan Dwight, "Individuality in Association," *Harbinger*, October 4, 1845, 264–65.

seems diametrically opposed to the one in "The American Scholar," where Emerson describes "a good finger, a neck, a stomach, an elbow, but never a man."[68] But in both cases, whether the members are "distorted" or "good," the assumption is that they depend on a preexisting state of social unity. And this assumption must ultimately devalue individual input into association and begin the transfer of the energies needed to fuel Brook Farm to a vaguer (but, ironically, more authentically Fourierist) program for the conversion of the people of America as a whole. In asserting that association can redeem our lives, the associationists have made it impossible for us to establish association in the first place, and have therefore lost the struggle to find individual purposiveness amid the wastefulness of the historical process.

Perhaps this verdict is just a cumbersome way of saying that, in the end, the Transcendentalist-Fourierist view was simply wrong. Nature was not organized in the way it claimed, and therefore did not have the capacity to bring history to an end. History moved on, and instead of a harmonious world what came about was the divided America of the Civil War. Moreover, the next important insight into the natural world, Darwin's theory of evolution, asserted that historical forces determined the structure of nature itself.

One does not, in any case, need to build a complex argument to explain the collapse of Brook Farm. The task is to understand how it managed to last for six years. It succeeded in doing so because of the energy of a remarkable man, George Ripley, along with that of many other like-minded and idealistic people. Equally important, it was established in accordance with a coherent vision, indeed a vision of coherence. These factors were enough to enable it to effect a break in the historical continuum for as long as it did.

In an excellent article titled "Christian Socialism and the First Church of Humanity," Charles Crowe has discussed the Boston church to which Channing ministered after the collapse of the enterprise at Brook Farm. It promoted the reconciliation of Fourierism and Christianity for several years in the late 1840s and the early 1850s. At the end of his piece Crowe explains this interaction: "While evangelical democracy with millennial overtones thrust men towards visions of the future Kingdom of Man, disquieting memories of sin and guilt remained to haunt the disciples of progress. . . . The official creed of American optimism came to birth in the presence of a receding Calvi-

68. Ralph Waldo Emerson, "The American Scholar," in *NAL*, 53.

nist consciousness. . . . For a few years an ardent band of New Englanders satisfied both memories of Christian tragedy and dreams of progress in the First Church of Humanity."[69] These remarks effectively identify the kind of contradictory impulses we have been exploring. But, as with his comments on the transition between Transcendentalism and Fourierism, Crowe tends to express this drama in the linear terms of historical development rather than in the lateral ones of philosophical accommodation.[70]

Nobody could show more consciousness of the tragic imperatives of history than the Transcendentalists, nor more ingenuity in formulating methods for circumventing them. The Brook Farmers demonstrated particular originality and persistence in their attempts to enable the individual to break free from the deterministic roles that his or her inheritance had created. This undertaking provided an admirable balance of individualistic and collective tendencies, since it involved the kind of coalescence between the one and the many that Emerson and the other philosophers of the movement continually searched for. The conversion to Fourierism seemed to set the seal on the enterprise, since this version of serial law was elaborated, formal, written—was in short historical, while at the same time revelatory, foreign, and intuitive, in other words, natural in the sense established in Emerson's poem "The Sphinx." But of course once inside the system, so to speak, we find that the equilibrium comes to an end and history resumes its sway. This problem is solved, on one level at least, by introducing the concept of Christian sacrifice, for that enables the conversion experience, the spontaneous awakening every morning to a new world, to become a part of the institutional structure, the myth of continuity.

The fact that this solution was in turn temporary seems inevitable, but perhaps that is also, ultimately, irrelevant. After all, continuity through time would affirm the priority of history, which was one of the terms of the equation, not its solution. If utopia partakes of *kairos* and operates outside the temporal process, it is hardly possible that we

69. Charles Crowe, "Christian Socialism and the First Church of Humanity," *Church History* 35 (1966): 104–5.

70. Anne C. Rose, in *Transcendentalism as a Social Movement, 1830–1850* (New Haven: Yale University Press, 1981), also sees a linear development, one that had been too rapid: "They had moved too quickly from spiritual to social reform to feel comfortable with the new idea." The millennium the Brook Farmers had strived for was one "of the head, not of the heart," but they could not ultimately escape from the fact that "deep down, they were still the children of evangelical Protestantism who could not help seeing signs of divine judgment on their presumption to redeem the world by themselves" (161).

could perceive it from our own historical perspective. The Brook Farmers' achievement may be of an invisible sort, requiring the agency of a transparent eyeball. Better perhaps to leave them under those pine trees where, as Codman shows in his account, they were perfectly aware of straddling a historical divide and consequently in their very awareness both embodying and transcending the historical process: simultaneously pilgrims and reformers in the old style and architects of a Church of Humanity that would cater to the future.

The architecture itself is significant: a circle made up of men and women with joined hands, at once structural and evanescent, spontaneous and ritualistic, achieving an "at-one-ment" that acknowledges alienation even while it affirms communion.

5

Fruitlands: Convergence

In "English Reformers," published in the *Dial* in 1842, Emerson cannot resist quoting in full an advertisement that had appeared in a London newspaper, the *Morning Chronicle*, three months previously: "Public Invitation. An open meeting of the friends of human progress will be held tomorrow . . . for the purpose of considering and adopting means for the promotion of the great end, when all who are interested in human destiny are earnestly urged to attend. The chair taken at three o'clock and again at seven, by A. Bronson Alcott Esq., now on a visit from America. Omnibuses travel to and fro, and the Richmond steam-boat reaches at a convenient hour."[1]

We have already come across the concept of *kairos*, the genius of the decisive moment. It is a testimony to a certain insistent literalness on the part of Alcott and his associates that the decisive moment—or, in this case, the decisive moments—should be so specifically defined. The great end was to be promoted at three o'clock and again at seven. Interested parties could be conveyed toward a confrontation with human destiny by omnibus or on the Richmond steamboat. On the one hand, the utopian ideal; on the other, the practical conveniences of public transport. Or, to put it in terms that have become familiar, a counterbalance is established between the spontaneous perception of a new world and the formal procedures, horse-drawn and steam-driven, of the status quo.

The balance represented by this proposal is, of course, a literary acci-

1. Ralph Waldo Emerson, "English Reformers," *Dial* 3 (October 1842): 241.

dent. In reality Alcott's life can be seen as a sequence of zeroings-in on an ever-retreating utopian possibility. He was, as we shall see, the sort of man whose vehicle would either fail to arrive on time or shoot off with its passenger's baggage. On a philosophical level his predicament can be seen as the result of an endless effort to reconcile the contingent and the ideal, or, to use terms more familiar to Alcott himself, a wrestle between circumstances and spirit. He characteristically undertook the task in a very direct, indeed empirical, fashion, carefully monitoring the cranial development of his baby daughters, for example, in order to record the interaction of spirit and matter. "The mind is modifying the head," he records of his daughter Anna at five months. "The organs which indicate intellectual and moral attributes are protruding themselves; and making the mind, as it were, externally obvious." Not that he is advancing an unequivocal doctrine that the child is, so to speak, mother to the woman, since at about the same time he records in his journal his intention to intrude his own intellectual and moral attributes into that mind: "Infancy seems to me the period when most good can be done for the improvement of the character, and this the period of life upon which I am inclined to spend my direct personal labours."[2]

The kind of contradiction apparent here, between the protrusion of the inner being into the external world and the intrusion of the external world into the inner being, characterized not merely Alcott's philosophical ruminations but also his life as a whole. The title of the biography that has done most to form our picture of the man, Odell Shepard's *Pedlar's Progress*, captures one aspect of the conflict but not the other. Certainly Alcott was a traveler who made what living he could from peddling his intellectual stock, projecting his interior preoccupations onto the world at large. Born into an impoverished rural community in Wolcott, Connecticut, in 1799, he began quite literally as a pedlar, making three trips to the South in his late teens and early twenties.[3] Yet, like Theodore Parker and his distant cousin Orestes Brownson, who began life in similar circumstances, Alcott also man-

2. A. Bronson Alcott, "Observations on the Life of My First Child, during her first year" (1831), MS, Houghton Library, 59M-306 (1), 109; *The Journals of Bronson Alcott*, ed. Odell Shepard (Boston: Little, Brown, 1938), 29, entry for July 31, 1831. In this and the following chapter on Fruitlands, I have made use, where appropriate, of material originally published in my article "Circumstances and Salvation: The Ideology of the Fruitlands Utopia," *American Quarterly* 27 (May 1973): 202–34. Reprinted by permission of the Johns Hopkins University Press.
3. See Odell Shepard, *Pedlar's Progress: The Life of Bronson Alcott* (Boston: Little, Brown, 1937), 44–71.

aged to educate himself to an impressive level, specializing particularly
in what we would now call developmental psychology and educational
theory, and immersing himself in the works of J. H. Pestalozzi. In the
1820s and 1830s he set up various schools of his own, first in Boston,
then in Germantown, Pennsylvania, next in Philadelphia, and finally
back in Boston again, where his Temple School was made famous, and
in some quarters notorious, by Elizabeth Palmer Peabody's published
record of his classroom methods. After this educational experiment
foundered in the late 1830s, Alcott relied for many years on the support of friends, the efforts of his wife, Abigail, and a tiny sporadic income from "Conversations" to make ends meet. In 1842, funded by
Emerson and his relatives, he went across the Atlantic to visit a group
of "English Transcendentalists" which had been established under the
leadership of James Pierrepoint Greaves. The following year, along
with Charles Lane, a member of that group, he founded the Fruitlands
community in central Massachusetts, which was financed by Lane, and
which lasted just six months. After that debacle he continued with odd
jobs and with his "Conversations," eventually embarking on a series of
relatively successful speaking tours to the West. In 1859 he received
some kind of institutional acknowledgment as an educator by being
appointed Concord's school superintendent, a position he retained until 1865. Toward the end of his life he established the Concord School
of Philosophy in a curious building, half shed, half Athenaeum, which
he had erected in his own garden.

It was a nomadic, unsettled existence, in which travel and questing
can be seen as indications of a mind, like that of little Anna, making
itself "externally obvious." But that was only half the story. Despite his
travels Alcott was deeply embedded in the cultural life of a small geo-
graphical area. He was also a man whose life can be seen to have been
determined by his relationship with his environment and with those
around him. Though something of a drain on the funds of his friends,
he was loyal to them and loved by them. It is probably fair to say that
he was the closest friend of both Emerson and Thoreau, two individuals who were fairly discriminating in their relationships. He was preoccupied by family concerns and devoted to his wife, children, mother,
and brothers. He was, in short, as stable and responsive as he was mo-
bile and impulsive. The struggle between opposing elements in his existence was never resolved. It was only his enormous capacity for hope,
necessary given the disasters to which he was prone, that enabled him
to convince himself at intervals that he had arrived at the point of
equilibrium, as though he, like Emerson's Sphinx, could unite movement and stasis and "stand Monadnock's head."

In his intellectual biography of Alcott, Frederick Dahlstrand tracks his subject's zigzagging trajectory with great meticulousness, but occasionally shows a tendency to endorse Alcott's own claims to have achieved a resolution of his dilemma. As early as 1829, we read, "whereas 'circumstances' had long been for Alcott the determining force in human development, by June . . . he had come to see them as a potential hindrance to the natural development of the divinity within." Five years later "the epistemological problem he had wrestled with for so long was solved," the solution being as before: "The spiritual principle . . . gave [human beings] the ultimate power to transcend all external circumstances."[4] In fact, as the process continues through Alcott's long life, it becomes clear that these moments are points of rest, of exhaustion, rather than epistemological solutions, though it is perhaps true that as time went on Alcott did find ways of accommodating his dilemma, even if he could not eradicate it.

It is important to stress Alcott's determination not to override the circumstantial world in his long struggle with what is, after all, one of the central issues of Western philosophy, the relationship between the ideal and the contingent. The most important episode of his life, the establishment of a "consociate family" at Fruitlands in Harvard, Massachusetts, has traditionally offered itself as a case study in hopeless defiance, by a set of incompetent idealists, of the intractable imperatives of the real world. Its remote situation, a small farmhouse overlooking the Nashua River valley, and its brief duration, the six months or so between the community's establishment in June 1843 and its breakup at the end of the year, provide an appropriately dramatic environment. There is something intriguingly hubristic about the community's uncompromising commitment to its principles, a belief in cold showers and abstention from the use of animal products, including eggs, fish, milk, butter, oil, and leather—as well as alcohol, tea, coffee, and cocoa. Grain and fruit, which—apart from water—were just about all that was left, were to be grown without the help of manure. "No hope is there for humanity," Lane and Alcott tell us in one of their manifestos, "while Woman is withdrawn from the tender assiduities which adorn her and her household, to the servitudes of the dairy and the flesh pots."[5] The double entendre of the last phrase makes sexual abstinence into a kind of ultimate vegetarianism.

4. Frederick C. Dahlstrand, *Amos Bronson Alcott: An Intellectual Biography* (Rutherford, N.J.: Fairleigh Dickinson University Press, 1982), 68, 102.
5. A. Bronson Alcott and Charles Lane, "The Consociate Family Life," *New Age*, November 1, 1843, 120; also published in *Herald of Freedom*, September 8, 1843, and reprinted in Clara Endicott Sears, *Bronson Alcott's Fruitlands* (Boston: Houghton Mifflin, 1915), 48.

The cast themselves do not disappoint. The supporting roles are filled by characters such as Samuel Larned, who claimed to have lived for a year entirely off crackers; Samuel Bower, a nocturnal nudist who finally went off to Florida where the climate was more suitable; and Joseph Palmer of No Town, Massachusetts, who had been imprisoned for wearing a beard. Fruitlands itself seems a No Place well suited to such exponents of negativity, people who defined themselves through what they weren't and didn't, like that Thoreau of Emerson's not completely eulogistic funeral eulogy, the "protestant *à outrance*" whose life contained so many renunciations: "He was bred to no profession; he never married; he lived alone; he never went to church; he never voted; he refused to pay a tax to the State; he ate no flesh, he drank no wine, he never knew the use of tobacco; and, though a naturalist, he used neither trap nor gun."[6] The Fruitlanders could rival this catalogue of negatives, renunciations, and refusals. But to attribute the failure of Fruitlands to the triumph of circumstances over idealism is to oversimplify the issues at stake in the establishment of the community in the first place.

This reductive explanation of the fiasco is often supplemented by an emphasis on the human drama involved. The star of the show is Abel Lamb, as Louisa Alcott calls her father in her memoir, *Transcendental Wild Oats*, who, "with the devoutest faith in the high ideal which was to him a living truth, desired to plant a Paradise, where Beauty, Virtue, Justice and Love might live happily together." As those abstract embodiments are trotted out, we feel an inevitable sense of contingency waiting in the wings for its cue. And if defiance of circumstances is not enough to trigger the drama, there is a villain also, Timon Lion, a.k.a. Charles Lane, intending "to found a colony of Latter Day Saints who, under his patriarchal sway, should regenerate the world and glorify his name for ever."[7] Moreover, at the heart of the action is an interesting version of the eternal triangle, with Abigail Alcott defying the interloper, defending her marriage, and, ironically in view of the community's high-flown asseverations about Woman, doing much of the hard work: taking, in short, the part of Reality Principle.

The dramatic genre being acted out here is of the portmanteau kind. The "Muse of Comedy," as Odell Shepard put it, hovered over the enterprise for the first few months, while the two philosophers interrupted their fruit and vegetable farming with frequent trips to other communities such as Brook Farm and the Harvard Shakers, and fellow

6. Ralph Waldo Emerson, "Thoreau," in *Lectures and Biographical Sketches, Works*, 10:392.
7. Louisa May Alcott, *Transcendental Wild Oats* (Boston: Roberts Brothers, 1876), reprinted in Sears, *Fruitlands*, 150.

luminaries in Concord, Boston, and New York, thereby missing most of the harvest, until replaced by the muse of near-tragedy when the weather grew cold, financial problems mounted, and tension deepened. In early January 1844 the community collapsed, Alcott went into a depression from which he nearly died, and Lane's son William fell into the clutches of the Shakers.[8]

Undeniably a tragicomic scenario was played out at Fruitlands, but things were not as simple as that. The members of the community were people, not caricatures. It is natural that there should have been no love lost between Louisa May Alcott and Charles Lane. *Transcendental Wild Oats*, though written over thirty years after the experiment took place, was inevitably informed by the perspective of the ten-year-old child who actually experienced life at the community and who, unlike her Brook Farm contemporaries, had no reason to look nostalgically back across the interval of time. From her point of view the energetic and forceful Lane had been a clear threat to the tight little family of which she had been, and remained, so integral a part. If her antipathy wavered, she had only to refer to her childhood diary: "Mr. L. was in Boston, and we were glad. In the eve Father and Mother and Anna and I had a long talk. I was very unhappy and we all cried. Anna and I cried in bed, and I prayed God to keep us all together."[9] Subsequent commentators such as Clara Endicott Sears and Odell Shepard have built on this version of things. The latter, for example, describes Lane as "the cold and logical theorist," "temporarily ridden, to the verge of insanity, by an idea."[10] More recently, however, Lane has been somewhat rehabilitated, as commentators have remembered that it was he who put up the money for the experiment in the first place, and that, despite the undeniable tensions that arose during the last days of the community, the Alcotts themselves were soon back on civil terms with him. Indeed, Dahlstrand emphasizes the unanimity of Lane and Alcott to such an extent that it is difficult not merely to sense any conflict but even to gain a picture of their separate personalities.[11]

Part of the problem is that Alcott characteristically lost the principal

8. Shepard, *Pedlar's Progress*, 367.
9. *Louisa May Alcott: Her Life, Letters, and Journals*, ed. E. D. Cheney (Boston: Little, Brown, 1939), 39.
10. Shepard, *Pedlar's Progress*, 377, 345.
11. The most sustained and sympathetic treatment of Lane is a doctoral dissertation by Roger William Cummins, "The Second Eden: Charles Lane and American Transcendentalism" (University of Minnesota, 1967). Cummins points out that Lane stayed with the Alcotts for several months in 1845, more than two years after the breakup of the community (193). Dahlstrand claims that it was only in late 1843 that Lane and Alcott began to have doubts about each other (*Alcott: An Intellectual Biography*, 201).

source of documentary evidence for one of the main episodes in his life, his journals for the years 1841–44, when in August 1844 the mail coach galloped away from him in Albany with his records of those years, plus some other effects. There is a kind of serendipity of loss. All his adult life Alcott wrote voluminous and minute diaries, large swaths of which, to his sorrow, nobody wanted to read, but the very volumes that could have been guaranteed close attention are precisely the ones that vanished. One commentator has even speculated, without a shred of evidence, that, presumably for some deep-rooted psychological reason, Alcott engineered the loss deliberately.[12] This explanation ignores not merely the man's acknowledged transparency of character but also the fact that six years later he was still writing to the superintendent of the railroad in New York City to ask if the material had at that late date happened to turn up, since he hoped his trunk "may have gone down the river and be stored at your deposit for lost baggage at New York."[13] When one relates this loss to the silence of Ripley and the other Brook Farm leaders on the subject of the ideology that underlay their own community, it hardly seems fanciful to connect such suspensions of discourse to those breaks in the fossil record about which Darwin complained, and which were perceived by Niles Eldredge and Stephen Jay Gould as an "expression," paradoxically enough, of the way evolution actually occurred by the process of "punctuated equilibria." One could argue that it would be inappropriate to have a substantial historical record of communities that were themselves intended to transform the historical process. Be that as it may, the loss of the Fruitlands material tempts the historian in one of two unsatisfactory directions: either toward resurrecting Alcott in the full glory of his eccentricities, or toward pitching the discussion at such a level of philosophical generality that it is almost impossible to get at the dynamics underlying the establishment, and rapid disintegration, of the community.

On one level, of course, one can just put the disaster down to incompetence; but that in itself can be seen as a reflection of confused objectives and deep-seated tensions. Nonetheless, it is possible to reconstruct the ideological interaction that took place. We can supplement the meager Alcott material that dates from the period of the community

12. See Anne C. Rose, *Transcendentalism as a Social Movement, 1830–1850* (New Haven: Yale University Press, 1981), 206.
13. "Eighty-Six Letters of A. Bronson Alcott," pt. 2, ed. Frederick Wagner, in *Studies in the American Renaissance, 1980*, ed. Joel Myerson (Boston: Twayne, 1980), 199, letter of December 7, 1850. He also wrote to his brother Junius on the same day, expressing "some hope of finding it": see *The Letters of A. Bronson Alcott*, ed. Richard L. Herrnstadt (Ames: Iowa State University Press, 1969), 160.

itself with what is known about his earlier and later positions, and about the general Transcendentalist concerns which he shared. He, too, was seeking to identify the perfect social unit, believing that once this was achieved the serial mechanism would do the rest. It thus becomes possible to see what the English reformers he met had to offer him, and in particular how their doctrine of circumstances—as defined, for example, in a document furnished by Charles Lane called "The Circumstantial Law"—could be perceived as providing the key to transforming the human universe by laying down how the ideal and the material, the spiritual and circumstantial realms, could be reconciled. As in the case of the Brook Farmers' response to Brisbane's translation of Fourier, both the transatlantic provenance of this ideology and its structural completeness provided Alcott with an immediate and exhilarating vision, a moment of revelation, while at the same time, coming as it did out of the institution James Greaves had set up at Ham in Surrey, it suggested an already established set of values, an implicit myth.

We can explore, too, the documentation that Lane has left behind—with care, of course, since in effect we are looking at only half of a dialogue, and a dialogue in which, moreover, the speakers do not always appear to have been listening to each other—in order to ascertain in some detail the course of *his* thinking as it led up to the founding of the community. By doing so we shall see in the next chapter how Alcott managed to overlook the fact that the circumstantial law had fundamentally different implications for Lane than for himself. Lane's view was that the *individual* provided the environment in which the forces of matter and spirit could achieve a synthesis. Once this synthesis had been accomplished, harmony would radiate outward and transform society. The consociate family merely provided an intermediate point in this process, a fulcrum by means of which the individual could gain leverage on society at large. Alcott does not appear to have argued with this view, at least at first; it is, however, clearly incompatible with his belief that the nuclear, indeed the biological, family in itself provided the instrument for the reconciliation of the polarities of the universe. For him the family was the fundamental unit of society, the microcosm or molecule, which when perfected—when, in his terminology, established as holy—would transmit its virtues along the serial chain through sheer force of example.

Fruitlands does indeed present us with a drama, but it is not some allegorical clash between the Lamb and the Lion. It is a drama of the mind, of ideology, in which two sincere and altruistic individuals found enough common ground, to use a convenient phrase, to build a community, only to discover that in their attempts to reconcile the ideal and the material, each had unintentionally taken on the role of an intractable circumstance that must confound the idealism of the other.

The old view of Bronson Alcott's philosophical allegiances was best expressed by Shepard: "His peculiarity was not that he was an idealist, for all true Americans are that. It was, rather, that he was nothing else."[14] Harriet Martineau, a century before Shepard, had gone even further, complaining that Alcott's antisensationalism, as exhibited in his educational practice, posed a problem for those (like herself) unlucky enough not to have the full use of their senses in the first place: the blind, deaf, and dumb are hardly likely to receive adequate care and appropriate educational facilities if able-bodied people are encouraged to think that the "interior being of these sufferers is in a perfect state, only the means of manifestation being deficient."[15] As we have seen, a modern commentator such as Dahlstrand, while conceding that Alcott tried to cope with circumstances, agrees that his essential position is that of an idealist. Certainly he adduces sufficient evidence for his claim, and it is unarguable that Alcott often thought of himself in that light. Alcott's instinct, however, like that of his fellow Transcendentalists, was to search for a way of apprehending the world in which circumstances were not to be transcended but identified as part of a system that joined polarities in a repetitive structure: a serial law, in short. His attitude toward the vexed subject of miracles, as expressed in his journals in 1836 at the height of the controversy, provides a good example: "The wonderful cures wrought by Jesus, were wrought in accordance with the action of certain immutable laws, *organic, and spiritual.* It is the part of the true organism to ascertain these laws, and, from the knowledge of these, to interpret the phenomena, that are the exponent of these laws—Truth to attempt this. *The philosophy of the miracles of Christ*—this is my aim—."[16]

Dorothy McCuskey, in her 1940 book *Bronson Alcott, Teacher,* suggested a useful way of regarding this structure of law. In discussing Coleridge's influence on Alcott during the period when he was teach-

14. Introduction to Alcott, *Journals*, xxvi.
15. Harriet Martineau, *Society in America*, 3 vols. (London: Saunders, Otley, 1837), 3:176–77.
16. "Bronson Alcott's Journal for 1836," in *Studies in the American Renaissance, 1978*, ed. Joel Myerson (Boston: Twayne, 1978), 39, entry for March 1, 1836.

ing at Germantown in Pennsylvania (1831–34), she remarks that the English poet established a "method of scientific thought" in which philosophy is considered "bi-polar," with Plato concentrating on truth as it manifests itself at the ideal end (*"de mundo intelligibili"*), while Bacon confines himself to the material (*"de mundo sensibili"*). Coleridge, she concludes, "thus corroborated Alcott's feeling (it was scarcely more than that) that Bacon was, in some way, related to the spiritual principle. . . . Alcott particularly delighted in Coleridge's eclecticism—his inclusion of Plato, Aristotle, Jesus, Bacon, and the German philosophers in one system."[17]

These philosophers are in one system because everything is in one system. As Alcott put it a couple of years later in his journals: "Body is Spirit at its circumference. It denotes its confines to the external sense; it individualizes, defines Spirit, breaks the Unity into Multiplicity and places under the vision of man parts of the great whole which, standing thus separate, can be taken in by the mind—too feeble to apprehend the whole at once and requiring all save an individual thing to be excluded at a single view."[18] Matter, in short, is spirit brought into focus. One can apparently have access to the totality only by way of an "individual thing" which acts as the definition—or, to use Emerson's term, representative—of spirit. The connecting structure, what Emerson called the over-soul, is modular and repetitive, its unity achieved by multiplying from its unit. At his most optimistic Alcott foresaw the possibility that someone might come across the actual "calculus" that conjoins matter and spirit and holds them together in a single system, the formula of series itself. In one of the "Orphic Sayings" he published in the *Dial* in 1840, he almost anticipates the late twentieth-century search for what Stephen Hawking has called "a complete unified theory of everything in the universe all at one go," telling us:

We need what Genius is unconsciously seeking, and, by some daring generalization of the universe, shall assuredly discover, a spiritual calculus, a novum organon, whereby nature shall be defined in the soul, the soul in God, matter in spirit, polarity resolved into unity; and that power which pulsates in all life, animates and builds all organizations, shall manifest itself as one universal deific energy, present alike at the outskirts and center of the universe, whose center and circumference

17. Dorothy McCuskey, *Bronson Alcott, Teacher* (New York: Macmillan, 1940), 74.
18. Alcott, *Journals*, 73, entry for December 21, 1835.

are one; omniscient, omnipotent, self-subsisting, uncontained, yet containing all things in the unbroken synthesis of its being.[19]

The single sentence acts like an elaborately woven trawling net in which totality might be captured. As Taylor Stoehr has said of the assumptions behind the "Orphic Sayings": "Bronson Alcott thought one need only find the right formula, the correct expression of the truth, and it would be immediately apparent to all. There would be no argument, only instant conviction."[20] And yet Alcott had but to review his own intellectual strivings to be aware that this "complete unified theory of everything" hardly seemed to relate to the clash of matter and spirit in life's daily round. In an unpublished passage of his journal for 1834, for example, he shows himself grappling with—and indeed to a surprising extent approaching a solution to—this problem.[21]

In talking about his pupils, he makes the point that writing, in the form of journals and correspondence, provides a good means of development for the young mind because the child finds in describing his environment that he "is himself extended over the circle around him."[22] We have seen how Emerson was to claim in "Circles" that "throughout nature this primary figure is repeated without end."[23] The linguistic colonialism of the children Alcott is describing here can accordingly be seen as the second stage of a process, the first being the formation of the skull's topography, the mind of a baby modifying her head. But, just as Alcott seems to counterbalance his observations of Anna's cranial evolution with remarks about his mission to improve infant character, so here he becomes aware that this educational doctrine implies a somewhat overproprietorial attitude toward the external world, for he goes on to remark a little later in the entry that "this was a *cloudy, dim* day," and as a consequence his pupils have not worked well. The admission leads to an interesting modification of his position. "Without asserting for *circumstances* the transcendent importance which they receive in the theory of *Mr. Owen*," he tells us (the ironic use of "transcendent" in the circumstantial context giving us some hint, perhaps, of the intellectual authoritativeness that Emerson and others found in

19. A. Bronson Alcott, "Orphic Sayings XXXI," *Dial* 1 (July 1840): 93; Stephen Hawking, *A Brief History of Time* (London: Bantam, 1988), 155.

20. Taylor Stoehr, *Nay-Saying in Concord: Emerson, Alcott, and Thoreau* (Hamden, Conn.: Archon Books, 1979), 18.

21. A. Bronson Alcott, MS journals, Houghton Library, 59M-308 (7), 25–40, entry for April 23, 1834.

22. Ibid., 26–27.

23. Ralph Waldo Emerson, "Circles," in *Essays 1*, 179.

Alcott as a talker), it is nevertheless true that to a large extent "the wisdom and happiness" of men is determined by their environment. "That men form and modify institutions is true; but it is equally true that these institutions, by a reflex influence, form men—shape individual and national character."[24] This balance of inner and outer had been crisply summarized in his "Observations on the Life of my First Child" three years previously, when he complained that "man and the universe have not been taken as forming a whole, mutually connected, existing as appulsive, and impulsive, influences upon each other, out of which human volition is born."[25] One cannot help noticing the similarity in sentiment, and even in wording, to that passage which William Henry Channing was to write fifteen years later in his *Spirit of the Age*: "In action and reaction, each impulse encounters circumstances which it moulds, or is moulded by, and from all combined experience of pleasure and pain is formed a reflected image of the harmonious conditions of Integral existence." Channing's point, too, is that this dialectical interaction provides a *willed* harmony.

Alcott goes on to describe this reciprocal process in more detail, concentrating particularly on how it leads people to accept the Baconian or Lockean universe as the whole truth. He explains that man possesses free will and thus has dominion over his environment. The temptations provided by his animal frame, however, and the influences of external nature make him lose his perspective in the course of time, and he becomes "a servile slave of his own folly; and having resigned himself to the perverted influences of his own institutions, he loses the original perceptions with which he was wont to behold things, and terminates his vision in the reflex image of himself on surrounding things. Then comes [*sic*] the half-visaged theories of materialism—the transcendental power of circumstances—the one-eyed philosophy of Experience—substituting effects for causes, and solving all mysteries by outward observation."[26] In other words, man makes his presence felt on

24. Alcott, MS journals, 29.
25. Alcott, "Observations," 277. His difficulty in negotiating this complex and potentially paradoxical idea is well illustrated by the passage that immediately follows: "Human vitality, not less than inert matter, is influenced by general laws. Man's constitution differs from inert natures, chiefly, in its internal power of self-movement. By volition, man become himself an agent—he gains the power of acting on himself, of influencing, in a secondary way, matter about him. This power is limited because it is the offspring of greater power, operating upon him, from the laws of vitality without him; and becomes efficient, in proportion as it coincides with the uniformity of these laws. He modifies his own being, by his own volition, but he does this in accordance with the actual influences which mean even volition itself" (278).
26. Alcott, MS journals, 32–33.

the external world and then is impressed by the evidence of his own manipulation of that world; consequently, instead of taking his superiority for granted, he becomes subservient to, and tries to learn from, the environment which he has, in part, created. Although in this respect he is deluded, and a victim of the historical process, nevertheless there is a bright side: "This is all well for the melioration of mans [*sic*] outward condition." Humility toward circumstances is unnecessary, but in its way it is educative. It "fits him up a more comfortable dwelling, opens communication with his brethren, developes and directs his manual skill and activity, and fits him up in life, provided with the means of entering upon the great vocation which he was sent to complete—*the right use of his free will.*"[27]

There is an extraordinarily fruitful kind of paradox here. Our dominance over circumstances leads, by the misunderstanding of later generations, to an increased respect for, and therefore knowledge of, our environment, and thence to even greater control. The materialistic approach gives humanity a stepping-off point for higher things:

> Human effort does not end in nature; it is the purpose of Heaven that it should mould and shape nature to the furtherance of its own ends—which springing from the mind, must return their fruits to the mind—as the germinating seed produces from the tree that is shaped out of it, its counterpart in return. Mind, unless it remade [*sic*] and mould the pliant elements of matter, into instruments for its own manifestations and growth, forfeits its divine mission, and degrades itself to a lower element—losing its attributes in the grosser forms to which it seeks affinity.[28]

To avoid confusion, it must be said that whereas in previous chapters I have been using "nature" in the Emersonian sense, as one of the names one can give to the total structure of the universe, Alcott is thinking of it more classically as referring to circumstantial or material reality. This train of thought—that the physical world provides a stage on which the spirit can manifest itself and grow before once more returning to its elevated plane—leads him, a little later, to formulate his own version of what has come to be known as the "organic metaphor." The figure is an important element in Transcendentalist writing since it is perfectly adapted to express an anti-Lockean stance—though, appropriately enough, it evolves through time to reflect the

27. Ibid., 33.
28. Ibid., 33–34.

movement's development and the shifting emphases of individual contributors.

Its debut, so to speak—certainly its first significant appearance—occurred in Sampson Reed's M.A. oration, "On Genius," delivered at the Harvard Divinity School in 1821 to an audience that included the eighteen-year-old Emerson, to whom it was a revelation. Reed begins by claiming, "There is something in the inmost principles of an individual, when he begins to exist, which urges him onward." The language is unobtrusive, perhaps, but it is being inscribed on the very surface of the tabula rasa. Reed gives this "something" the name of love, but clearly feels uncomfortable with the implication of that term as far as free will is concerned, since it inevitably preempts human decision in just the sort of manner that Calvinist election does. He goes on to stress, rather peculiarly, that love here is a morally neutral concept, a sort of life force that can be harnessed to either good or evil. He then introduces his metaphor: "The mind of the infant contains within itself the first rudiments of all that will be hereafter, and needs nothing but expansion, as the leaves and branches and fruit of a tree are said to exist in the seed from which it springs." Again, he is eager to stress that, despite the fact that the seed is a "given," the path of its development and growth is not preordained. People retain the option of over-reaching, as Reed makes clear by launching an attack on great men: "There prevails an idea in the world that its great men are more like God than others. This sentiment carries in its bosom sufficient evil to bar the gates of heaven." In fact, he goes on to claim, "there is something which is called genius that carries in itself the seeds of its own destruction." What he is objecting to is what one might call the Carlylean version of the hero, though of course the oration predates it. His basic argument is that "the intellectual eye of man is formed to see the light, not to make it," that the organism's task is ultimately to experience a revelation of what lies beyond itself.[29]

In the preceding chapter we saw Channing provide a later example of the organic metaphor—in his case, in effect, *two* organic metaphors. In his 1843 pamphlet *A Statement of the Principles of the Christian Union*, he, like Reed, talks of a seed developing into a tree: "Its germ of life, its organizing principles, its growth, is from God." But just as Reed introduces a gulf between man and God by claiming the moral neutrality of this life force, and establishing a distinction between seeing and mak-

29. Sampson Reed, "On Genius," in George Hochfield, ed., *Selected Writings of the American Transcendentalists* (New York: Signet, 1966), 67–68.

ing (or trying to make) the light, so Channing feels it necessary to plant another tree, so to speak. He goes on to discuss the current eclecticism, which may lead to a barren "vanity of knowledge," and then refers to the "tree of knowledge, of good and evil," which "may again fill our minds with seeds of death." This second tree counterbalances the one "organized" by God in having that ambivalence that Reed attributes to his first and only one. Knowledge for Channing, like love for Reed, is a quality that can be either good or evil.

What we are seeing in these contrasting examples is two men coping, each in his own fashion, with the problem of reconciling a Godhead who is somehow or other immanent in his world with the possibility of free will, and beyond that with the dilemma of how to relate the material and spiritual planes to each other. It is interesting to see how Alcott manipulates the organic metaphor in order to cope with this issue in his 1834 journal entry, thirteen years after Reed (the oration circulated in manuscript form among Emerson's friends until finally being published in Elizabeth Peabody's *Aesthetic Papers* in 1849)[30] and nine before Channing.

According to Alcott, right-thinking people know that

> they are but the heart, and external nature is the woody bark of that great tree, whose life is from another sphere; whose roots penetrate the depths of nature, whose trunk ascends into the clouds, and through whose ample leaves, and numerous tubes, it imbibes the precious nutriment upon which it feeds from heaven and earth!—evolving itself out of eternity to manifest itself in space, and mark the duration of time by its annual rings! and that when decay shall have laid it low, behind, in the soul which it had so long overshadowed, are left the symbols of its strength, in the acorns which another generation shall behold expanded into a child like itself.[31]

What Alcott has succeeded in doing—and, alas, this is not to make any broad claims for his literary accomplishment—is to find a way of establishing an even balance between the material and spiritual worlds in his use of the metaphor. The tree's "life" comes from "another sphere" though its roots are in nature. Its nutriment is both from the earth itself and from the divine light above. His exclamatory invocation of the tree's annual rings once more anticipates Emerson's claim that

30. Elizabeth Palmer Peabody, ed., *Aesthetic Papers* (New York: G. P. Putnam, 1849), 58–64.
31. Alcott, MS journals, 35–36.

"around every circle another can be drawn": we visualize the progressive pulsations of a spiritual force in a material world.

The imaginative interpenetration of the two terms continues into the later stages of the cycle. It is not clear whether "soul" for "soil" is a slip of the pen, though that is quite possible. Some imp of the perverse favored this particular substitution, which is also evident in the errata at the beginning of Brisbane's *Social Destiny of Man*: "Page 387 line 27—for souls, read soils."[32] Alcott's pun, whether accidental or deliberate, suggests a Codmanesque doubleness at the heart of existence and provides us with a simultaneous apprehension of opposites, not torrid and frigid zones but divine and earthly ones. On the one hand, we envisage an accumulation of spirituality, a fertile stockpile of the values that underpin individual existence and accumulate during the history of civilization. On the other, we have the self-renewing system of the natural world, that cycle of decomposition and growth (without, however, the addition of manure, of which more later) which was to be the basis of Whitman's optimism in "Song of Myself." Thus, the acorns, products of the two domains, can grow up and maintain that exactly inbetween stance established by the parental oaks.

It is perhaps a little anticlimactic to have to admit that this reconciliation is not sustained in Alcott's passage. In fact, he goes on to discuss why it is that the balance between the halves of our being so frequently tips over to the physical side. His final attitude seems to be that life is but a testing ground to prepare us for our entrance into a higher state of being. Yet enough of his earlier vision of a harmonious and self-perpetuating state on earth remains to make him sound at least equivocal about the nature of the test we are to undergo: it will be good for our souls, he claims, whether we are "influenced happily or unhappily, by external nature—by the institutions of society—by men—science, philosophy, or art."[33] Again, we must note that when he talks here of "external nature," he is quite happy to equate it with the historical world, "the institutions of society," and so on. They are all, in their various ways, embodiments of contingent reality, as opposed to the spiritual or ideal domain, his point being that to concede the power of the material world is not necessarily to admit its malignancy.

In any case, the optimism about the possibilities of life on earth which finds expression in his use of the organic metaphor can be found in other places in his early writings. What we discover is not

32. Albert Brisbane, *Social Destiny of Man; or, Association and Reorganization of Industry* (Philadelphia: C. F. Stollmeyer, 1840), xvi.
33. Alcott, MS journals, 40.

simply a hopeful doctrine but a doctrine that addresses the nature and significance of hopefulness. In *The Doctrine and Discipline of Human Culture*, for example, published two years after the journal entry, we find Alcott prophesying the advent of what amounts to a heaven on earth: "It is the mission of this age . . . to reproduce Perfect Men. The faded image of Humanity is to be restored, and Man to reappear in his original brightness. It is to mould anew our Institutions, our Manners, our Men. It is to restore Nature to its rightful use, purify Life; hallow the functions of the Human Body, and regenerate Philosophy, Literature, Art, Society. The Divine Idea of Man is to be formed in the common consciousness of this age and genius mould all its products in accordance with it."[34]

It is characteristic of Alcott's maddening insistence on having his cake and eating it too (though he might not have appreciated the greedy metaphor) that he foresees the accomplishment of this mission in terms of the collective transformation of human expectations and standards ("the common consciousness of this age") and at the same time as the product of genius. Perhaps the two can be reconciled if we assign "genius" the alternative meaning of spirit of a people. Although in the "Orphic Saying" which I quoted earlier on the subject of a spiritual calculus the word seemed to be used in its individual sense, the context was a search for the "daring generalization" that would unify the phenomena of the world, and one might suppose some sort of corporate intelligence to be the appropriate instrument for such an achievement. The whole point of the law of series is that it makes distinctions between the one and the many ultimately irrelevant, as we have seen in Emerson's claims concerning the averageness of great men. Nevertheless—and this will become an important issue when the subject of Fruitlands itself is broached—as far as having a utopian programme is concerned, the matter needs to be resolved because it requires us to deal with simple causality: the extent to which the community was and was not the product of individual rather than collective intention becomes a key to understanding what happened to it.

In the meantime, up until his visit to England in 1842, a program was what, among many other things, Alcott simply did not have. Indeed, the only constructive action toward the creation of a better world which he took in the four years between the end of his teaching career and his meeting with Lane was adherence to a strict diet, and in a

34. A. Bronson Alcott, *The Doctrine and Discipline of Human Culture* (Boston: Monroe, 1836), 4.

lesser man this might well hint of nothing more significant than a realistic assessment of the meagerness of his funds. "The hunger of an age," he says in one of the "Orphic Sayings," "is alike a presentiment and pledge of its own supply," and hunger Alcott could readily provide.[35]

It is easy to miss the point here, to assume that his attitude toward diet represented a kind of philosophically based anorexia. Whereas Emerson would probably have regarded it in that light ("A man cannot free himself by any selfdenying ordinances, neither by water nor potatoes"), Alcott clearly did not.[36] Dieting for him was a means not of minimizing his hold on the material world but, as we shall see, of putting that relationship on the right track to "reproduce Perfect Men." One of the most touching of his journal entries, dating from 1839, describes an errand to the butcher's to buy supplies for the family (he had given up meat himself four years previously). "Not speaking the dialect, nor having the air of the market," he was a soft touch for the butcher, who, "well knowing what I wanted, took me literally," and palmed him off with some unlikely cut of meat: "Any revision of the carnal code was above his morality."[37] Alcott describes being summoned home later to "survey the strange flitch as it lay on the table," and being forbidden to do this part of the shopping in future. He goes on to talk of his feelings about the incident: "What have I to do with butchers? Am I to go smelling about markets? . . . Cruelty stares at me from the butcher's face. I tread amidst carcasses. I am in the presence of the slain. The death-set eyes of beasts peer at me and accuse me of belonging to the race of murderers. Quartered, disembowelled creatures on suspended hooks plead with me. I feel myself dispossessed of the divinity. I am a replenisher of graveyards."[38]

The correlation between meat and a low morality is a direct and literal one, established through cruelty. It was, quite simply, because he *was* a butcher that the butcher gave him an unwanted cut of meat. As far as Alcott is concerned, in repudiating a flesh diet he is rejecting death and affirming the values of life. And within the Christian tradition bread is a spiritualized version of flesh, thus serving to fulfill the needs of body and soul simultaneously. Moreover, Alcott finds "that power that pulsates in all life" in the pattern of growth and harvest, and indeed explicitly relates this rhythm to the sort of historical pulsa-

35. A. Bronson Alcott, "Orphic Sayings XXIV," *Dial* 1 (July 1840): 91.
36. Emerson, *JMN*, 8:282, entry for October 1842.
37. Alcott, *Journals*, 115, entry for February 5, 1839.
38. Ibid.

tions identified by Hedge: "When there is a general craving for bread, that shall assuredly be satisfied; bread is even then growing in the fields. Now, men are lean and famishing; but, behold, the divine Husbandman has driven his share through the age, and sown us bread that we may not perish; yea, the reapers even are going forth, a blithe and hopeful company, while yet the fields weep with the dews of the morning, and the harvests wave in yellow ripeness. Soon shall a table be spread, and the age rejoice in the fulness of plenty."[39] The juxtaposition of weeping fields and bright harvests catches the paradoxical nature of a doctrine of punctuated equilibria very nicely, and more particularly picks up the combination of hope and despair in Alcott's own predicament.

In 1837, as Alcott's pedagogical career declined, an odd seed had been planted in the form of a letter from an English Transcendentalist, James Pierrepoint Greaves, a strange document containing twenty-nine questions, as many maxims, and an account of Greaves's life. Greaves, who had come to hear about Alcott from Harriet Martineau, was presumably sufficiently Neoplatonic to discern the ideal man lurking behind this accidental source of information, and therefore began a correspondence with him, eventually naming his community-cum-school Alcott House in his honor. The effect this long-distance admiration must have had on Alcott as his fortunes went from bad to worse in the late 1830s and early 1840s can readily be imagined, constituting a bright touch of yellow in the midst of weeping fields, particularly since Greaves and his circle shared Alcott's views about the literal as well as the metaphorical harvest, as Greaves's dietary advice to his follower Alexander Campbell reveals. The consumption of dead meat, he says in a letter of 1840, means the accommodation of dead, and therefore deathly, circumstances: "In fruits, in uncooked vegetables, the vital force is operating, and the Spirit's conditionating combinations are there for Life sustenance, for Light organism, for Love essentiality. With dead elements this cannot be. He who feeds upon them, feeds only upon the husk, the visible, the tangible, and corruption is the inevitable consequence: essence and esse are fled—only the coarsest materiality remains."[40] Part of the benefit of vegetarianism is that it makes possible the consumption of raw, indeed living, food, thereby allowing the life force to flow directly into the eater. It is ironic that

39. Alcott, "Orphic Sayings XXIV," 91.
40. *Letters and Extracts from the MS Writings of James Pierrepoint Greaves*, 2 vols. (Ham Common, Surrey: Concordium Press, 1843–45), 1:206, letter of September 11, 1840. Alcott's own copy of this collection of Greaves's letters is in the Houghton Library.

Greaves manages to make this austere and principled diet savor faintly of cannibalism.

Given the parallels between Greaves's theories in this area and his own, the approach from abroad must have suggested to Alcott a change of fortune. In due course (and with the assistance, as was so often the case, of Emerson), he went over to England to see what harvest might be gleaned from this burgeoning relationship.

As in the case of those members of the public who were to respond to the advertisement that would shortly be placed in the *Morning Chronicle*, this visit was a voyage by public conveyance to a confrontation with utopian destiny, and it is typical of Alcott's luck that his ship was too late—by a margin of three months, that being the interval that had elapsed since Greaves's death when Alcott turned up at Alcott House in the summer of 1842.[41]

Alcott House was a school, run on strict principles of cold showers and vegetarianism and in accordance with Pestalozzian methods, by a young member of the Greavesian group called Henry Gardiner Wright. It must have been enormously flattering to Alcott to have such an institution named after him. All around was the buzz of reforming activity, amusingly detailed by Emerson in "English Reformers," as he itemized the material Alcott was sending him from England: "Here are Educational Circulars, and Communist Apostles; Alists; Plans for syncretic associations, and Pestalozzian Societies, Self-Supporting Institutions, Experimental Normal Schools, Hydropathic and Philosophical associations, Health Unions and Phalansterian Gazettes, Paradises within the reach of all men, Appeals of Man to Woman, and Necessities of Internal Marriage illustrated by Phrenological Diagrams."[42] Alcott was to spend a busy summer in the company of the authors of these documents, people such as Hugh Dougherty, J. J. Heraud, Francis Barham, Robert Owen, J. W. Marston, and John Goodwyn Barmby.[43] But the most important relationship he struck up was with the man generally conceded to be the heir to Greaves's philosophical estate and to the leadership of the Transcendentalists at Ham: Charles Lane.

The two men immediately discovered that they had a great deal in common. Indeed, like a true Transcendentalist, Lane even had a doctrine of instant recognition to give a basis to the occasion: "The mind

41. Greaves died on March 11, 1842.
42. Ralph Waldo Emerson, "English Reformers," *Dial* 3 (October 1842): 227.
43. For Alcott's activities in England, see Alcott, *Letters*, 69–91, and Shepard, *Pedlar's Progress*, 303–42.

which is already new natured, like a true mason, at a glance hails a brother." This assertion occurs in Ham House Tract no. 5, *The Old, the New Old, and the New*, published in 1841, a copy of which is pasted into Alcott's "Autobiographical Collections" for 1840–44.[44] In this piece, intriguingly, Lane also offers his own version of evolution by default.

Lane points out that we are always being told we are on the brink of a great political, religious, and scientific crisis, but it somehow never seems to lead to permanent and ultimate change. Beneath this layer of "momentary agitation," however, there is an "*under current* of public opinion," by which thinking people "endeavour to attract us from the puppets to the men who move the wires." This effort, too, proves disappointing: "If they sometimes approach Socialism, they are not more than Socialists." But, there is yet another level, that of the Main Flood. I have mentioned that Tuveson's metaphor of a "forward drift" in history fails to incorporate collapse or regress in the pattern, unlike the models produced by the Transcendentalists and the Fourierists. Lane, like the latter, manages to structure discontinuity, providing an ingenious tissue of reverse causality to connect the unconnected: "If the grand exploits of our own day are only of an ephemeral nature, which is, doubtless, the fact, we shall learn this fact daily more and more rapidly; until the experience becomes so immediate and intense, and such a small portion shall serve us, that little shall be put into so small a portion of space and time, that our experience and our intuition shall become almost one, and the consummation be fulfilled. A child's top, at the extreme height and velocity of its spinning, appears to stand still."[45]

What this passage does is to make transformation the product of disillusionment. We discover—what would ring bells in the mind of a "failure" like Alcott—that much of the daily fuss and agitation is about nothing and gets nowhere. As we grow more experienced, we come to that conclusion more readily; our response accelerates exponentially until it becomes more or less instantaneous. But the unexpected bonus of this process is that experience (in Emerson's terms, history) and intuition (nature) are reconciled. Outer and inner worlds are united, albeit through the apprehension of the negative. "The really new man, the really new-natured, or true-natured, or good-natured, individual"

44. Charles Lane, *The Old, the New Old, and the New* (Leeds: Joshua Hobson, 1841), 7; A. Bronson Alcott, "Autobiographical Collections" (1840–44), 10 vols., Houghton Library, 59M-307 (4), 5:133.
45. Lane, *The Old*, 3, 5.

comes into being.[46] Lane's image of this revolution, like Emerson's vision of standing Monadnock's head, insistently combines extreme activity with motionlessness. He thus gives a practical legitimacy to the Transcendentalist claim that, in Alcott's words, "the voice of the private, not the popular heart, is alone authentic."[47]

An excellent case study of the compatibility and complementariness of Lane's and Alcott's ideas occurs in an article written by the former on the subject of the latter and published in the *Dial* a year after they met. Lane devotes some of his space to explaining why Alcott House was not a completely satisfactory experiment (here he is doing some essential loin girding for the imminent Fruitlands enterprise), and talks illuminatingly about the problem of the ideal and the circumstantial. It is not enough for us simply to follow inspiration, he claims, because of the

> difference between genius and the generator: between God and man. The *idea* is unquestionably impregnated by the divine mind on the human soul at *a flash*; at an instant of time whose duration is too short to be capable of measurement; and it may therefore be more truly said to be conceived in eternity than in time. But the outworking of the idea is a temporal work; and assiduity is constantly an attribute in true genius. The seed, buried in the dark earth, germinates, under the favorable conditions of spring, at some inappreciable point in time. Of the radiant sun at noon, while we say it is, it is not. Thus of every deific manifestation. But to man is awarded another course. Through the law of industry he is to elaborate those divinely generated conceptions, to whose inbirth time is not attributable.[48]

What we see here is the programmatic facet of Lane, and it takes us beyond the "instant of time" into which, to return to the earlier passage, an "immediate and intense" experience can be fitted. Indeed, he is now intent on separating what was previously bound together, and he does so by means of the organic metaphor, though he develops Sampson Reed's image a stage further than Alcott did.

Alcott stressed the fact that if a tree's branches were in the air, and its general tendency was upward, its roots were nevertheless in the ground. Future generations would benefit from this even balance be-

46. *Ibid.*, 6.
47. Alcott, "Orphic Sayings XVII," 89.
48. Charles Lane, "A. Bronson Alcott's Works," *Dial* 3 (April 1843): 21–22.

tween the spiritual and the circumstantial. Lane similarly acknowledges the role of the "deific manifestation," the sun, but at the same time he tells us that "while we say it is, it is not." He has a knack of rattling off slightly inaccessible epigrams, though in this case that may be the point. He seems to be saying that the sun is there, but we cannot reach it, so we might as well cultivate our gardens and concentrate on what we *can* engage with. The latency of the eternal in the present, the prospect of *kairos*, is all very well, but we have to operate in the historical domain. The focus is on the earth below, not the heavens above, and he emphasizes that people have their own distinct role to play in the evolutionary process. It is their duty to obey the "law of industry," to "elaborate" what they have received from God. His train of thought is moving inexorably toward an attempt to reach an accommodation of the circumstantial world as it presented itself on the Fruitlands farm in central Massachusetts.

This programmatic side of Lane's philosophy is worth mentioning because it is often assumed that the Greavesian thinkers based their notions of philosophic good on the principle of more or less total inertia. To some extent the circle's vocabulary laid it open to this sort of interpretation, but it is nonetheless one that is not wholly fair. Lane, Oldham, and Wright summed up their master's "peculiar practical doctrine" as "the eminent superiority of Being to all knowing and doing." It is easy to slide over the word "practical" in this claim, and to fail to pick up the full resonance of what comes a little later: "Out of this feeling he constantly inculcated not so much that practice should coincide with theory as that a depth of Being should be realized capable of supporting both theory and practice."[49] We are in the realm of the Main Flood here, of the spinning top, where movement is so comprehensive that it is not necessarily ascertainable. The new man, Lane tells us in his Ham House tract, "demands no price, he can receive no recompense, for his payment is involved in every act. He is at war with none, though all may war against him; he works for all, though all may work against him; his system includes all, though other systems may exclude him."[50]

Emerson, revealingly, chose to interpret this doctrine as a commitment to opting out, acknowledging in "English Reformers" that "the remedy, which Mr. Lane proposes for the existing evils, is his 'True Harmonic Association,'" but going on to claim that "he more justly

---

49. Quoted in Shepard, *Pedlar's Progress*, 334. Shepard does not name his source.
50. Lane, *The Old*, 6.

confides in 'ceasing from doing' than in exhausting efforts at inadequate remedies. . . . His words come to us like the voices of home out of a far country."[51] Amusingly, less than a year after these words were published in the *Dial*, Lane criticized Emerson in a letter to Oldham for exactly the reason Emerson had praised *him*: "Mr Emerson is, I think, quite stationary: he is off the Railroad of progress, and merely an elegant, kindly observer of all who pass onwards, and notes down their aspect while they remain in sight; of course when they arrive at a new station they are gone from and for him."[52] The new station at which Lane had now arrived was, of course, Fruitlands, and Lane catches very precisely that particular stance of the Sage of Concord, smiling benignly, but with a suggestion of ironic detachment, at the various experiments undertaken by his friends: Brook Farm, Fruitlands, Thoreau's hut.

But in fact Emerson's stationariness was no more complacent than Lane's "ceasing from doing." Emerson's objection, after all, was that action—or perhaps one should say activism—as such was not radical enough. Associationists try to "arrange a heap of shavings of steel *by hand* in the direction of their magnetic poles instead of thrusting a needle into the heap, and instantaneously they are magnets."[53] *Doing* for him meant fussy, ineffectual manipulation, a tinkering with the processes of history rather than an endorsement of the method of nature, a myth-oriented commitment to outmoded forms of thought and behavior rather than a revelation of the underlying or overarching structure of the world. Yet, as we have seen, Emerson's belief that utopia could be reached instantaneously—"It is and will be magic"—is an essential component of Transcendentalist reforming ideology, and the fact that Lane in his turn downplayed it was to be one of the causes of structural tension in the Fruitlands community. True, Lane acknowledged that the original impulse toward transformation was instantaneous, "an instant of time whose duration is too short to be capable of measurement." But he also supplemented that revelation with a doctrine of gradual amelioration, and it is this latter process that he wishes to stress. The flash, the pulsation, is all very well, though—and this is a

---

51. Emerson, "English Reformers," 236–37.
52. The original letter is now lost, but a copy of it is included in a selection of letters gathered together in an article by William Harry Harland, "Bronson Alcott's English Friends." Written in 1906, it was not published at the time; the MS is at the Fruitlands Museums in Harvard, Mass. In 1978, however, it was edited by Joel Myerson in *Resources for American Literary Study* 8 (September 1978): 24–60; see letter of September 29, 1843 (55).
53. Emerson, *JMN*, 8:210. The associationist in question was Albert Brisbane.

sign not merely of a different philosophical emphasis from Alcott's but of a different, more pragmatic and impetuous temperament, too—he rather pooh-poohs it: "While we say it is, it is not."

The most sustained account we have of Lane's views on the route, and the engine, of "the Railroad of progress" occurs in "The Third Dispensation," an article originally published in 1841 as an introduction to the English edition of *The Phalanstery: or Attractive Industry and Moral Harmony* by the French Fourierist Mme. Gatti de Gamond. Lane does in fact use a number of Fourier's terms in his article, but the main tenor of his argument differs radically from Fourier's with its assumption that man was designed from the beginning, like a fine piece of machine tooling, to operate efficiently within the phalanx. The introduction was republished in pamphlet form by the Pestalozzi Press later in 1841 (Alcott glued a copy of this edition into his "Autobiographical Collections" for the following year) and it reappears as an anonymous contribution in the *Present* for November 15, 1843.[54] It is also discussed by Emerson in "English Reformers."[55]

Lane begins with a quick look at human history to date. There have so far, he says, been two "dispensations." The first was "the form of family union, or connexion by tribes," which had a divisive effect and was followed by a "loftier idea . . . the state of union called national." The second dispensation, however, has not been able to emancipate mankind from the "narrowness" of the first; the survival of the family unit continues to break society down into small cliques and arrests the infinite ramification of human relationships that will take place in an ideal social order. This problem must be solved, since "association is an essential development, and to the coming age its development is assigned."[56]

The problem is that to achieve the perfect society, we need to possess the correct social attitudes; but to develop the correct attitudes (as opposed to selfish familial ones), we need to be members of a perfect society. As Lane puts it, "The difficulty consists in this, that the unitary external arrangements which appear absolutely indispensable *for* the evolution of the unitary spirit, can alone be provided *by* the unitary spirit. We seem to be in an endless circle, of which both halves have lost their centre connexion; for it is an operation no less difficult than

54. [Charles Lane], "The Third Dispensation," *Present*, November 15, 1843, 110–21. This is the most accessible version of the essay. See also Alcott, "Autobiographical Collections," 5:171.
55. Emerson, "English Reformers," 235–37.
56. Lane, "Third Dispensation," 110–11.

the junction of two such discs that is requisite to unity. These segments also being in motion, each upon a false centre of its own, the obstacles to union are incalculably multiplied."[57] Rarely in the history of utopian thought can this fundamental problem have been so lucidly expressed. It is not difficult to imagine a sense of excited recognition on reading this passage from the man who had written that while "men form and modify institutions," it is "equally true that these institutions, by a reflex influence, form men."

Even more important than this identification of the problem is Lane's proffered solution. He goes on to show how the two "halves" are to be fitted together, and does this by means of a further elaboration of the "organic metaphor":

There is, however, a power discovered at work in outward nature, whereby the greatest changes and the highest terrestrial beauty are reached. Thus the soil is softened from rocky fragments to impalpable mould, the forest is transformed into a garden, by the annual decadence of the vegetation nourished in its own primeval rudeness. The wind, the rain, the heat, the cold, magnetism and electricity, are combined by one uniting power to this result. There must be a power superior to the elements elaborating them to this end. Chymical combinations cannot be effected without a chymist. . . .

Is it not constantly present to the feelings and convictions that there is an operant of this kind, setting the various natures in man one to work upon another, in modes analogous to those of the physical world? There are the sunshine and the rain to the soul, as to the soil, the heat and cold, the electricity, and the magnetism, agitating the mind to act upon the body, as vegetation upon the rocks, softing and meliorating, and rendering it still more useful in the elaboration of the higher nature.[58]

This process of friction, interaction, and development obviously resembles that described in the series of rhetorical questions posed by Channing (the *Present*'s editor), in which the point is made that men have to experience isolation and opposition in order to learn how to cooperate.[59]

There is an important distinction to be made, however, between Lane's analysis and Channing's. Channing, as a Fourierist, saw the ma-

57. Ibid., 112.
58. Ibid., 113.
59. William Henry Channing, "Heaven upon Earth," *Present*, March 1, 1844, 298.

terial world as a manifestation of the law of groups and series which
distributes the harmonies of the universe. Humanity alone was out of
tune, though Channing was able to collect an ethical bonus from this
anomaly, demonstrating that the evolutionary process necessary to enable us to harmonize with our surroundings also served the purpose of
giving our experience a moral dimension. Lane, meanwhile, holds that
both the human and the "physical world" are engaged in identical and
simultaneous processes of evolution. It is a perspective much more in
tune with the forthcoming Darwinian breakthrough than the ones I
have explored hitherto. For Lane the harmony of both the world of
nature and that of history is still unfolding. He links the two domains
by making the same pun on "soul" and "soil" that Alcott stumbled into
in his own version of the organic metaphor. Moreover, when he talks
of an operant "setting the various natures in man to work upon one
another," he is thinking not about the development of society but
about that taking place within the individual human mind, supplementing his anticipation of an evolutionary perspective with an account of the human interior that seems to grope toward a psychological vocabulary. Certainly he is unabashed about using a scientific frame
of reference to convey human motives and attitudes. Within each of us,
he says, is a battlefield on which a number of warring factions meet in
order to resolve their differences. Lane's image is that of a crucible in
which the chemicals—one's needs and desires—have been placed by
the almighty chemist so that they will react with one another: "Man is
not, then, in the hopeless position to which the idea of strict self-eleva-
tion would consign him. This self is not a simple ultimate element,
containing no ingredients for human chymical activity. The varied elements are in him, the various natures are in him, and the chymist,
operant, or causer, is no less present in man than in the material
world."[60]

The chemical metaphor is not, as it happens, as much of a metaphor
as it looks. Although the elements of the soul combine and modify one
another in exactly the same way as those of matter, what this fact establishes is not parallelism between the two domains but intersection. It is
at this point that Lane's exposition of Greavesian theory meshes with
Alcott's belief that in some way diet could provide a bridge between
the external circumstantial world and humankind's inward, spiritual
health.

Lane claims that the chemical reaction within the human mind can

60. Lane, "Third Dispensation," 113.

take place only in the context of an appropriate relationship between the individual concerned and his or her external environment. Indeed, the actual ingredients for "human chymical activity" are provided *by* the material world:

> The substance of cerebral organs may differ elementarily as much as their application. If each organ in the brain is designed for a different object, may not the spirit require different nervine elements for the healthful growth of each? Benevolence, Ideality, Constructiveness, being organs altogether so varied, must have not only mental supplies altogether varied, but physical supplies as varied also. For, although interiorly all organs are connected with the one organizer, exteriorly there is a material relation, in which conditions for the organ exist, as the organ itself is a condition to the spirit. If the lowest conditions are disharmonic, the lowest nature must be disharmonic; and man's lowest nature cannot be unharmonized, without the whole instrument vibrating out of tune. Flesh, farina, and fruit cannot be equally suitable means of nourishment to faculties so distinct as those of Veneration, Causality, and Combativeness.[61]

He is of course using the language of phrenology, but his main concern is to relate the development of the brain's different organs to a specialized diet.

Alcott had become interested in phrenology in the early 1830s and in the dietary theories of Sylvester Graham not long afterwards, but he saw them as alternatives, with the Grahamites having the edge, since they gave priority to the soul over the body rather than, as in the case of the phrenologists, vice versa. Phrenologists themselves were aware that in declaring that the topography of the brain provided an explanation for character and behavior they were opening the door to determinism. O.S. Fowler, one of the leading American exponents, calls fatalism "the great gun of the opposition" to his "science," one that he himself tries to duck by claiming that the "exercise of particular mental faculties" leads to the enlargement of "corresponding portions of the brain," and hence to the strengthening of the original faculties.[62] There is a certain unhelpful circularity about his argument: in order to increase one's faculty of benevolence, one must be benevolent. But if the problem with phrenology lies in its suggestion that the individual is

61. Ibid., 116.
62. Dahlstrand, *Alcott: An Intellectual Biography*, 173; O. S. Fowler, *Practical Phrenology*, 3d ed. (New York: O. S. and L. N. Fowler, 1844), 382.

internally programmed (predestination), by the same token the problem with dietary theory is that it suggests that the individual is a product of the environment (the deterministic tendency of the doctrine of the tabula rasa). In short, one could argue that phrenology and dietary theory embody the two fundamental threats to the freedom of the will. In fusing the approaches, Lane was able to suggest to Alcott the possibility of resolving the deterministic difficulties that plagued each of them. The organs of the brain need their appropriate nourishment in order to function correctly; once that has been achieved, however, their interaction is still the responsibility of the "organizer." And of course that "organizer," or individual, has to select the diet that will nourish (or otherwise) those cerebral organs in the first place.

The most formal presentation of Greavesian orthodoxy in respect of the relationship between outer and inner environments, the circumstantial and the spiritual worlds, occurs in a table that was originally drawn up by Greaves himself on a visit to his friend and disciple Alexander Campbell in Stockport in 1840, and which was published by Lane in a slightly revised form in an 1842 issue of the *Healthian*, a journal of the Alcott House group.[63] The material is glued into Alcott's "Autobiographical Collections" for that year, and also copied out in Abigail Alcott's diary, so it obviously had an impact, and can clearly be seen to herald the Fruitlands regime.

We can see from the introduction to the table that the Greavesians were well aware that the whole issue of causality and determinism was a minefield, and that it was safest to proceed on tiptoe. "Circumstances" do not have absolute sway over human identity because, when the roots of the word are explored, they "STAND ROUND" something already created; thus etymology joins logic and truth, a formidable trio, in preventing us from asserting "that circumstances form the character." At the same time, however, they have an influence on what is there already: "we may safely affirm that the END, or the CAUSE in CIRCUMSTANCES produces RESULTS." In a letter to Campbell, Greaves makes some revealing remarks about "conditions": "The love and intelligence in every being will respond in a surprising manner when they are intelligently and lovingly conditionated, that is, when conditionated with their own conditions, and the physical conditions kept as subordinate as possible."[64] The tortured passive at the heart of this sentence, in which beings are to have conditions provided for them, but those con-

---

63. For the original table, see Greaves, *Letters*, 2:80–81, letter of December 28, 1840. For the 1842 version, see Alcott, "Autobiographical Collections," 5:139, reproduced overleaf by permission of the Houghton Library; A. M. Alcott, Diary (1841–44), Houghton Library, MS 59M-311, entry for October 8, 1842.
64. Greaves, *Letters*, 1:162, letter of July 12, 1840.

The True Practical Socialist, being aware that Man is not a simple, but a compound, or, rather, a complex Being, whose threefold Character is formed by the threefold Law in the sympathetic, intellectual, and physical Circumstances, or Conditions, by which he is constantly surrounded, is desirous of presenting to such Law, in its several spheres, the circumstances most conducive to Man's harmonious development.

Though it be true that the CREATIVE POWER cannot properly be attributed to the CIRCUMSTANCES, because the latter term is used to designate the things which STAND ROUND something already created, yet, for as much as RESULTS can never be attained without circumstances, or conditions, and it is only over these that Men individually, or socially, have any interfering power, the furnishing of suitable conditions, is a subject demanding the deepest consideration. While neither etymology, nor logic, nor truth, permits the assertion, that Circumstances form the Character; we may safely affirm that the END, or the CAUSE in CIRCUMSTANCES produces RESULTS.

The following Table is submitted as a Scheme, attempting to show the sort of conditions which should be offered in the Physical Sphere, according to the intention or desire for developing the higher or the highest natures. As a consequence it serves as a key to the interior state of any individual. Each one becomes in this manner a condition to others, for the evolution of the like nature, to that of which such conduct is an exhibition.

For the better understanding of the pure conditions, there is subjoined a hint of the present prevailing errors in each department.

Table No. 1. PHYSICAL CIRCUMSTANCES.

	AIR.	FOOD.	CLOTHING.	HABITATION.	EMPLOYMENT.	EDUCATION.	RELIGION.	MARRIAGE.
Best, for the Spirit Nature. Love Conditions.	Pure Balmy Atmosphere.	Ripe uncooked Saccharine Fruits.	Linen Robes	The Tent. An unfixed Locality.	The Orchard.	Progressive Gymnastic Exercises. Growth of Nerve.	Active Benevolence. Love for the unlovely.	Union of Spirit-selected pairs in sympathetic harmony.
Better, for the Soul, or Human Nature. Light Conditions.	Pure Temperate Atmosphere.	Green, or Succulent Vegetables.	Pervious and Flowing Cotton Garments; undyed.	The House: Social and scientific conveniences.	The Garden.	Progressive Gymnastic Exercises. Growth of Muscle.	Thoughtful benevolence. Thought for the thoughtless	Co-education, or betrothment of Spirit-selected pairs.
Good, for the Body. Life Conditions.	Pure Bracing Atmosphere.	Farinaceous Grain & Pulse.	Cotton or Hempen Dress, undyed.	The Public Hall. Accomodation, Rest and Amusement.	The Field.	Progressive Gymnastic Exercises. Growth of Bone.	Practical benevolence. Bread for the hungry.	Social intercourse of Families, Races and Nations.
Bad, for all Nature. Prevailing erroneous Conditions	Ill ventilated apartments; atmosphere corrupted in coal-dust, smoke, tobacco, &c.	Fermented and Cooked Fruits, Vegetables and Roots. Flesh of Animals. Fermented Liquors	Woollen fabrics, tight and impervious to perspiration; Animal skins; Metal decorations, &c.	Towns and Cities; dirty, dense & dark; luxurious Mansions and dilapidated Cottages.	Exchange of Commodities, useful & useless. Factory & other Slave-Labour.	Treatment of the Being as a passive blank. Routine of discipline.	Physical representations and deadening Ceremonies.	Legal Bonds. Animal Lust.

Charles Lane

ditions are nevertheless to be their own conditions, represents an attempt to achieve on a grammatical level what the rubric to the circumstantial table tries to effect on an etymological one, and which Lane's comparison of soul and soil seeks to accomplish on an evolutionary one: that reconciliation between inner and outer, intuition and structure, nature and history which was the Holy Grail of Transcendentalist thought.

Whatever the contortions surrounding it, the table gave the Greavesians a chart to follow along their way, and it must have reassured the Alcotts just as the "Table of the Movement of Civilization" or the "Analytical and Synthetical Table of the Passional System" in Brisbane's *Social Destiny of Man* would have clarified the position of the Brook Farmers. It encouraged one to choose the particular circumstances that would then be associated with a specific spiritual accomplishment. Its very existence as an inclusive structure gave testimony to the reality of the overarching law which the Transcendentalists sought. As in the case of the Fourierist blueprint, its transatlantic provenance (its quality as a "given"), coupled with its definiteness and particularity, combined revelatory perception with mythic substance. As in the Fourierist schema, moreover, there is a mysterious divide between waste and progress, represented here by a double line.[65]

In "The Third Dispensation" Lane's advocacy of "melioration" comes up against the problem of "an illogical expectation, that antagonistic society should give birth to harmonic society," since "philosophy is in error, in seeking new results from old results." His solution is to make a distinction between chronological and causal sequence, and to construct a theory of historical change through impulses or pulsations: "Events undoubtedly follow events in time, as material bodies bound material bodies in space; but they are not therefore sequences from each other. On the contrary, they are all sequences of an antecedent power, which alike resolves them all from its own ever living newness." He then goes on to use an analogy with the family which would have had particular significance for the Alcotts. Actually it is not an analogy but an example (when the serial law is being described, we tend to move out of the realm of metaphor and into that of metonymy): "In a family, the children are born one after the other, links in the generative chain; but they are not consequences one of another, but each separately and distinctly is the consequence of a parental act in the parents. So it is with universal progress in the human race. Event fol-

---

65. In Greaves's original version the good and evil axis is reversed, with bad at the top of the page and best at the bottom (Greaves, *Letters*, 2: 80–81).

lows event, state bounds state, alternate links of gold and iron succeed each other; but they are not generative consequences one of another. No; they are each and severally distinctly referable to an antecedent generative *causant*, from which all flow." He goes on to suggest that "the better idea seems to be that of a perpetual refunding and referring of man to this *operant*, in order to the evolution of the new state."[66]

On the face of it this account seems to be inconsistent with the passage I quoted earlier, also from "The Third Dispensation," in which Lane describes a gradual evolutionary development, but there is in fact no contradiction: the serial energy (or, in theological terms, grace), which in terms of the organic metaphor plants the seed and provides the light toward which it aspires and from which it gains one part of its nutriment, comes from a single transcendental source ("This Unity, this Uniter, this One"),[67] while the equally necessary material development involves the progressive interaction of the components of the circumstantial world. The table of the circumstantial law shows a development from bad, through good and better, en route to best: implicitly a process of evolutionary amelioration. At the same time, each stage in that process seems to be a little plateau, and we find in the accompanying rubric the suggestion that they are all available simultaneously so that the individual may select the one he or she would feel most at home with. It is through such a structure as this circumstantial table that ahistorical transformation in the Emersonian sense ("It is and will be magic")—or, in Lane's terms, that *flash* which lies beyond human control and even the bounds of language because "while we say it is, it is not"—can be reconciled with history, to create a system of punctuated equilibria.

Interestingly, Greaves offers a similar structure in the form of a numerical scale which prefaces one of his letters to Alexander Campbell.

								1	The absolute maker includes the 45; but the 45 does not include the maker, or absolute, or one.
							2	2	
						3	3	3	
					4	4	4	4	
				5	5	5	5	5	
			6	6	6	6	6	6	
		7	7	7	7	7	7	7	
	8	8	8	8	8	8	8	8	
9	9	9	9	9	9	9	9	9	
9	17	24	30	35	39	42	44	45	

66. Lane, "Third Dispensation," 117–18.
67. Ibid., 118.

"I send you a scale," he writes, "in which you will see that the man who declares 17 to be his standard, is right, because he can do no better; but 24 says somewhat more, and includes 17; 30 includes 24; and so on." Each link in the serial chain has its own integrity and identity; nonetheless, it is possible to move along it, to develop: "You may declare yourself to be where you will, 39 or 42, waiting to be progressed"—there is the passive again, straddling that difficult terrain between free will and determinism—"to 45."[68] In the same way, each of the levels in the circumstantial table represents a state of equilibrium, but their hierarchical ordering suggests overall progress.

From Alcott's point of view, what the table provides is the longed-for *given*, the structure that justifies his claim that the divine Husbandman has "sown us bread that we may not perish." Lane is able to provide the "spiritual calculus" for which Alcott had been searching, "a novum organon, whereby nature shall be defined in the soul, the soul in God, matter in spirit, polarity resolved into unity," and which is able to tap "that power which pulsates in all life, animates and builds all organizations."

What is important about the circumstantial law is its precision. There is nothing whimsical, improvised or faddish here; we find instead a careful gradation and accumulation of those external factors that signify the different states of spiritual well-being. The chart is as precise as a railway timetable, like those arrangements whereby at three o'clock and again at seven interested parties could board public conveyances to take them to their rendezvous with utopia. As in the case of Brisbane's exposition of the law of duality of movement with respect to passional development, the Greavesian account of circumstances defuses the issue of cause and effect with the ingenuity one associates with covenantal theology. Circumstances provide a "key to the interior state of any individual" just as for a Calvinist justification gave empirical evidence of salvation. Circumstances are neither merely a symptom nor the ultimate cause but somewhere in between. The point of intersection between inner and outer worlds does not allow for priority, since the two developments exactly coincide.

Nevertheless, as a result of this balance benefits can flow into the community: "Each one becomes in this manner a condition to others, for the evolution of the like nature, to that of which such conduct is an exhibition." Person A's spiritual nature is exhibited by means of a sort of circumstantial index, which provides an environment in which per-

68. Greaves, *Letters*, 1:179–80, letter of August 10, 1840.

son B's spiritual nature can develop along the right lines. That environment does not itself provide the spark, or to use Lane's word the *flash*; but it can offer the "favourable conditions of spring" to enable divine growth to reach upward from the "dark earth."

The complexity of the relationship between circumstances and the individual's moral status is difficult to grasp imaginatively, but that is not the only challenge the circumstantial law brings with it. We also have to deal with the paradox of absent (or at least minimal) circumstances. As in the famous Sherlock Holmes case of the dog in the night-time which was significant because it did *not* bark, so here: as we rise up the circumstantial table, the circumstances themselves get fewer and more restricted. The utopian—the Fruitlander to be—breathes a pure atmosphere, eats raw fruit, dresses in linen robes, lives in a tent,[69] works in an orchard, engages in progressive gymnastic exercises, loves the unlovely, and participates in spiritual marriage. As Alcott put it in a letter of February 15, 1843, "The entrance to Paradise is still through the straight gate and narrow way of self-denial."[70]

In the next chapter I explore in more detail the problems facing Lane and Alcott in negotiating this narrow entrance. As they set about the task of establishing a utopian community, they had to formulate specific policies in relation to circumstances. I begin by discussing in some detail their views on diet, manure, and sexual relations, concerns that are more closely linked than might seem likely. This discussion in turn leads to an analysis of their perspectives on the structure of the family and its role in the larger social scene, issues that take us to the very heart of the assumptions on which the community was founded and in fact brought about its destruction a few months later.

69. Interestingly, Lane has intensified this requirement in his version of the table. Greaves merely advocates "buildings cheerful, light and spacious, adapted to Genetic natures" (Greaves, *Letters*, 2:80–81).
70. Alcott, *Letters*, 99.

6

Fruitlands: Divergence

On July 21, 1843, only a month after the founding of Fruitlands, Isaac Hecker itemized the community's failings in an entry in his journal. Point four encapsulates the ironies and ambiguities that, as we have seen, permeated the ideological background of the enterprise and were to dog the community itself during the few months of its existence: "The place has very little fruit upon it, which it was and is their desire should be the principal part of their diet."[1] His phrasing accidentally captures the leaning toward the negative that so often seems to characterize the thinking of both Lane and Alcott by suggesting that the main crop of the farm coincided with their main dietary requirement: to wit, very little.

But, as we have seen, there was also a positive side to Lane's and Alcott's attitude toward circumstances, and it was this side that was—or should have been—brought to the fore by the establishment of a community. Although, as Greaves's table of circumstantial law tells us, evil circumstances must be eliminated, the circumstantial world itself cannot finally be discarded. Negative circumstances are the historical legacy; purified ones are the utopian prospect. There is inevitably a built-in tendency toward deprivation, as Greaves claims ironically that "good circumstances are to be found associated with superficial thinkers," among whom he numbers "novel-readers, play-goers, horse-racers, and all such external externalists," going on to assert that "a well-fed man is

---

1. Isaac Hecker, MS diary, Paulist Fathers' Archives, New York, entry for July 21, 1843, quoted in Walter Elliot, *The Life of Father Hecker* (New York: Columbus Press, 1891), 85.

never a central thinker."[2] The point, of course, is to feed off centrality itself, and even the self-flagellation of cold water and flesh brush can be seen as forms of consumption. Greaves declares: "There are needed everywhere baths for health, but in the third dispensation they are indispensable. Shower baths for the skin, and rubbing with a coarse towel and a flesh brush all over, is necessary for health. Man feeds greatly by the skin, and particularly out of the aromal atmosphere. The purer man is in Love, the less heavy solid food he needs, at least so little as to be only fruits of the finest quality."[3]

We move, in short, from a restriction on oral gratification to the concept of the whole body as orifice, from a diminished menu to the fructification of diminishment, from a repudiation of the gross to a great feeding on the rarefied. In a passage of his journals written seven years after the demise of the Fruitlands community, Alcott provides perhaps the most intense and moving example of the gratuity—indeed the grace—that can be achieved in this kind of regimen, recreating the mystical sensations implicit in deprivation, the positive delights forthcoming to a traveler on the *via negativa*:

During the extreme cold of the winter of 1844, I was at Fruitlands, and kept within doors, and at my pen from early sunrising to midnight and sometimes on toward dawn. . . . I fed on fruit, biscuit, and drank water, exclusively, and often. Sometimes I was unable to relinquish my studies, so delicious was thought to me, and sat up all night. I bathed in cold water, dunking head and shoulders for several times successively to the bottom of the capacious tub in which I stood; and poured water by pailsful over the whole body, rubbing down briskly afterwards with crash towels, and practiced friction with the flesh brush. In the coldest mornings, there was a crackling and lambent flash following the passage of my hand over the pile of the skin, and I shook flames from my finger ends, which seemed erect and blazing with the phosphoric light. The eyes, too, were lustrous, and shot sparkles, whenever I closed them. On raising my head from the flood, there was heard a melody in the ear, as of a sound of many waters, and rubbing the eye gave out an iris of the primitive colors, beautiful to behold, but as evanescent as a twinkling. It was not easy to write prose, while thus exalted and transfigured. I tasted mannas, and all the aromas of field and orchard scented the fountains; and the brain

2. *Letters and Extracts from the MS Writings of James Pierrepoint Greaves*, 2 vols. (Ham Common, Surrey: Concordium Press, 1843–45), 1:95, letter of May 1, 1840.
3. Ibid., 2:242, letter of November 9, 1841.

was haunted with the rhythm of many voiced melodies. I enjoyed this state for a couple of months or more, but was left somewhat debilitated when spring came, and unfit for common concerns. Most of what was written in this season of efflorescence, is now lost; but the sweetness was secreted in the memory, and abides as a honey-combed era of my spiritual history.[4]

It is perhaps appropriate that this "era" of Alcott's spiritual history is somewhat adrift in time and space. Because he associates it with Fruitlands, it is likely that the regimen at least began there (the farm was snowbound from December), but if it continued till spring it must have done so elsewhere, since the Alcotts moved from Fruitlands to their neighbor J. W. Lovejoy's on January 16, 1844.[5] In short, the mystical interaction of spiritual and circumstantial worlds proves to be divorced from the historical continuum. Alcott himself acknowledges the incompatibility of such epiphanic experience with the prosaic by confessing his inability to do justice to it in prose—and reminding us that the prose itself was lost on that ill-fated Albany coach.

Alcott's raptness of tone and the relationship he establishes between ecstasy and deprivation are reminiscent of Emerson's account of the joy of crossing a bare common on a winter's day. That exhilarating connection between inner and outer which Emerson experienced is a function of the common's very bareness, an equation of zeroes that leaves us with nothing but the formal integrity of the equation itself: "«No» is «no»," to quote Jakobson's tautology. Nevertheless, although Alcott's account celebrates the absence of adverse circumstances, it lays its principal stress on the presence of favorable ones. He partook of his minimal diet not merely "exclusively" but "often." The ecstatic tone of the passage can be fully accounted for only if we see it not as a response to what is *not* there—balanced meals, comforting beverages, warmth—but as a celebration of what *is*: fruit, biscuits, water, cold. When the circumstantial table advocates "pure air," the adjective is intended to emphasize not the minimal but the maximal possibility. Air free of impurities is air in its most heady and concentrated form. At the same time, purity is a moral as well as a physical category, the crossover having been legitimized in Emerson's "Divinity School Address" with the balancing of gravity against purity of heart, an equation seized

4. *The Journals of Bronson Alcott*, ed. Odell Shepard (Boston: Little, Brown, 1938), 240–41, entry for February 9, 1851.
5. Bronson Alcott, "Memoir, 1878" (covering the period 1834–55), MS, Houghton Library, 59M-306 (23), n. p.

upon by Andrews Norton as an example of "incoherent rhapsody."[6] Thus, Lane can claim in "The Third Dispensation" that "pure air must be furnished, before pure thoughts and pure sentiments can pervade the inner being."[7] The purity of absence has been balanced off against the purity of presence, lack of pollution against moral and sentimental integrity.

The passage from Alcott's journal is perhaps the clearest account possible of that *flash* which occurs when inspiration is "impregnated by the divine mind on the human soul." As we have seen, however, there is a strong pull toward the pragmatic and the quotidian in the thinking of Lane and Alcott, a concern with the historical process that follows— or precedes, or is periodically invaded by—the light of divinity. And in the period leading up to the founding of Fruitlands, the practical implications of circumstantial doctrine had to receive due attention. An extract from Alcott's diary, published in the *Dial* in 1842, and dealing with the advantages of a restricted diet (it is titled, of all things, "Banquet") celebrates the "small demands on foreign products" that a "Pythagorean diet" implies, and anticipates the time when Alcott will be able to achieve "entire independence."[8] In the *Dial* a year later Lane criticizes the Shakers for the fact that, since many of them consume flesh, milk, tea, and coffee, they have to trade, and these "proceedings require more extensive interchanges of money, and more frequent intercourse with the world, than seems compatible with a serene life."[9] In the previous issue of the *Dial* Lane complains in very Emersonian fashion that the problem with civilization is that "everything, every person is vicarious." By this he means that "no one lives out his own life, but lives for all." One of the consequences of this lack of self-reliance is the necessity for manure, since intensive farming is needed to make up for the failure of subsistence: "The farmer applies fresh quantities of foul animal manure to force heavier crops from his exhausted fields, which, when consumed, generate a host of diseases as foul as the manures to which they are responsible."[10] But since external purity is balanced by, or provides an index of, the internal variety (one must avoid lapsing into the vocabulary of simple cause and effect), then spiritual corruption must also be widespread. Alcott, in "Days from a Diary," makes the

6. Ralph Waldo Emerson, "The Divinity School Address," in *NAL*, 93; Andrews Norton, "The New School in Literature and Religion," excerpted in Perry Miller, ed., *The Transcendentalists* (Cambridge: Harvard University Press, 1950), 195–96.
7. [Charles Lane], "The Third Dispensation," *Present*, November 15, 1843, 13.
8. A. Bronson Alcott, "Banquet," *Dial* 2 (April 1842): 427.
9. Charles Lane, "A Day with the Shakers," *Dial* 4 (October 1843): 167.
10. Charles Lane, "Social Tendencies," pt. 1, *Dial* 4 (July 1843): 71, 72.

connection explicitly, telling his readers that "the narrow covetousness which prevails in trade, in labor, and exchanges, ends in depraving the land; it breeds disease, decline, in the flesh,—debauches and consumes the heart." Whitman, in "Song of Myself," makes a similar connection: "I keep as delicate around the bowels as around the head and heart."[11]

Hawthorne, as we have seen, grew to resent the time he spent working in the Brook Farm "gold mine," but his objection was the opposite of Lane's: he came to the conclusion that it hindered the exercise of his specialized vocation, that of writer. Lane, by contrast, sees manure as part of an economy of specialization, as a result of which "every one looks abroad to every other one; no one looks within to himself;—a universal representative life, in which the legislator represents the conscience, the judge the gravity, the priest the piety, the doctor the learning, the mechanic the skill of the community; and no one person needs to be conscientious, grave, pious, learned and skilful. Out of this grow those monstrous and dreadful conditions which large cities, the very acme of civilized life, without exception, exhibit."[12] Once again we are reminded of Emerson's claim in "The American Scholar" that "the state of society is one in which the members have suffered amputation from the trunk and strut about so many walking monsters,—a good finger, a neck, a stomach, an elbow, but never a man." Whereas Emerson is concerned about the incompleteness of the specialized, Lane— like John Sullivan Dwight in the passage discussed in Chapter 4—condemns the exaggeration and intensification of the characteristics involved, as his example of manure suggests. Moreover, for Lane the alternative to this state of affairs is not the representative man, for that role suggests avoidance of reality rather than participation in it. The elevation of a few does not point toward the potential of the many but deprives the many of their chance of fulfillment: "Exalted intellect on the part of a few, . . . at the expense, frequently, of moral and physical life, elevates national renown, with extreme ignorance of all that really concerns them, on the part of the masses. A few intense spots of wealth, learning, or heroism, amongst an endless range of poverty, ignorance, and degradation, accumulated, apparently, for no higher end than the meretricious employment of the three opposite qualities."[13]

11. A. Bronson Alcott, "Husbandry," in "Days from a Diary," *Dial* 2 (April 1842): 426; Walt Whitman, *Leaves of Grass*, ed. Harold W. Blodgett and Sculley Bradley (New York: New York University Press, 1965), 53.
12. Lane, "Social Tendencies," pt. 1, 72.
13. Lane, "Social Tendencies," pt. 1, 72.

Those "few intense spots" are an abstract equivalent of the compacted nutriment of manure.

What differentiates Lane's view of representation from Emerson's is precisely the doctrine of circumstances. Emerson expects the right-minded individual to rise *above* circumstances, so that "neither his age, nor his breeding, nor company, nor books, nor actions, nor talents, nor all together, can hinder him."[14] For Lane, with his extraordinary capacity for relating the application of foul manures to the achievement of exalted intellect, such Neoplatonic elevation is a sure indication of a parasitic or excremental manipulation of circumstances rather than of release from them. Manure represents a sort of concentration (indeed, it represents a sort of representativeness), and a concentration of pure materiality at that.

It also embodies the past. It is a substance quite literally composed of the status quo ante: treasure, to use Hawthorne's ironic term. The Greaves–Lane–Alcott group would agree with Lévi-Strauss that utilizing the accumulated "treasury" represents a mere reorganization of the cultural set; what is required is spiritual cleansing and a new start. Rerouting waste back into the system would undo the sort of purgation that Greaves advocates at the conclusion of some dietary advice to Alexander Campbell: "Disease will die in the constitution when you do not feed it, and when you suffer Spirit almost uninterruptedly to act in it. Joyful experiences will begin as soon as the painful experiences have been worked out."[15]

In another letter Greaves locates manure in the actual cooking and consumption of food itself, using imagery of dilation and distortion that is closely related to Lane's:

Food has in it three natures and an excrementitious residuum. By cooking we dislodge two natures, the Spirit and the Spiritual, and feed on the physical and the excrementitious, and eat by far too much of this gross earthy residuum or sediment. The bowels are extended beyond their proper size, and the digestive power has rather to digest corruption than Spirituality. There is nothing in cooked food for the affections, nothing for the mind; but in undressed food there is provision for both. Boil an orange, and what is it worth? All that is Spirit and Spiritual is drawn out of it by the fire, and a lifeless gross mass remains."[16]

14. Ralph Waldo Emerson, "The Over-Soul," in *Essays 1*, 169.
15. Greaves, *Letters*, 1:162, letter of July 12, 1840.
16. Greaves, *Letters*, 2:230, letter of October 19, 1841.

His complaint is that a diet involving the consumption of meat and the process of cooking (the example of an orange suggests that he did not possess the English taste for marmalade) creates a lack of balance between the elements of food, leading to the exaggeration of some features and the elimination of others. Spirit and spirituality go by the board, leaving only the physical, which combines with the excrementitious (not properly an element of food at all: from this perspective meat and manure are indistinguishable) to diminish the consumer's higher qualities and enlarge his bowels.

A subsistence economy, both materially and spiritually, involves a holistic, balanced view of the individual and the environment and a living relationship between the two. Crops do not need to be forced because a surplus is not required for trade. Manure therefore has no part to play. Similarly, vegetarianism means that the nutritional concentration represented by meat (parallel to that of manure) is not being relied on either, in turn preventing the individual from developing exaggerated bowels or those "few intense spots" of learning and heroism. As a result, both individuals and communities can achieve a nonhierarchical relationship with nature, with one another, and with the world in general.

Nowhere can the relationship between oneself and the external world be more significant—not to say more complex and problematical, more prone to loss of balance and intrusions of hierarchy, more in danger of unwanted concentrations and excess—than in the sexual sphere. The sexual economy evolved by Greaves and his disciples at Alcott House is perhaps the most intriguing and enigmatic element in their ideology. It is also the area where the circumstantial philosophies of Lane and Alcott proved, ultimately, to be incompatible.

In his 1906 article "Bronson Alcott's English Friends," William Harry Harland, using primary material that is now lost, recounts the sad tale of English Transcendentalism versus sex. Two of the leading members of the group, Lane and William Oldham, had contracted unhappy marriages, and the former had spent three years in litigation in order to extract himself from his entanglement. Greaves himself never married but demonstrated a wonderful knack of arousing the "platonic affections of women."[17] The story of Henry Gardiner Wright, who was responsible for running the Alcott House school, provides a useful index of Alcott House sensitivity on the subject. In 1841, when he was

---

17. William H. Harland, "Bronson Alcott's English Friends," ed. Joel Myerson, *Resources for American Literary Study* 8 (September 1978): 30.

twenty-seven, Wright fell in love with Elizabeth Hardwick, a trainee teacher at the school, and married her. The reaction of his colleagues, whom he had understandably enough not notified beforehand, is illustrated by a letter Greaves sent to Oldham: "I wish to be no party to anything, to retire from all things . . . thank God I can close my room door and lay me down in peace to die. . . . If Mr Wright be spirit aided he will be able to clear his way out of all predicaments he is in and if he be not he must sink into misery."[18]

In the light of this extreme reaction it might seem surprising that the English Transcendentalists did not forbid marriage and sex; indeed, under certain circumstances—a key word for them—they actively advocated it. Just as the negative aspects of dieting could be counterbalanced by enthusiastic consumption of the rarefied, so abstemiousness in sexual matters could finally give way to union. The Greavesian courtship ritual unfolds as follows:

> The man and the woman ought to be betrothed, and live together until the prophetical union is consolidated, as well as the metaphysical; and at a given state, when the woman demands it, not the man, the physical marriage should take place. . . . In no case are passions to be allowed to enter the affair. The woman, with the love in her feelings, must win the man's affections, and the man, with his wisdom, must exercise and direct the woman's understanding. When the two invisible unions have taken place, the third then, under the spirit law, may take place. What is to be suspended is the physical union, until the higher elements are generated. . . . The two uniting parties must be considered not as seed but as ground; and as is the ground, so will the seed flourish.[19]

The passage enshrines certain nineteenth-century assumptions about gender: that only the woman can be trusted to be custodian of a strangely unimpassioned passion, and that she is the source of the affections, while man is the fount of wisdom. Greaves's doctrine certainly makes hard work of sex, and it seems appropriate that its concluding metaphor should be of tilling the soil rather than the more obvious one of planting the seed. He is concerned with the adjustment of circumstances, not with the germination of new life, since without the necessary preparation of the ground new life would be not new at all but, as in the case of manure-fed crops, a pernicious bodying forth of

18. Ibid., 35–36.
19. Greaves, *Letters*, 1:32, letter of February 22, 1840.

the status quo ante. (That this comparison is not stretched or provocative can be seen by the vocabulary Alcott chooses to employ in a passage of "Days from a Diary," significantly titled "Husbandry": "The
soil, grateful thus for man's generous usage, debauched no more by
foul ordures, nor worn by cupidities, shall recover its primeval virginity.")[20]

As in the case of Lane's similarly sexual description of the way in
which "the idea is . . . impregnated by the divine mind on the human
soul at a *flash*," there is a radical discontinuity between the temporal
dimension in which work is done and the mystical moment in which
being is transformed. We are in effect dealing with the relationship
between history and *kairos* once more, and that relationship cannot be
other than an equivocal one. Both Greaves and Lane make their obei-
sance to the transforming moment, which in the latter's account precedes the "temporal outworking" and in Greaves's follows the preparation of the ground, though both place their emphasis on hard work in
the here and now rather than on the transcendental donnée. In the
words of Eliot's "The Hollow Men," "Between the conception / And
the creation . . . Between the desire / And the spasm . . . Falls the
Shadow."[21] It is in that shadow—in the "dark earth," as Lane expresses
it—that invisible unions can take place, and the "divinely generated
conception" can be elaborated.

It is fair to say that, up until Wright's marriage in 1841, Greaves's
vision of future harmony depended on the relationship between the
sexes. "If God's will is to be done on earth as it is in heaven," he asks
Campbell in a letter of 1838, "must it not be done in marriage, as the
very root of all well-doing?" One may detect an implicit reference to
the transgression in Eden as he goes on to put his next question: "Can
there be any real well-doing on earth, until the well-being begins in
marriage, where the evil-doing began and continues?"[22] The trouble
with Greaves's writings is that they are bogged down in repetition and a
jargon of his own creation, which preclude any coherent presentation
of the utopian future toward which he yearns. Nevertheless, successful
pairing is clearly all-important, not simply because a new seed can then
be planted but also because the true spiritual unit turns out to be the
couple: "If I say man needs woman," he explains two years later, "I
mean the intellectualized soul requires its deficient half, or Love na-

20. Alcott, "Husbandry," 426.
21. T. S. Eliot, "The Hollow Men," in *The Complete Poems and Plays* (New York: Harcourt,
Brace and World, 1952), 59.
22. Greaves, *Letters*, 1:6–7, letter of August 13, 1838.

ture, in which are enshrined all the Love qualities, not merely the organized matter; and the same when woman and her half nature are spoken of. The masculine nature must be blended or united with the feminine nature—the feminine nature must be blended or united with the
masculine nature. Of these two essences, the Spirit makes one whole
Being."[23] Greaves is envisaging not just a sort of allegorical process of
spiritual completion but an actual social order based on such pairing.
"It is not designed for our nature to walk *alone*," he tells Campbell in a
letter of the following week, going on to contrast the proposed pairing
with the larger (and for him soulless) structures advocated by the
Owenites: "The divinity, in its own region, has arranged its workman-
ship to be consciously realized only by 'pairs,' and not by dead massive
co-operative associations."[24]

It might seem a trifle anomalous, then, that Greaves did not merely
remain single himself but became distraught when Henry Wright and
Elizabeth Hardwick got married. Odell Shepard offers what is prehaps
the most satisfactory explanation of this inconsistency when he suggests
that Greaves "had come to the sad conclusion that although this sancti-
fication of marriage was necessary it was also practically impossible; and
so he believed, as a logical consequence, that there ought not to be any
marriages whatsoever."[25]

Once again—in sex as in diet and husbandry—the utopian ideal is
liable to be compromised by caveats and negativity. The Greavesian
doctrine of generation is really an extraordinary combination of Calvinist and Owenite determinism which somehow manages to give the
child the worst of both worlds. The infant inherits his vices not just
from his first parents but also from his immediate ones; and those vices
are not just abstract and metaphysical but also physical and social. They
are diseases. As Greaves put it in his notebooks:

> Diseases proceed altogether from generation, let the conditions be
> what they may.
>
> Man's first duty is to have the curse removed from his existence,
> and to generate offspring without the curse; and this he can only do
> by a marriage in, from, and for God.
>
> It is obvious, that man's uncursed existence, and his properly exer-

23. Ibid., 1:42–43, letter of March 6, 1840.
24. Ibid., 1:50, letter of March 15, 1840.
25. Odell Shepard, *Pedlar's Progress: The Life of Bronson Alcott* (Boston: Little, Brown,
1937), 331.

cising it, would entirely alter the state of society in every nation in the world.[26]

Generation is not just the problem: it has to be the solution also. When Greaves coyly speaks of "properly exercising" an uncursed existence, what he is referring to is reproduction in a world in which the curse of the Fall has been remitted in, so to speak, a *post*-postlapsarian context. On the basis that two negatives make a positive, such an environment can equally well be conceived of as *pre*lapsarian, as Greaves makes clear. "Our progress," he tells Campbell, "let it be what it may, is from the pre-is, that is, ever with us." The disclaimer registers his awareness of the paradox involved, since "progress" is to be made only by tracking backwards. Moreover, whatever the spiritual characteristics of this state of pre-isness, it is to be achieved not as a consequence of moral choices but through the process of generation. Thus, when a stranger asks Greaves to help him write something on the subject of education, the master makes a cutting riposte: "I asked him if he thought he could change a fox-dog into a fox by education; if not, why think of re-generating man by education."[27]

As is often the case with the thinking of Transcendentalists, an apparent metaphor—"re-generation"—turns out to be a metonymy. Inner and outer are not connected analogically but operate as a single system. If parents achieve their sexual union in the appropriate context, with negative circumstances such as the passions omitted and pure ones such as love and wisdom prevailing, their offspring will be free of both physical and moral defects. The problem is almost literally that of the chicken and the egg: the prescription calls for a perfect chicken to lay a perfect egg, and a perfect egg to hatch out into a perfect chicken. As Lane writes in "The Third Dispensation": "The difficulty consists in this, that the unitary external arrangements which appear absolutely indispensable *for* the evolution of the unitary spirit, can alone be provided *by* the unitary spirit."[28]

At the heart of this dilemma, indeed at the heart of the conflict between Lane and Alcott, lies the institution of the family. We have seen that in theory the Greavesians endorsed marriage and procreation; and that to some extent Greaves's own utopian vision rested on a concept of spiritual pairing. The vision is a vague and contradictory

---

26. Quoted from Greaves's notebooks by Lane in "James Pierrepoint Greaves," *Dial* 3 (January 1843): 294.
27. Greaves, *Letters*, 2:145, letter of April 2, 1841; ibid., 2:136, letter of March 31, 1841.
28. Lane, "The Third Dispensation," 112.

one, however. The circumstantial table represents the pairing as incorporeal, somewhat compromising the prospect for regeneration. Given that Shepard is probably correct in surmising that the sexual solution had come to be seen by the Greavesians as a lost cause, it is hardly surprising to find Greaves in due course suggesting a mechanics of social renewal that seems to involve a direct interaction, of a rather Emersonian kind, between the one and totality. The individual provides the basic link in the serial chain only when invaded by the transforming powers of that totality, thus becoming aware of his or her participation in some sort of over-soul:

If a societarian result be wanted, no quantity of individuals, as individuals, can produce it. A universe community nature must activate these individuals, and by them manifest the same. . . . Let it then be clearly understood that, for a true societarian result, true being must be generated; no number of selfish individuals can produce it, however they may congregate, or whatever verbal principles they may put forth. Men have been sadly mistaken in attributing to congregated numbers results which belong to a nature that works in and by them, and holds them in exterior union as long as it is suitable to the end proposed.

The notion that congregation represents an ideal in itself attracts the same contempt as excrement does elsewhere, and for good reason: such trust in numbers creates an effect of exaggeration and distortion, and establishes hierarchy, "intense spots" of community rather than "a true societarian result." Nevertheless, Greaves was willing to concede that small groups which maintained an awareness of the nature that "works in and by them" might prove efficacious where selfish clustering would not. Alcott House, after all, was an example. In one of his letters to Campbell, Greaves envisages the desirability of a group of half a dozen as an effective unit of association. "To make an association of hundreds seems to be something, but to make only six persons declare this wrong, would be more efficient."[29] There is no mention of any biological basis for this family-sized unit of half a dozen, however. Two years have elapsed since Greaves advocated pairing, and in that interval Henry Wright had married Elizabeth Hardwick.

Greaves is perhaps most comfortable when he can universalize sexually charged imagery:

29. Greaves, *Letters*, 2:119, letter of March 10, 1841; ibid., 2:195, letter of June 22, 1842.

That man can be baptised in his constitution, and breathe the universal vital fluid, is demonstrated constantly in magnetism; and what is done medically for the relief of physical diseases, may be done for the elevation of man in his causal nature. As a result of the Spirit's own magnetism, he can be transferred into the warm vital fluid, and has to suffer it willingly, that it may not have to meet with too many incoming obstacles from the cold air without. The sublime Spirit must be cordially invited to magnetize us within, and must be welcomed in its working against the cold world's air. Our universal hopes must all be transferred to the Spirit, that with them, as spiritual warm means, it may work magically against the cold world's ends."[30]

In this rapt and poetic evocation of the modus operandi of serial law, Greaves insists on a parallelism between the physical and the spiritual, combining the Stoics' concept of the pneuma with the phenomenon of magnetism. There are erotic undercurrents—"warm vital fluid," "spiritual warm means"—but they simply form part of a process that involves the interaction of the unit with everything else. That unit modulates from "he" to "us," but without any suggestion that pairing has taken place. The adverb Greaves chooses in the last sentence to evoke the completeness and efficacy of the identification of the one with the totality, the process of serial transformation, once more brings to mind Emerson's claim: "It is and will be magic." The family is given no part to play in this abrupt transformation.

We have seen that in "The Third Dispensation" Lane was also aware of the problem of "too many incoming obstacles," and numbered the family among them. Even under the second dispensation the family unit continues to break society down into small cliques, the social equivalent of that concentration represented by manure, and thus prevents the infinite ramification of human relationships that will take place in the third and final social order.[31] At this stage of his thinking,

30. Ibid., 2:217–18, letter of August 14, 1841. See Stephen Toulmin, June Goodfield, *The Architecture of Matter* (London: Hutchinson, 1962), for a concise and helpful account of the Stoics' concept of the pneuma: "Every ordered system is the manifestation of a psyche, and every psyche is carried by a pneuma, which holds the parts of the system in their order. The cosmos is an ordered system, in which all things are interlinked. *Ergo*, the universe itself must have a psyche: and this 'World-Soul' must be carried by a universal pneuma, which binds all the objects of heaven and earth in a common destiny. . . . The last step in the argument united the individual human with the cosmos. All life comes from the World-Soul, and eventually returns to it. . . . Having entered the individual at conception, the pneuma remained there throughout his life, sustaining itself on draughts of warm air from the surrounding atmosphere" (109–10).
31. Lane, "The Third Dispensation," 110–11.

Lane's view of the family was that it constituted an unnecessary and obstructive middle term between the two extremes of the serial process. In short, although the English Transcendentalists had initially been willing to pay lip service to the possibility of pairing (on a spiritual level at least), and to the purification of the race through some sort of uncursed sexual congress, there is no evidence that they saw any role for, or had any imaginative sympathy with, the conventional nuclear family structure. In this respect their position differed radically from Alcott's.

On May 22, 1836, Alcott recorded the baptism of his three children, Anna Bronson, Louisa May, and Elizabeth Peabody. This occasion led him into a meditation on the subject of naming, and on the significance of the family: "Beautiful as an historical fact, is this union of spirits in the significant imagery of names. Our genealogy is inscribed on the appellations of our children; and the spirit's ancestry finds embodment [*sic*] in terrestrial parentage. The family of souls, inheriting one common name, and mingling together in the familiar relation of the flesh, are brought into one significant appellation, and History saith the Record thereof."[32] It is clear that Alcott sees the family as the institution that enables nature to be reconciled with history, the absolute with the temporal. At the center of the process the act of reproduction itself is presented in terms that would provide common ground with Greaves (the passage dates from before the transatlantic approach). The "Spirit's ancestry" (what Greaves was to call the "pre-is") finds "embodment" (the spelling points up the fact that in this context the term is used literally rather than metaphorically or abstractly; indeed, its sense is the exact opposite of abstraction) in "terrestrial parentage." The unified structure of spirit—"the family of souls"—thus achieves a metonymical unity in this smaller-scale "mingling," the "familiar [in modern usage, *familial*] relation of the flesh." Inheritance, genealogy (significantly, Elizabeth's was the only second name that was not a family one, an omission later rectified when it was changed from Peabody to Sewall), and, most important, history as both fact and record are invoked. The great Transcendentalist cleavage between "isness" and continuity, nature and history, is thereby bridged.

Alcott goes on to elaborate the serial continuity between his terms, to emphasize the strength and efficacy of the familial bridge. Here he parts company with Lane's position that family represents an obstacle

32. "Bronson Alcott's Journal for 1836," ed. Joel Myerson, *Studies in the American Renaissance, 1978* (Boston: Twayne, 1978), 59, entry for May 22, 1836.

to social transformation: "The Universal spirit floweth through every form of humanity, never losing its own essential life; yet assuming, to the external sense, every variety of manifestation, without marring, or fracturing, the Divine Unity. The flesh containeth the same Blessed Spirit—only in the forms thereof lyeth our particular individuality. *Family* is but the name for a larger synthesis of spirits united by one common tie of the flesh, like the leaves and flowers, the buds and branches, that shoot forth from the same stem!"[33] The clincher here is the use of the organic metaphor. We have seen how Alcott used the example of a tree to show how nutriment could be obtained from both heaven and earth by means of "ample leaves" and "numerous roots," respectively; here we see a *family* tree providing the same reconciling function. The characteristic of the spiritual realm is unity, that of the earthly realm, variety. The point is that these polarities can be related to each other without fracturing, and the family is perceived as an intermediate term, larger than the individual, smaller than humanity, in which such unity with variety can be maintained. It is, to revert to imagery I have used earlier, a molecular version of the serial form which must underlie the structure of a coherent universe. No wonder that in a journal passage three years later Alcott can celebrate the sexual act with an unalloyed enthusiasm which the Greavesians could never match: "Fluids form solids. Mettle is the Godhead proceeding into the matrix of Nature to organize Man. Behold the creative jet! And hear the morning stars shout for joy at the sacred generation of the Gods!"[34] The uncomplicated immediacy and frankness of this passage emphasizes the element of strain in Greaves's use of innuendos such as "universal vital fluid" and "spiritual warm means." It is not wholly surprising that in his unpublished "Tablets in Colours: Disposed on Twelve Tables," written in 1849, Alcott was to make the most daring suggestion yet for nature's ultimate serial form: not the leaf or the vertebra but the egg, which he finds in the testicle and in the brain ("Seminal vessels are brains secreting rudimental forms of animals, by the Spiritual alchymy of the animating soul. . . . Brains are oval; because Eggs. The brain is the Egg of the future state)."[35]

Of course, there is a downside to Alcott's version of the generative cycle. In his unpublished volume "Psyche, an Evangele" he paints a gloomy picture of the organic consequences of lustful behavior on the

33. Ibid.
34. Alcott, *Journals*, 121, entry for March 31, 1839.
35. A. Bronson Alcott, "Tablets in Colours: Disposed on Twelve Tables" (1849), MS, Houghton Library, 59M-306 (11), 667.

sinner's children: "His own uncleanness doth flow in their corporeal members. . . . So jealous is God, over lineage, visiting sins, or virtues, of parents, upon children, unto third or fourth generation." But even here virtue balances sin, and elsewhere in the book he praises the whole cycle of "espousal, wedding, birth," proclaiming that "a Family is the heaven of the Soul."[36] Indeed, Alcott's fervent advocacy of the family as fundamental serial unit, the place where heaven and earth merge, continued right up to the founding of Fruitlands, as this letter to his daughters, written only a few months before the community was inaugurated, demonstrates:

> It is pure and happy; a kind and loving family—a home where peace and joy, and gentle quiet, abide always. . . . This is the Jewel—the Pearl of priceless cost.
>
> The heavens above, the Earth beneath, can witness nothing more glorious than this—nor can one cover, nor the other support, a more comely Building than such a Home. 'Tis a Holy Spot—a consecrated Hearth—a Temple wherein to God himself enters and there abides with his angels. 'Tis Heaven and Earth in substance—that, indeed, of which the blue vault above, and the broad world around, are but vanishing and nothingness shadows.—Come then, my Children and abide in this imperishable mansion which I would prepare for you.[37]

It is worth bearing in mind that only two years had elapsed since Lane (who, even as this letter was being written, was residing with the Alcotts) had claimed in his introduction to Mme. Gatti de Gamond's book that the family was divisive and would fragment the national dispensation into small, selfish units. Nevertheless, by 1843 his position—probably under the influence of Alcott himself—had softened considerably.

In his two-part article "Social Tendencies," published in the *Dial* in July and October 1843 (from which I have already quoted in relation to the excremental side of his concerns), Lane makes the point that radical social transformation is a gradual process:

> With the sincerest wish for the success of any programme having for aim the bettering of man, or his conditions, we still can entertain but faint hopes where we perceive the scheme rather than man is placed

36. A. Bronson Alcott, "Psyche, an Evangele" (1838), MS, Houghton Library, 59M-306 (9), 24, 17.
37. *The Letters of A. Bronson Alcott*, ed. Richard L. Herrnstadt (Ames: Iowa State University Press, 1969), 96–97, letter of February 1, 1843.

first in importance. That there is to be a gradual outworking of society, a vast progress for mankind, cannot be doubtful to the steady
observer. A sufficient arc is known to prove the fact of a concentric
orbit. But that circular track cannot be calculated by the moral astronomers, who are not centralized beings. It is a calculation, too, which
cannot be put beforehand into books, and systems, but must be realized, day by day, from the centre itself, as are the planetary motions.[38]

This suspicion of schemes, systems, and the written word may seem
to sit somewhat awkwardly with, for example, Lane's promulgation of
the circumstantial table. But it is worth noting that social transformation itself is seen to have a regular and potentially predictable structure: the problem is simply that observers—the "moral astronomers"—
cannot be trusted to make the calculations aright. What Lane is talking
about is not the provisional or relative nature of truth but the pragmatic and practical stance necessary for understanding and implement-
ing it.

Lane goes on to point out that the family is the ideal instrument for
gentle and organic change. On the one hand, the family will make it
possible for "human emergence" to be achieved "by easier transition
than is presented in extended scientific arrangements"—such as, presumably, Fourierism or Owenism. On the other hand, the communication of the circumstantial law cannot be left to the random processes of
individual interaction since "divine justice would scarcely be perceptible in making the improvement and health of one individual wholly
dependent on the improvement and health of every other." The family, he claims, provides a solution to this impasse. In this environment
the individual is most susceptible to the force of a good example, since
"man, though he loves all objects with the same love," cannot "love
them all in the same degree." The family, he tells us, "need not be a
hindrance to a love for the whole human race." He goes on to explain
how the new order will crystallize around the human solidarity that the
family makes possible:

Practically the steps will be gained somewhat after this manner. More
and more recruits will daily be enlisted from the old crowd, and swell
the orderly ranks of the new phalanx; but let it not be forgotten that
the family relation cannot be lightly or irreverently treated. Not in
public halls, but around the hearth-stone it ever has happened that
improvement has been first discussed. Not in the noisy bustle of life

38. Lane, "Social Tendencies," pt. 1, 86.

where they are preached, but in the quiet recesses of home, all high, dignified, and heroic actions have their origin. In the family, the last, the noblest, the redeeming secret lies hid. Perhaps it is true that in this circle man's fall originated, and in it is perpetuated; but logically and retributively that fact should at least not preclude, if it does not confirm the prognostic, that in the family are to be sown the permanent seeds of new life.[39]

There is something in the tone of this passage that suggests a modification of Lane's position under the influence of Alcott. The first mention of the family's role interrupts his vision of gradual but massive change, the establishment of a "new phalanx." The phrasing almost suggests another speaker coming in with a note of warning: "Let it not be forgotten that . . ." Then, after a panegyric on the family, the perspective switches again. The extreme caution of the wording of the final argument—"but logically and retributively that fact should at least not preclude, if it does not confirm"—provides a full measure of Greavesian doubt about the likelihood of the family's achieving a redemptive role. In any case, one gathers that the family's contribution will be only a temporary one, that of providing a way station on the route to a new life. The family is the progenitor of change, not the fundamental unit of a utopian society. The implication is that when it has completed its role it will wither away, as social classes were expected to do in Marxian theory once they had completed their interaction.

It is probably true that even in terms of this practical and transitional role the family's identity, so far as Lane is concerned, is primarily as an intellectual and spiritual unit rather than a biological one. The process of development that he is envisaging appears to involve attracting new adherents, one by one, around a central core, until eventually the "family" becomes coextensive with society as a whole. Lane's series is progressive—it goes from the individual to the family to society—whereas Alcott sees the family itself as a perfectible unit, the primary form of social life. Lane had gone as far as he was able in Alcott's direction, and it is clear from his article "A Day with the Shakers," published in the *Dial* in August 1843, a couple of months into the short life cycle of the Fruitlands community, that he continued to take a grudging attitude toward the sexual relation. What the Shakers exemplified for him, in fact, was a way of reinstating Greaves's notion of spirit pairing without the awkward concomitant of sexual union.

39. Lane, "Social Tendencies," pt. 2, *Dial* 4 (October 1843): 200, 203.

The Shakers had a community near Fruitlands, and the article describes one of a number of visits Lane made to what were, in many ways, his natural allies. He restates the Greavesian position that sex is allowable so long as it is not fun: it is necessary to "lay the propensities of lust entirely aside, and enter upon that work [sexual intercourse] without the influence of any other motive than solely that of obeying the will of God, in the propagation of a legitimate offspring" (so much for the morning stars shouting for joy). But at the same time he was impressed by the number of biblical authorities the Shakers were able to muster in defense of their doctrine of celibacy, and even more by the way in which their social organization demonstrated that the lack of a maternal role frees the woman for other activities and gives her a chance of achieving equal status with the male: "The union of the two sexes in government, in influence, in religion, in chaste celibacy, is an achievement worthier of renown than many works of greater fame. The extent of its operation, and its important consequences, are yet but faintly discernible. It is also worthy of remark, that the most successful experiment of associate life, and community of property, was founded by A WOMAN." More important to Lane than the practical issue, though, was the spiritual one. He is fascinated by the status afforded to the Shaker founder Ann Lee as "female principle or supplementary nature to Jesus Christ." There is no second best implied by the term "supplementary," since Christ himself is defined as the "male complement."[40] For Greaves, Christ's "humanity was of the universe virgin nature."[41] Thus celibacy, somewhat ironically, serves to link the two great manifestations of gender.

It is interesting to see how Margaret Fuller addresses this topic in the previous issue of the *Dial*. In her article "The Great Lawsuit: MAN versus MEN. WOMAN versus WOMEN," expanded into *Woman in the Nineteenth Century* the following year (and favourably reviewed by Lane),[42] she too gives woman a separate set of qualities which incline toward the elevated: "The especial genius of woman I believe to be electrical in movement, intuitive in function, spiritual in tendency." That is, woman is more attuned to the life force than man: "She is great not so easily in classification, or re-creation, as in an instinctive seizure of causes, and a

40. Charles Lane, "A Day with the Shakers," *Dial* 4 (October 1843): 171, 172, 169.
41. Greaves, *Letters*, 2:137, letter of March 31, 1841.
42. See Charles Lane, review, *Herald of Freedom*, September 5, 1845, n. p. Lane emphasizes that it is "not by inviting Woman more into the male world" that she can be enabled to make her contribution, but by allowing her to contribute her specifically womanly (i.e., spiritual) virtues, and especially by her role of barring "the door against licentiousness."

simple breathing out of what she receives that has the singleness of life, rather than the selecting or energizing of art." The contribution of "Femality" is dynamism, and the verbs Fuller marshals to describe the operations of soul in or through this principle are reminiscent of those Emerson put at the disposal of *his* female embodiment, the merry Sphinx: "It flows, it breathes, it sings, rather than deposits soil, or finishes work, and that which is especially feminine flushes in blossom the face of the earth, and pervades like air and water all this seeming solid globe, daily renewing and purifying its life." In short, Fuller, like Ann Lee and like the Greavesians, believes that "male and female represent the two sides of the great radical dualism." The nature of femality complicates the issue, however, since because it is fluid it will not stay put. "Fluid hardens to solid," Fuller tells us, using almost the same words Alcott uses in describing the function of "mettle." For her, though, the transformation is not that of reproduction as such but a kind of transsexuality, at least as far as gender values are concerned. If woman is liquid, well, water can freeze; by the same token, "solid rushes to fluid." The genders have distinctive qualities, but they are not stable entities: "There is no wholly masculine man, no purely feminine woman."[43]

The fluidity of the female breaks down not merely the barrier *between* the sexes but also the one bisecting her own gender, freeing her for a double role in life. Fuller quotes a "profound thinker" to the effect that "no married woman can represent the female world, for she belongs to her husband. The idea of woman must be represented by a virgin." For her, as for the Shakers, virginity is not an aspect of male ownership but an indication of female autonomy. "The very fault of marriage, and of the present relation between the sexes, [is] that the woman does belong to the man, instead of forming a whole with him." Fuller therefore maintains the virginal ideal but subsumes this most uncompromising of values in the metaphor of fluidity: "Woman, self-centred, would never be absorbed by any relation; it would be only an experience to her as to man. It is a vulgar error that love, *a* love to woman is her whole existence; she also is born for Truth and Love in their universal energy. Would she but assume her inheritance, Mary would not be the only Virgin Mother. Not Manzoni alone would celebrate in his wife the virgin mind with the maternal wisdom and conjugal affections. The soul is ever young, ever virgin."[44] As Emerson put it, "The soul looketh steadily forwards, creating a world before her, leaving worlds behind

43. Margaret Fuller, "The Great Lawsuit: MAN versus MEN. WOMAN versus WOMEN," *Dial* 4 (July 1843): 43.
44. Ibid., 47.

her."[45] In Santayana's terms, the soul is able to confront each morning with "fresh sincerity." At the same time, Fuller asserts that this virginal outlook or approach is compatible with the mature values of motherhood, with the mythical accumulation of "maternal wisdom." Nature and history can, after all, be reconciled.

Hers is, understandably, a vision short on detail. Indeed, in the next and final paragraph of her piece Fuller rather touchingly suggests that the resolution of the problem may have something to do with the young queen of England: "And will she not soon appear? The woman who shall vindicate their birthright for all women; who shall teach them what to claim, and how to use what they obtain? Shall not her name be for her era Victoria, for her country and her life Virginia? Yet predictions are rash; she herself must teach us to give her a fitting name."[46]

This rhetorical solution is not available to a utopian community. The degree to which Lane and Alcott confronted, and solved, the problem of virginity versus motherhood, along with the competing values those terms carry in their wake, can be seen in a joint letter they composed in response to an inquiry by A. Brooke of Oakland, Ohio. The letter is headed "The Consociate Family Life" and signed "Charles Lane, A. Bronson Alcott, Harvard, Mass., August 1843," so it was actually written during the brief lifespan of the Fruitlands community, and can therefore be taken as providing a fair cross-section of its ideology. A copy, cut out of the *Herald of Freedom* for September 8, 1843, is inserted in Alcott's "Autobiographical Collections."[47] The title, like the letter itself, maintains the ambivalence we have already seen over the nature of the serial unit in social regeneration. A consociate family could readily be construed as a group of utopians who have come together to provide a transitional stage en route to a complete overhaul of society. But the phrase "family life" in the title rings a more traditional bell, suggesting a particularly intense, and socially idealistic, version of the nuclear family structure, a suggestion that appears to be supported by a passage near the beginning in which Lane and Alcott proclaim the family to be the most important social unit precisely because it centers on the procreative act:

45. Emerson, "The Over-Soul," 163.
46. Fuller, "The Great Lawsuit," 47.
47. Charles Lane and A. Bronson Alcott, "The Consociate Family Life," *Herald of Freedom*, September 8, 1843, 113–14. This letter is inserted in Alcott's "Autobiographical Collections" (1840–44), 10 vols., Houghton Library, MS 59M-307 (4), 5:293–95.

Let it be admitted as the embosoming of the most vital, and only creative of all human acts, and we are convinced of the absorbing importance of family life. The next age depends much for its character, its modification, its happiness, on parents in this generation, as they have depended on their parents, by the relative opposition or concurrence of their wills with the Divine will. In a deep sense, all human conduct may be said to centre in this act. As birds migrate to our latitude in the warm season, build and use their nests, sing a song or two, and as the cold approaches depart to a warmer zone, so man is sent from balmier climes to breed upon the earth, and all other actions should be but preparative to this of securing an off-spring unprofaned by any self-will, untinctured by lust.[48]

Of course, there is nothing here that formally contradicts the Greavesian position, and indeed the final austere phrases authentically resonate with it. Nevertheless, the tone of the rest of the passage is much more optimistic than one would expect from Lane, with the rather charming reference to birds in their nests presenting an unmistakable image of the nuclear family. Above all, there is a hint that the family institution has already shown what it can do, and that at least some among the previous generation of parents have achieved "concurrence of their wills with the Divine will." (Interestingly, the nesting simile is omitted from the version of the letter published in the *New Age and Concordium Gazette* for November 1, 1843, where authorship is attributed to Lane alone.)[49]

A little later, however, we get a different story altogether. The Shakers, we are told, have achieved "harmonic results" by the "bringing together of the two sexes in a new relation." Near the end of the piece the question "Shall I become a parent?" figures among a number of others which are answered rhetorically: "To how many of these questions, could we answer them deeply enough, could they be heard as having relation to our eternal welfare, would the response be 'ABSTAIN'?" So much for the birds in their nests. The authors are aware

48. *New Age*, 294.
49. Ibid., pp. 116–20, see 117. This is taken from the version in the *New York Evening Tribune* 3, no.124 (1 September 1843): 1, though the *New Age and Concordium Gazette* gives the reference incorrectly. The *Tribune* version is also signed by Lane alone, though it does give the nesting simile. It begins in Lane's first-person singular, and after a few paragraphs moves into the plural. One can infer that Lane penned the letter himself with Alcott's assistance, but later edited it for publication in the English *New Age* to reflect his own more austere position.

that the views expressed are not exactly coherent. They mention that the "narrative . . . has undergone some changes in its personal expression which might offend the hypercritical," but go on to claim somewhat coyly that at least they have produced an "unartful offering."[50]

Perhaps in the end one should not condemn Alcott and Lane for their lack of dialectical ability. Their two central assertions, that "man is sent from balmier climes to breed upon the earth" and "ABSTAIN," cannot produce a synthesis to give their letter, and indeed their community, a consistent basis. One could argue that the structure of dialectic is itself related to that reproductive act which the Fruitlanders found so problematic. The question whether Fruitlands should cultivate fruit or fruitlessness was, finally, an insoluble one.

Emerson, that most perceptive of observers, perhaps picked up on the fact that two points of view lay in suspension in the community just as they did in the letter to Brooke, since they also appear side by side in his journal entry for July 8, 1843, in which he describes a visit to Fruitlands. He begins:

> The sun & the evening sky do not look calmer than Alcott & his family at Fruitlands. They seem to have arrived at the fact, to have got rid of the show, & so to be serene. Their manners & behaviour in the house & in the field were those of superiour men, of men at rest. What had they to conceal? What had they to exhibit? And it seemed so high an attainment that I thought, as often before, so now more, because they had a fit home, or the picture was fitly framed, that these men ought to be maintained in their place by the country for its culture. Young men & young maidens, old men & women, should visit them & be inspired. I think there is as much merit in beautiful manners as in hard work.[51]

This passage perfectly reflects that stationary Emerson of whom Lane was to complain a mere two months later in his letter to Oldham. Nevertheless, it also has relevance to the legendarily serene Alcott, whose "beautiful manners" were explored in F. I. Carpenter's famous 1940 article "Bronson Alcott, Genteel Transcendentalist."[52] The vision behind these words is of exemplary or repetitive seriality whereby a perfected social unit transforms the surrounding structures into its own

50. Lane and Alcott, "Consociate Family Life," in "Autobiographical Collections," 5:294.
51. Emerson, *JMN*, 8:433, entry for July 8, 1843.
52. F. I. Carpenter, "Bronson Alcott, Genteel Transcendentalist: An Essay in Definition," *New England Quarterly* 13 (1940): 34–48.

configuration. Emerson is describing the home celebrated in Alcott's letter to his daughters, a place of "peace and joy, and gentle quiet." What is important about such a unit is what happens *inside* it; it is a place of "quiet recesses," to quote Lane in "Social Tendencies."[53]

Nonetheless, Emerson's inclusive and intuitive sensibility does not allow him to leave the matter there. Without any acknowledgment of a shift in perspective, he goes on to suggest that the utopians will win acceptance only if they are outward-looking and interact positively with the community around them: "If they will in very deed be lovers & not selfish; if they will serve the town of Harvard & make their neighbors feel them as benefactors, wherever they touch them; they are as safe as the sun."[54] In short, hands must reach out beyond the picture frame and clasp the surrounding citizenry. We have moved from the security of enclosure to that of total public exposure, the safety of the sun; from a conception of family as nuclear entity to one of family as provisional and transitory social arrangement mediating between the individual and society at large, from selfishness to love, discreteness to engagement; from manners to benefaction, crystal to fluid.

Interestingly, Abigail Alcott, writing in her journal a month earlier—only three days after the founding of the community—quite explicitly identifies the same alternatives:

> Walked over our little territory of woodland, vale, meadow, and pasture. Hill, grove, forest—all beautiful, the hills commanding one of the most expansive prospects in the country. The Escutney, Wachusett, Monadnock, all visible from the same eminence. One is transported from his littleness and the soul expands in such a region of sights and sounds. Between us and this vast expanse we may hold our hand and stand alone, an isolated being occupying but a foot of earth and living but for ourselves; or we may look again, and a feeling of diffusive illimitable benevolence possesses us as we take in this vast region of hill and plain.[55]

The Transcendental dilemma, whether to "stand alone" or to succumb to a "feeling of diffusive illimitable benevolence," could hardly be put more clearly. Moreover, the extent to which the problem is implicit in the very structure of the Transcendentalists' vision of the

53. Lane, "Social Tendencies," pt. 2, 203.
54. Emerson, *JMN*, 8:433.
55. Selections from Abigail Alcott's journals for 1842–44 are given in Shepard's edition of Bronson Alcott's journals by way of compensating for the missing volumes of the latter's work; see Alcott, *Journals*, 153, entry for June 4, 1843.

world is revealed by the casual and unaffected way it arises out of Abigail Alcott's perception of the surrounding landscape. On the one hand, the Fruitlands domain is "our little territory"; on the other, it commands "one of the most expansive prospects in the country" (the "eminence" on which the farmhouse is situated is called Prospect Hill). It was not only Emerson who could be moved by the sight of Mount Monadnock to a consciousness of the juxtaposition of static and dynamic solutions to life's riddle. And if Abigail Alcott's phrasing of the great question suggests that she favors a particular answer, the rest of her journal entry demonstrates a pragmatic talent for leaving the options open: "I gathered an apron of chips while the children collected flowers. Like provident Mother Earth I gathered for use, they for beauty. Both gave pleasure. It was very characteristic in me, and most natural in them."[56]

The two Fruitlands models lie side by side on the page in Emerson's journals as they do in Abigail Alcott's and in the letter to Brooke, Emerson having digested the incompatibility between Alcott and Lane without, apparently, being fully aware of what he had actually swallowed. Nevertheless, he obviously experienced certain rumbles, and had to admit that "they [Lane and Alcott] have yet to settle certain things," remarking ominously (and prophetically), "We shall see them in December."[57]

If Fruitlands provides us with an allegory, it is not one of the conflict between Good and Evil, as Louisa May Alcott in effect claimed in *Transcendental Wild Oats*, but rather that of a much more authentically Transcendentalist struggle between the forces of Nature and History, as embodied in Alcott and Lane, respectively. Although the two main protagonists of the Fruitlands drama shared a perhaps unfortunate capacity for latency, as is suggested in the letter to Brooke and mirrored in Emerson's remarks, this means not that they were unconscious of contradiction but only that they had not succeeded in resolving it, as Emerson also reveals in his remark about their unfinished business. There is, however, some evidence that both men made an effort to cope with the gulf between their positions. In January 1843, about five months before the inauguration of the community, when Lane and his son William were staying with the Alcotts in Concord, Abigail Alcott instituted a domestic post office in order to relieve the tensions that were already beginning to divide the household. The idea was that

56. Abigail Alcott, ibid., 153.
57. Emerson, *JMN*, 7:433.

members of the consociate family could explain their feelings to one another in notes, which would be distributed after the evening meal each day. Two letters from Lane to Mrs. Alcott, both aimed at clearing up a misunderstanding between them, are glued into the appropriate pages of the latter's diary.

In the first, dated January 30, 1843, Lane writes: "In coming to this hospitable land I hoped to enact only a fractional part of some larger work, or rather I should say I anticipated something of that kind, but if it be ordained otherwise I am happy." Two days later he writes, even more revealingly: "I confess I do not see my way very clearly, and had I been aware of the real state of things here, the probability is that I should not have come, yet no one has deceived me nor do I think that I have deceived myself. It seems that we can only actually know things by acting, and though I expected I should have had to fill some very subordinate part in a large affair, I cannot say I feel disappointed that it is otherwise and that we are left to work our way in comparative solitude."[58] In other words, the man with an allegiance to history ("some very subordinate part in a large affair") has had to reconcile himself to nature ("comparative solitude").

The evidence in the other direction is more scanty, simply because for this period all Bronson Alcott evidence is scanty. We do, however, find—again in the invaluable Abigail Alcott journals—a vignette of him inveighing in Greavesian fashion against sexual indulgence. This entry is for July 2, 1843, a month into the Fruitlands experiment: "Mr. Alcott most beautifully and forcibly illustrated on the blackboard . . . the † on which the lusts of the flesh are to be sacrificed." Her combination of adverbs perhaps suggests the extent to which this stance was an acquired and even an imposed one. Certainly she herself remained skeptical about the benefits to be derived from living according to the celibate principles of the Harvard Shakers: "Visited the Shakers. I gain but little from their domestic or internal arrangements. There is a fat sleek comfortable look about the men, and among the women there is a stiff awkward reserve that belongs to neither sublime resignation nor divine hope."[59] It may not be surprising, given her commitment to her own nuclear family and her refusal to take the sentimental view of Shaker life, that by November she was threatening to leave the community.

This information is contained in a copy of a letter from Lane to

58. See Abigail Alcott, Diary (1841–44), Houghton Library, MS 59M-311 (1), (January, 22 and February 6, 1843).
59. Abigail Alcott, in Alcott, *Journals*, 153, 154, entries for July 2 and August 26, 1843.

Oldham dated November 26–29, 1843, which Harland appended to his article. Lane goes on to say that if Abigail left, he would not be able to stay with Bronson because "to be 'that devil come from Old England to separate husband and wife,' I will not be, though it might gratify New England to be able to *say* it." (Only a month after his letter this demonology was established by the eleven-year-old Louisa's diary entry.) Lane complains that it has been made next to impossible for new members to join the community, and claims that Mrs. Alcott, "who vows that her own family is all she lives for or wishes to live for," more or less kicked a certain Anna Page out of the community.[60] This is obviously the "Jane Gage" of *Transcendental Wild Oats*, who, according to Louisa, fled Fruitlands after being humiliated by *Lane* for eating a piece of fish tail. Whatever the rights and wrongs of this matter, Lane's broad claim about Abigail Alcott corresponds with her own account of her feelings, in her journal for January 7, 1843, the day after Lane finally left the community: "The arrangements here have never suited me, and I am impatient to leave all behind and work out my way in some more simple mode of life. My duties have been arduous but my satisfaction small. The family since our residence here has been variable and uninteresting. The care of Mr. Lane and William has been at times exceedingly arduous. My children have been too much bereft of their mother, and she has murmured at a lot which should deprive her of their society."[61] As though to maintain a certain degree of ambiguity to the end, Abigail Alcott uses the word "family" to refer to consociation and "society" in relation to her own children, but the general disposition of her loyalty is clear and corresponds with Lane's diagnosis.

Lane goes on to make a specific claim that Bronson Alcott misled him about his own views and intentions:

> In conversation the other day Mr. A. put it to me thus—"You think that before the outlay of money began I expressed certain high moral principles, that during the expenditure these principles were for lower and selfish ends suppressed; and that now the money is all expended I recur to the higher moral principles formerly avowed." I trust it was mere speculation and not consciousness which suggested this thought to him. His conduct is certainly liable to such interpretation, but I deem him rather wayward and notional than wicked or acquisitive, and more borne down by his wife and family than wishful to abandon any affirmation he may make. He one day spontaneously

60. Harland, "Bronson Alcott's English Friends," 58.
61. Abigail Alcott, in Alcott, *Journals*, 156, entry for January 7, 1844.

put this question to me—"Can a man act continually for the universal end while he cohabits with a wife?" How different a state of mind must this thought have issued from to that which caused him to shed tears on the same subject eighteen months ago at Ham!! Hopeful prospect![62]

Even a sketchy acquaintance with Bronson Alcott's character establishes that financial considerations would never have had any influence on his behavior, though the thought might have occurred to him that his own swings of attitude could be construed in that light, particularly if Lane had given him a cue by expressing some (unrecorded) bitterness on the subject. There is a certain circumstantiality about Lane's account that rings true. Isaac Hecker confirms Alcott's failures from the communitarian point of view in that July entry in his diary which lists reasons for his own precipitate flight from the fruitless farm: "1st, his [Alcott's] want of frankness; 2nd, his disposition to separateness rather than win cooperators with the aims in his own mind; 3d, his family, who prevent his immediate plans of reformation."[63]

It is not hard to reconstruct the misunderstanding that must have taken place between Alcott and Lane, on both the psychological and the ideological levels. It is worth emphasizing, for example, Alcott's state of mind when he became exposed to English Transcendentalism. He had been made aware of transatlantic interest in, and respect for, him at just the moment when his spirits were most in need of a lift. The Temple School had folded, and he was facing, with great courage and dignity, a torrent of public abuse, the main charges being that he was blasphemous and immoral and had no idea how to teach. It is not surprising that when, in 1842, Emerson offered to finance a trip to England for him, he should have made a beeline for Ham in Surrey. As Abigail Alcott put it in her journal for April 1, 1842, "These transatlantic worthies will be more to him, in this period of doubt, than anything or anybody can be to him here."[64]

The first thing that must have struck home was that Alcott House was continuing to function adequately, a success story that belied the nomenclature it had acquired. The school itself was in the charge of Henry Gardiner Wright, who immediately impressed Alcott as being an even more gifted teacher than himself: "Mr. Wright has more genius for education than any man I have seen: and not of children alone, but

62. Harland, "Bronson Alcott's English Friends," 58–59.
63. Elliot, *Life of Father Hecker*, 85.
64. In Alcott, *Journals*, 141.

he possesses the rare art of reaching men and women. What I have dreamed and stammered and preached and prayed about so long, is in him clear, definite; it is life, influence, reality."[65] The emphasis, significantly, is on the sharper focus and greater practicality of the Englishman, his capacity for actually achieving what Alcott only thought about.

Apart from Wright and Lane, "a man of the deepest, sharpest, intellect I have ever met," Alcott got to know a wide circle of other reformers.[66] Something of the atmosphere of that summer is conveyed in the resounding advertisement inviting "the friends of human destiny" to a public meeting on Richmond Common; the fact that only sixteen or twenty such friends in fact materialized would hardly put a damper on things, since, whatever their differences, both Lane and Alcott subscribed to the doctrine of small beginnings.[67]

It is not to be wondered at that, amidst all this hectic activity, Alcott should listen with enthusiasm to his admirers' plans and feel that the reforming impetus he had come across was likely to achieve practical results. In one of the first letters he wrote from Alcott House, he says that "England is in advance of America in the province of thought and action wherein I have dwelt so long, and with so little company to cheer me in my work." By August 16 he is claiming that "many persons are becoming interested in our purposes. . . . I have hopes now that Mr Lane and his little boy will return with me. . . . And Mr and Mrs Wright would go at once, but for the Babe. . . . Mr Wright has a brother too who is unwilling to stay behind; And his sister . . . is expected here early in September, with Mr Bennett. . . . I have heard from him and shall meet him with hope. Miss Parsons too, inclines to unite with us." These people, together with some Americans, "Mr David and the Greens," were to form the basis of the new community.[68] (In fact, of those mentioned only Lane, his son, and Henry Wright actually came over, and Wright did not join Fruitlands.) The logical conjecture is that Alcott was seduced by English enthusiasm into taking up a much more radical stance than his faith in redemption through a virtuous family life really permitted: that is, he provided a mirror image of the reforming zeal he encountered.

At the same time, the English Transcendentalists would have been predisposed to look long and hard in the mirror that Alcott provided.

65. Alcott, *Letters*, 72, letter of June 17, 1842.
66. Ibid., 70, letter of June 12, 1842.
67. The occasion is described, and the attendance given, in an unattributed letter quoted in Ralph Waldo Emerson, "English Reformers," *Dial* 3 (October 1842): 241.
68. Alcott, *Letters*, 71, 89–90, letters of June 12 and August 16, 1842.

For one thing, they would no doubt have assumed, like many Europeans, that America was the place where true social progress was most likely to be made. Moreover, though they hardly lacked self-confidence—and certainly not faith in their leader, James Pierrepoint Greaves, that "gigantic mind," as Lane described him, "bestriding the narrow world of literature like a colossus"—the English Transcendentalists must have felt that their American opposite numbers were the leaders of the movement and had created rather larger social, religious, pedagogical, and literary ripples than any of the activities at Ham.[69] And Alcott's legendary capacity for enthusiasm, no doubt at full throttle in the excitement of his trip, would have made it easy for the English to imagine that some big enterprise was under way. The fact that the recently deceased Greaves admired Alcott would further have encouraged his disciples to demonstrate their zeal to him and to be responsive to the excitement he showed in return.

What would have helped to clinch this mutual psychological susceptibility on the ideological level was the built-in tendency of Transcendentalists to respond to revelations from across the water. I have already discussed the Brook Farmers' vulnerability to a translated ideology (Brisbane's rendition of Fourier's French), which had the force of a revelation of the structure underlying the world while at the same time suggesting an already established set of values arising from, and geared toward, the historical process. Essentially the same process can be seen at work in the transatlantic interaction between Lane and Alcott. In this case, of course, one is using the word *translation* in a metaphorical sense, but there must have been a powerful shock of recognition, for both of them, in encountering in an alien context ideas with which they were so conversant. The combination of alienation and familiarity, of myth (culture) and revelation (sunrise), charges Alcott's account of the experience with a religious rapture: "I waited long for the man to come who should take an interest like mine in the demonstration of the true culture; I sought him amidst my own country men; for a time I postponed my own work, and despaired almost of my Hope; but now from this darkness that well-nigh swept my Sun from the heavens, rises my Genius again in this East, and I return to my own land to dwell in its rising light."[70]

As we have seen, both Alcott and Lane proposed the two central Transcendentalist approaches in their programs for millennium, and

69. Quotes from Shepard, *Pedlar's Progress*, 333.
70. Alcott, *Letters*, 87, letter of August 2, 1842.

this doubleness helped to enable their ideologies to interlock. At the same time each had his characteristic emphasis. And although these differences would have enforced the original attraction by giving each protagonist a belief in the complementary allegiance of the other, they would also have been responsible for creating the strains that brought the community to its rapid collapse. For a short time the two perspectives overlapped sufficiently to provide a sense of utopian possibility. Perhaps the best example occurs before the Fruitlands experiment even began.

In a letter to Oldham dated February 21–March 1, 1843, Lane describes in extraordinary detail the routine of life in the Alcotts' house in Concord. He explains how they all get up at about six, and Bronson Alcott goes downstairs to light the fires, bathe the baby, Abby May, and get breakfast. They then wash all over with cold water, having bored a hole through the sometimes inch-thick ice to get at it. No mention is made of electrical epiphanies while this is taking place, though Lane does tell us that the water is so cold "it freezes round the basin while we sponge." Then they sit before the fire to take breakfast: "Each has a small red napkin or D'Oyley, in the lap, and the water, unleavened bread, apples and potatoes are handed round by one who is Ganymede on the occasion." After breakfast Mrs. Alcott tidies up Lane's room while he gives a music lesson. He then gets on with his writing until the next meal, while Bronson Alcott brings in the water, wood, and "school apparatus," Mrs. Alcott does housework, and the children work or play. At ten school begins, though Bronson Alcott sometimes takes time out from his pedagogical duties to bake bread. Lunch, along the same lines as breakfast, is taken by one, and afterwards there is a recess until two, followed by more lessons. At four William Lane (who was eleven) shovels paths in the snow, while Lane writes and collects letters and reads. At six-thirty they all sit around the fire for their supper. "The post office is then opened, which consists of a small basket hung all day in the passage, and if there is a lamp the letters are read, but as we disuse all possible animal products, oil is a rare article and candles are scarcely used in all the land." Lane then plays his violin, and they dance and sing until eight, when the children go to bed. The grownups talk for another hour or so, while Abigail Alcott does her knitting, and Bronson peels the potatoes for breakfast.

Rather oddly, Lane completes this account of the day with a plan of the seating arrangements around the fire, which Harland has copied.[71]

---

71. Harland, "Bronson Alcott's English Friends," 42–43.

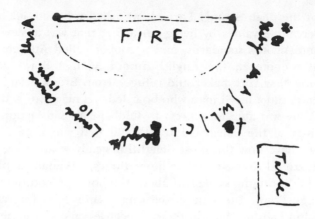

One cannot help but think that the precision of this account, and especially of the diagram, reflects not just the confidences of friendship but a faith in the utopian destiny of the community being described. The fact that the structure of hearth and home, as Lane has sketched it out, coincidentally reproduces the form of the Fourierist serie, inevitably, even if accidentally, reinforces the point. Of course, the question remains as to what kind of a community this one actually is, and it is probably because of this ambiguity that the setup has achieved a shaky equilibrium. Around the fireplace, from right to left, are the baby Abby May, Bronson Alcott, William Lane, Charles Lane, Elizabeth Alcott, Louisa May Alcott, Anna Alcott, and Abigail Alcott. The scheme is all a matter of parents and children, but of course there are *two* sets of parents and *two* sets of children. The group is poised exactly between being a nuclear family and a transitional social arrangement. Even at this point, though, Lane's own allegiance is clear: he goes on to ask Oldham about recruits, since "there is grand work here to be done."[72]

There are probably a number of reasons why no equivalent vignette of (apparent) domestic harmony is available at Fruitlands, though all indications point in the same direction: to the dominance of the Lane view of the family as transitional social arrangement over the Alcott emphasis on family as a biological unit. In May Lane cleared up Alcott's Concord debts, which probably amounted to $300, and paid $1,500 of his own money and an additional $300 that he had borrowed for land on the Wyman farm near the town of Harvard, some dozen miles west of Concord. On June 1 the Fruitlands community began in the farmhouse which had been provided rent-free for a year

72. Ibid., 44.

as part of the deal. Samuel Larned, who had rebelled against his father's mercantile values by living on a diet that was austere even by Lane's and Alcott's standards, and a cooper called Abraham Everett joined at the outset; the English nudist Samuel Bower and Isaac Hecker, the New York baker and refugee from Brook Farm, arrived a little later, as did a hired man who boarded at a neighbor's. By the end of June Lane was able to express to Oldham his satisfaction with the busy activity of the consociation: "Would that you were here for a month; we have now the most delightful steady weather we can conceive; we are all dressed in our linen tunics, Abraham is ploughing, Larnard [*sic*] bringing some turf about the house, Alcott doing a thousand things, Bower and I have well dug a sandy spot for carrots, the children and Lady are busy in their respective ways, and some hirelings are assisting."[73]

This first flush of enthusiasm for life on the land seems to have dissipated rapidly, however. In late July Lane writes that he and Alcott have just returned from a walking trip to Boston and Brook Farm. A month or so later they went to Providence with Anna Page, who had joined the community in July, in order to make arrangements about her furniture. When there the two men got the chance to catch the steamboat to New York, and promptly made the rounds of the city's radicals and reformers. Lane was so impressed by the inhabitants of a boarding house who followed the strict dietary principles of Sylvester Graham that he declared some of them were "half if not quite alive." On the way back from New York they visited New Haven, and then Spindle Hill in Walcott, Connecticut, Alcott's birthplace. No sooner had they arrived back at Fruitlands than they set off again, this time to New Ipswich in New Hampshire to visit a Mr. Hamond, expert workman and able portrait painter, who was married to "an exoteric wife of some good household qualities." By September 29 Lane could confess to having been a "gad-about" for the past month. As it was harvest season, this gadding about seems to have amounted to a sort of agricultural suicide. The only compensating factor was that the community had been joined in August by Joseph Palmer, "the man with the beard," as Lane called him, who owned, in defiance of Fruitlands principles, an ox-and-cow team, and did the farm work "for love." Even he was not exactly a stabilizing influence, however, for he was continually trying to persuade the Fruitlanders to start afresh in Leominster, though ironically he bought the Wyman farm himself after the collapse of the com-

73. Ibid., 49, letter of June 28, 1843.

munity and continued to keep a sort of open house there. It is hardly surprising that by October 30 Lane was admitting that "the crops . . . will not discharge all the obligations they were expected to liquidate."[74]

One would almost think that the community's two leaders suffered a catastrophic loss of concentration at the crucial moment, though this does not exactly chime with what we know of the qualities of the men in question. Lane proved most able at conducting a conventional career both in his early days and after his return to England. The same cannot be said of Alcott, though he was energetic enough in his way, and he proved after the collapse of the community that he could devote long hours to gardening, summer-house building, and the like. The fact that Lane had invested all his assets in the community and that Alcott nearly died of grief after its failure also makes it unlikely that the two men were simply being careless or lazy in the way they ran it, or ran away from it.

A more likely explanation is that Lane's expansive philosophy prevailed for the time being. Just as the Fourierist Brook Farmers began to look toward a national arena, so Lane was impatient to widen the scope of his utopian adventure. His particular vision of the social millennium emphasized serial development rather than the serial repetition of the exemplary unit. Indeed, there was a kind of claustrophobia interwoven into the very texture of his utopian theorizing. A few years after the Fruitlands community's demise, he wrote a series titled "Popular Music" for the *Spirit of the Age* (he was an accomplished violinist) in which he praised music because it "is the least concrete, the most living, subtle, and evanescent of all the varied forms of art." Since music is not capable of "fixation" in time or space (unlike art or architecture), "the living human voice, the living human hand must be always present. . . . [M]anifestations of the harmonic law in its highest department, cannot be embossed in frozen representations, and nailed upon the wall."[75]

Lane was not the only communitarian to despise the concrete and architectural qualities that are necessarily associated with a fixed habitation. A century later Charles Olson would adopt a policy of selling off parts of Black Mountain College until the community finally moved altogether into the realm of pure value. As Olson's biographer Martin Duberman explains, "Like Rice [the original founder of Black Mountain College], Olson believed . . . in not becoming an 'institution.' Rice didn't want to build one; Olson, inheriting one, dismantled it, sold it

74. Ibid., 45, 49, 50, 52–57.
75. Charles Lane, "Popular Music," *Spirit of the Age*, November 17, 1849, 310.

off in bits so that something else, not 'it,' might live—the people there, the life in them."[76] Once again there is the awkwardness of negative principles (Olson believed "in *not* becoming an 'institution'"), but at least Olson was positioned on the ideal side of a quantum process, switching from materiality to the "living, subtle and evanescent" rather than the other way around (and he was also able to deploy the vocabulary of mid–twentieth-century physics). But Fruitlands represented an attempt to create just that sort of "frozen representation" of the ungraspable flow of life that in another context Lane despised. Why, if you do not believe in nailing things to walls, would you want to go about acquiring walls in the first place? In this context it is of the utmost significance that Lane's main modification of Greaves's circumstantial table was to change his optimum habitation ("Buildings cheerful, light and spacious, adapted to Genetic natures") to "The Tent. An Unfixed Locality."[77]

One might conjecture, therefore, that Lane's dedication to an unfixed locality may have caused him to persuade Alcott to accompany him on their various peregrinations. Certainly Alcott seems to have been somewhat bemused at times. When Lydia Maria Child asked, "What brings you to New York?" Alcott is alleged to have replied, "I don't know. It seems a miracle that we are here."[78] Perhaps this tendency to wander off just when there was important farming work to be done was an attempt to avoid fixation in space and frozen representativeness. Indeed, at the apex of Lane's circumstantial prospectus lies an intractable agricultural irony: the nomadic life, fluid and unrestricted though it may be, is associated with hunting or animal husbandry, whereas a fruit and vegetable diet requires a fixed and static mode of existence.

Even if Alcott quite literally went along with Lane, this did not mean that he had surrendered his microcosmic and exemplary perspective for a proselytizing and nomadic one. Lane complains frequently about Alcott's "despotic manner," in very much the way Hecker did.[79] This intolerance is not characteristic of other periods in his life, and though it may reflect some of the stress he experienced during the Fruitlands episode, it also suggests an instinctive yearning for a small-scale, per-

76. Martin Duberman, *Black Mountain: An Exploration in Community* (London: Wildwood House, 1974), 334.

77. For Greaves's version, see his *Letters*, 2:80–81, letter of December 28, 1840.

78. Shepard, *Pedlar's Progress*, 370.

79. Hecker to Oldham in Harland, "Bronson Alcott's English Friends," 56, letter of October 30, 1879.

fectible, exemplary community (the sort that could be provided by a nuclear family). Indeed, Lane concedes as much in a most revealing passage in a letter to Oldham of September 29: "Mr Alcott makes such high requirements of all persons that few are likely to stay, even of his own family, unless he can become more tolerant of defect. He is an artist in human character requiring every painter to be a Michael Angelo. He also does not wish to keep a hospital, nor even a school, but to be surrounded by Masters—Masters of Arts, of the one grand Art of human life. I suppose such a standard would soon empty your Concordium as well as every other house, which I suppose you call by insinuation 'Discordiums,' or more elegantly 'Discordia'."[80] It is almost as if Lane is glossing that very entry in Emerson's journals which I discussed earlier. Alcott has eschewed that activism which would enable the communitarians to "serve the town of Harvard & make their neighbors feel them as benefactors, wherever they touch them." He is not interested in founding hospitals and schools; instead, he is aiming for mastery of the art of life, establishing a "fit home," a picture that is "fitly framed."[81]

Lane and Alcott ultimately held two irreconcilable views about the nature and purpose of the Fruitlands community, so it is little wonder that the enterprise became a Discordium after a very short time. In the autumn William Lane was ill for a whole month and required constant attention. Money worries became acute. Samuel May, Abigail Alcott's brother, had co-signed a note for the $300 loan Lane had needed to make up the $1,800 required for the Wyman farm, but he now refused to pay his share of the first installment. Given his consistent generosity to the Alcotts, he most likely did so at the request of his sister, since within a couple of sentences of complaining about May's refusal to pay, Lane tells Oldham that "Mrs Alcott gives notice that she concedes to the wishes of her friends and shall withdraw to a house which they will provide for herself and her four children."[82] In January 1844 the community disbanded.

The explanation for its rapid demise lies not in any allegory about Timon Lion and Abel Lamb but in an honest disagreement about the operation of serial law as it applied to the creation of the social millennium. Does it work expansively, from the perfected unit outward, or repetitively, through the exemplary force of "a kind and loving family . . . the Pearl of priceless cost"? Retrospective confirmation of this reconstruction of the fundamental ideological disagreement can be ob-

80. Ibid., 55.
81. Emerson, *JMN*, 7:433, entry for July 8, 1843.
82. Harland, "Bronson Alcott's English Friends," 58, letter of November 26–29, 1843.

tained by looking at the principals' reactions to the collapse of Fruit-lands.

Lane states his conclusion about family life in that letter to Oldham in which he speaks of the danger of being blamed for splitting up the Alcott family: "Everything about me, both within doors and without, convinces me more and more that the individual family life must soon cease. Common sense, economy, and good feeling must put an end to the separation of man from man which only the grossest selfishness and ignorance could tolerate for one hour, especially in a country where human action is so free as here it is."[83] In view of this disillusionment with "individual family life" it is hardly surprising that Lane went on to join the consociate family that he admired so much: the Shakers. He had been contemplating such a step since October 1843, and took it immediately after Fruitlands collapsed. His residence lasted somewhat longer on this occasion, but he still had not found his spiritual home, and left in August 1845.[84] At this point a strange reversal took place when he found himself unable to extricate his son William from their clutches.

In fact, the problem could have been anticipated. The Harvard Shaker journals are full of accounts of court cases involving the disputed guardianship of children who were left in the community's custody. One passage gives a good insight into the Shakers' attitude:

Nov. 1844 Fri. 1st. A man and his wife belonging to Providence come here and bring two of thier [sic] children to leave. Sat. 2nd. The Providence man and woman leave here and take their children with them because the woman refused to singn [sic] the Indenture. Simon carried theme [sic] to Acton Depot with the Ministrys horses. When they are got to the Depot they are concluded to sign the Indenture and let Simon bring the children back but after they are gone the woman is so distressed to part with her children that her husband hires a horse and carriage to obtain them but Simon had not arrived so he turns back and meets him and takes his children who are glad to see their father and go with him. Thus it is seen how much trouble the overweening affections of these irresolute parents for their children caused them and us and finally effected nothing.[85]

83. Ibid., 59.
84. See Priscilla J. Brewer, "Emerson, Lane, and the Shakers: A Case of Converging Ideologies," *New England Quarterly* 55 (June 1982): 269–72.
85. Harvard Shaker Journals, library of the Fruitlands Museums, journal no. 2 (1843–45), n.p.

It is hard to imagine how an observer capable of detailing the intricacies of this family's distress could sum up the moral of the story with the heartlessness of that final sentence, but the reaction firmly establishes the Shaker community's position in the context of the debate I have been exploring. In a series of letters written between 1846 and William's release in 1848, Lane expresses his anguish at the entrapment of the product of his biological marriage in the toils of a consociate family. The very incoherence of this passage provides an index of his frustration:

> I cannot think the melancholy principles of the Shakers will last long, but they may continue long enough to kill him. What should I do? Ought not society to move in such a business and since I lack energy undertake that William shall not be crushed between my passivity and Shaker machinery? If I am incapable of doing him justice, they are less so. If I appeal to the law as they now stand upon it, they having more money and device than I have will blind the eyes of justice. But society itself is incapable of entering into such subjects, and that is my only court of appeal.[86]

The complex tensions in Lane's mind between entities such as society and family, passivity (presumably the reference is a bitter restatement of a charge that had been laid at Lane's door) and machinery, law and justice, are here caught in the process of decay. Two years later he is repudiating asceticism: "My connection with the extremely plain philosophers has opened my eyes more clearly to the utility, aye necessity of the beauteous element in every human institution. Privation leads to sensibility. A period of darkness deeps our consciousness of the beauty of light."[87] After his return to England, Lane married again and had five more children. When he died in 1870, his old colleague Oldham, who had taken up spiritualism, reported to Alcott that he had succeeded in communicating with Lane beyond the grave, and discovered that he had not gone straight to heaven because "he cannot forget his money affairs and his family."[88]

Alcott proved much more able, both temperamentally and philosophically, to accommodate the contradictions and complexities of the

86. Lane to Emerson, May 20, 1846. See also Lane's letters to Emerson of September 8, 1846; January 3, 1847; October 7, 1848; September 29, 1849, September 16, 1851. All MSS in Houghton Library, bMS Am 1280 (1810–38).
87. Lane to Emerson, October 7, 1848, Houghton Library, bMS Am 1280 (1831).
88. Oldham to Alcott, March–September 1870 (letter begun in March and resumed in September), MS, Fruitlands Museums.

serial law than his former partner. At the heart of his beliefs there was allegiance to the biological family, which had never really wavered. Abigail Alcott reported to her brother on January 11, 1844, that her husband's "conjugal and paternal instincts were too strong" to allow Lane to "disunite" the family.[89] Within a year Alcott was trying to establish a community again, but significantly his overtures were directed at his own brother, Junius, and what he clearly envisaged was not a consociation of individuals into a "family," but a consociation of biological families that would presumably act as the agency for extending domestic virtues out into society at large. Through the kind offices of Emerson (along with a legacy from his father-in-law, Joseph May), Alcott purchased a property in Concord called Hillside. A letter of January 2, 1845, shows how Alcott was not merely susceptible to disaster but actually capable of advocating it. "There is land," he tells Junius, "*not quite sufficient* for the support of several families."[90] In his proposal Alcott makes it quite clear that he is thinking of the biological family as the redemptive unit: the question is that of replicating redeemed households. In his next letter he suggests that in addition to Junius and his family, their mother should join them as well. Not only are his proposals directed at his own blood relatives, but he emphasizes the need for domestic boundaries even within that context: "The apartments are privated and distinct: private and sacred as we please to make them." And, needless to say, the mode of outreach is to be exemplary:

> It is quite unlikely that others will unite with us, especially at first. Few, perhaps not a solitary soul, is [*sic*] ready for such an enterprize; How far we are ourselves remains to be proved to us by actual trial. If a Holy Family is beyond us, we may, at least, exclude much that annoys and renders uncomely the Households on which we cast our eyes whersoever we turn—on the world around us. To aim at simplicity and purity, amidst the profusion and corruption every where about us, and none the less amidst indigence and rags, is, in itself, the noblest and most needful lesson we can teach our fellows.[91]

It is the old story: exclusion and purity.

The most practical and important proposal Alcott makes is that these aims can be achieved through gardening: "It seems fit for us to occupy these gardens of the soil and the soul, for the growth and ornament of

89. Abigail Alcott to Samuel May, January 11, 1844, in Bronson Alcott, "Memoir, 1878."
90. Alcott, *Letters*, 117; emphasis added.
91. Ibid., 119, letter of January 28, 1845.

both."[92] There we have those two antagonists, soil and soul, never more than a misprint apart, now reconciled through labor, as he pithily describes in a journal entry for April 30, 1846:

> Sodding is the tug of the sinews with ideals—the wrestle of the mind with earthly mould.
>
> > I deem sodding
> > A sternest Godding
> > Bone and muscle
> > In mundane tussle.[93]

That wrestling, however, is to take place within the tight boundaries of a garden, not in the more indefinite expanse of a farm's fields. The Holy Family is to be fitly framed, and the emphasis throughout is so squarely on growing for domestic consumption that, in a subsequent letter to Junius, Alcott actually manages to sound greedy: "The garden is now luxuriant and yields abundantly of melons, corn, squashes, beets, tomatoes, beans, carrots, turnips, and your favorite oyster plant, which we are waiting for you to show us how to prepare for the table. This week I am designing to sow some rye: the buckwheat is now fast ripening for our winter cakes."[94] Junius, perhaps wisely, did not accept these blandishments. But Alcott devoted much of his energy during the remainder of his long life to cultivating both his garden and his Holy Family, an endeavor that received its reward in 1868–69, when his daughter Louisa published her great celebration of American family life, *Little Women*.

For Alcott, of course, gardening and family life were a single entity, involving an interpenetration of mind and mould, a perfect unit of existence. Family, as we have seen, "is but the name for a larger synthesis of spirits united by one common tie of the flesh, like the leaves and flowers, the buds and branches, that shoot forth from the same stem!" As for gardening, his most mature thinking on the subject is evident in this passage from his journal for January 4, 1862:

> Gardening, properly considered, is the blending of man's genius with natural substance. It is the intermingling of mind with matter, and a conversion of the earth into man through the mind, the hands assisting. The gardener thus distinguishes himself as man cultivating the

---

92. Ibid., 118.
93. Alcott, *Journals*, 177.
94. Alcott, *Letters*, 122–23, letter of August 1845.

ground by choice, not from necessity and in bondage to his wants. He deals duteously with it by humanizing it, so to speak, and subdueing it to his designs and taking it into his picture. The woods do not belong to art or civility till they are brought into keeping with his thoughts, nor may they encroach upon us by nearness.[95]

In this account the frame is what counts most of all: the ground has to be taken into the human picture. There is perhaps a slightly defensive quality about the passage. The synthesizing process is elegantly described, but far from predicting the replication of this molecule, Alcott seems more concerned with its capacity for keeping darker forces at bay: the woods will not "encroach upon us by nearness."

Nevertheless, it must not be implied that Alcott ever lost his evangelical fervor. His taste for cultivating his garden was balanced by that urge to travel, both mentally and physically, which he achieved through the medium that became most dear to him, and at which, as Emerson acknowledged, he most excelled: conversation.[96] Indeed, Alcott himself asserted both the cultural centrality of this art, and his own credit for it, in his journal for April 10, 1856:

> Garrison made the Convention,
> Greeley made the Newspaper,
> Emerson made the Lecture,
>   and
> Alcott is making the Conversation.

"These are all purely American organs and institutions," he goes on to say, "which no country . . . can claim as we can."[97] What gives these media their Americanness—certainly what they have in common—is presumably their combination of informality, immediacy, and engagement with the community at large. Moreover, all are elements in an ongoing process rather than end-stopped or definitive in themselves, a point given emphasis in Alcott's own case by the use of the present continuous tense. In *Tablets* he emphasizes that conversation needs to have the qualities of improvisation and exuberance in order to do its business: "Any amount of sense, of logic, matter, leaves the discourse incomplete, interest flags, and disappointment ensues. None has command of himself till he can wield his powers sportfully, life sparkling from all his gifts and taking captive alike speaker and hearer, as they

95. Alcott, *Journals*, 344–45, entry for January 4, 1862.
96. Emerson, *JMN*, 11:19.
97. Alcott, *Journals*, 281.

were docile children of his genius and surprised converts for the moment."[98] Later in the book he establishes the scope and significance of conversation even more clearly when he explains first the relationship between thought and nature and then the relationship of speech to thought:

> Thought is the Mercury; and things are caught on the wing, and by the flying spectator only. Nature is thought in solution. Like a river whose current is flowing steadily, drop displacing drop, particle following particle of the passing stream, nothing abides but the spectacle. So the flowing world is fashioned in the idealist's vision, and is the reality which to slower wits seems fixed in space and apart from thought, subsisting in itself. But thought works in the changing and becoming, not in the changed and become; all things sliding by imperceptible gradations into their contraries, the cosmos arising out of chaos by its agency. Nothing abides; all is image and expression out of our thought.
>
> So Speech represents the flowing essence as sensitive, transitive; the word signifying what we make it at the moment of using, but needing life's rounded experiences to unfold its manifold senses and shades of meaning.[99]

What we see here is a picture of a pattern on the move, of a total structure in which even contraries can be seen to have a serial relationship with each other, of a fundamental parallelism between the "flying spectator" and the natural flux. Alcott footnotes his remarks on speech with a table.[100]

*CATEGORIES OF SPEECH.

	BEING:	
Flowing,		*Fixed,*
Subjective.		Objective.
I.	III.	II.
Actions,	*Participles,*	*Things,*
Verbs.		Nouns.
	IV.	
	Qualities,	
	Adverbs, Adjectives.	
	V.	
	Relations.	
	Prepositions, Conjunctions, Pronouns.	

98. A. Bronson Alcott, *Tablets* (Boston: Alfred Mudge and Son, 1868), 75.
99. Ibid., 174–75.
100. Ibid., 175.

Here we have the flowing and the fixed, the subjective and the objective, the dynamics of perception and the apparent stasis of the world set against one another. Between them is "BEING," comprising the grammatical functions of participles, qualities, and relations, all terms that create a mediating web between pure energy on the one hand and pure materiality on the other—the machinery required for standing Monadnock's head, in fact. In his discussion of conversation Alcott speaks of the effect of metaphor and conveys his elation at the unifying perception that can be achieved when the "pentecost of tongues" touches "the chords of melody in all minds": "What chasms are spanned with a trope, what pits forded, summits climbed, prospects commanded, perspectives gained,—the tour of the spheres made at glance, a sitting; the circle coming safely out of the adventure."[101] One cannot help thinking of Codman's similar adventure, when a pun took him from torrid to frigid zone and back again.

Conversation became steadily more important to Alcott, especially after 1853, when he began his tours to the West. Its attraction clearly lay in its mediating role between the flowing and the fixed, the historical process and the unchanging laws of the universe. The spiritual rapport that one can achieve through conversation is a "gift of divine grace," but at the same time it is achievable only through participation in a cultural tradition. The ability to receive the gift has to be earned. "Nothing in the world is so rare and precious as this grace of free and elegant discourse," he writes; "but it is the late and loveliest flower of all civility, and takes time to ripen."[102]

Conversation might seem to be at the opposite end of the spectrum from gardening. But it can accommodate the organic metaphor just the same, for it represents a combination of preparation and cultivation on the one hand and the spontaneous generation of life on the other. Lane perhaps identified this in-betweenness most perceptively in "A. Bronson Alcott's Works," published in the *Dial* for April 1843: "True conversation seems not yet to be understood. The value of it therefore cannot be truly prized. Its holy freedom, equidistant from hot licentiousness on the one hand, and cold formality on the other, presents constantly to the living generous mind a sphere for enquiry and expression, boundless as the soul itself."[103]

Although they exist on different levels of the serial hierarchy, both conversation and gardening provide a balance between mind and

101. Ibid., 76.
102. Alcott, *Journals*, 222–23, entry for February 7, 1850.
103. Charles Lane, "A. Bronson Alcott's Works," *Dial* 3 (April 1843): 430–31.

body, spirit and earth. And in between these two syntheses—between the villager working his plot and the peripatetic philosopher endeavoring "to belt the continent with talk"[104]—lies a middle point that synthesizes the two: the family. This institution completes the chain. Like the others it is composed of equal portions of the ideal and the material, but unlike them it is located in a completely stable position between the two worlds, tending neither upward like conversation nor downward like gardening. Alcott's approach, unlike Lane's, was not a dynamic one; it did not emphasize struggle and evolutionary growth. Instead, in a manner so characteristic of the New England Transcendentalists, he concentrated his efforts on the paradigm that lay to hand, and lived long enough to see his own family, through Louisa's success, become one of the most famous in America. It is the family— and ultimately that means the traditional, biological family—which provides the fundamental unit of society, of civilization, as Alcott's imagery of generation, physical as well as spiritual, makes clear: "The family is the sensitive plant of civility, the measure of culture. Take a census of the homes, and you have the sum total of character and civilization in any community. Sown in the family, the seeds of holiness are here to be cherished and ripened for immortality."[105]

104. Alcott, *Journals*, 411, entry for June 7, 1870.
105. A. B. Alcott, *Concord Days* (Boston: Roberts Bros., 1872), 86, journal entry for May 23, 1869.

7

Walden:
The Community of One

At Capon Springs, Virginia, on June 26, 1851, Daniel Webster gave a speech in defense of his support for the Fugitive Slave Act in which he made elaborate fun of the conception of a higher law. "Gentlemen," he said, "this North Mountain is high, the Blue Ridge higher still, the Alleghanies higher than either, and yet this 'higher law' ranges further than an eagle's flight above the highest peaks of the Alleghanies! No common wisdom can discern it; no common and unsophisticated conscience can feel it; the hearing of common men never hears its high behests; and, therefore, one would think it is not a safe law to be acted upon in matters of the highest practical moment."[1]

These words, which Webster reiterated at numerous other speaking engagements throughout 1851, were deeply shocking to Transcendentalist sensibilities, in part because of the way in which the Fugitive Slave Act brought the issue of slavery into their frame of reference. In "Self-Reliance" Emerson had emphasized the primacy of the immediate and the local: "If an angry bigot assumes this bountiful cause of Abolition, and comes to me with his last news from Barbadoes, why should I not say to him, 'Go love thy infant . . . and never varnish your hard, uncharitable ambition with this incredible tenderness for black folk a thousand miles off.'"[2] The act had precisely the effect of dragging slavery into the realm of the immediate, the arena of the local, as Emerson

1. Quoted by Theodore Parker in "Discourse Occasioned by the Death of Daniel Webster," in *Historic Americans* (Boston: American Unitarian Society, 1908), 228.
2. Ralph Waldo Emerson, "Self-Reliance," in *Essays 1*, 30.

himself pointed out: "I have lived all my life without suffering any known inconvenience from American Slavery. I never saw it; I never heard the whip; I never felt the check on my free speech and action, until, the other day, when Mr. Webster, by his personal influence, brought the Fugitive Slave Law on the country." What gave Webster's words a peculiarly ironic sting was that in the very process of bringing the slavery issue within the Transcendentalist orbit, they contrived to jeer at the alleged Transcendental preference for what was inaccessible and far away. Emerson's response to Webster's attempts at justification was one of freezing contempt: "He did as immoral men usually do, made very low bows to the Christian Church, and went through all the Sunday decorums; but when allusion was made to the question of duty and the sanctions of morality, he very frankly said, at Albany, 'Some higher law, something higher existing between here and the third heaven,—I do not know where.' And if the reporters say true, this wretched atheism found some laughter in the company."[3]

Of all the Transcendentalists Theodore Parker was the one most horrified by Webster's campaign against the "higher law." Part of the problem was that as a country boy from Lexington, Massachusetts, who had taken his Harvard examinations without being able to afford the courses that led up to them, he felt a certain rapport with Webster, who had begun life on a farm in Salisbury, New Hampshire, and achieved a Dartmouth education on less than two hundred dollars. Webster's words, particularly those distinguishing the exponents of the "higher law" from the "common people," aroused him to a pitch of indignation and fury. He referred to them repeatedly in his sermons and other writings for the remainder of his life; and when Webster died in 1852, Parker denounced his views in a memorial address that is an amazing combination of admiration and vituperation.

Webster's words struck home precisely because they reflected the Transcendentalists' anxiety about the possibility of a structural fissure in their vision of the world. We have seen how Bronson Alcott and Charles Lane tried to construct a vision of life and a model community in which the gulf between the ideal and the circumstantial could be bridged. Thoreau plays with the problem in his own way, using the phrase "Higher Laws" as the title of one of the chapters of *Walden* (1854), and then subverting the expectations thus aroused by opening with a shocking admission of blood lust: "As I came home through the woods with my string of fish, trailing my pole, it being now quite dark, I

3. Ralph Waldo Emerson, "The Fugitive Slave Law", in *Miscellanies, Works,* 11:219, 228.

caught a glimpse of a woodchuck stealing across my path, and felt a strange thrill of savage delight, and was strongly tempted to seize and devour him raw; not that I was hungry then, except for that wildness which he represented." Of course, this opening is something of a rhetorical trick. Thoreau is making the point that human beings are amphibious between two domains: "I found in myself, and still find, an instinct toward a higher, or, as it is named, spiritual life, as do most men, and another toward a primitive rank and savage one, and I reverence them both." Despite his claim he is obviously uneasy about the whole situation, and spends most of the chapter in Lane-Alcott mode, extolling the virtues of a vegetarian and water diet. He concludes with the image of John Farmer sitting on his stoop after a day's hard wrestling with the circumstantial world, trying "to recreate his intellectual man," rather as Hawthorne might have done after a day's shoveling at Brook Farm. John Farmer hears a flute playing, and its notes "gently did away with the street, and the village, and the state in which he lived." The question that then arises is, How to migrate to that "different sphere" from which the music is coming? In the last sentence of the chapter Thoreau makes it clear that he is dissatisfied with the one solution that seems available, the repudiation of the circumstantial: "All that he could think of was to practise some new austerity, to let his mind descend into his body and redeem it, and treat himself with ever-increasing respect."[4]

Elsewhere Thoreau shows more confidence in the possibility and desirability of repudiating one world for another. Indeed, in a letter of May 21, 1856, he eliminates the sarcasm from Webster's imagery and endows it with an extraordinarily poetic momentum: "It is not that we love to be alone, but that we love to soar, and when we do soar, the company grows thinner & thinner till there is none at all. It is either the Tribune on the plain, a sermon on the mount, or a very private *extacy* still higher up."[5] Confusingly, however, in a famous passage in *Walden* we discover that the higher law can also in fact be located *below*: "Let us settle ourselves, and work and wedge our feet downward through the mud and slush of opinion, and prejudice, and tradition, and delusion, and appearance, that alluvion which covers the globe, through Paris and London, through New York and Boston and Concord, through church and state, through poetry and philosophy and religion, till we come to a hard bottom and rocks in place, which we

4. Henry David Thoreau, *Walden* in *Writings*, 210, 221–22.
5. *The Correspondence of Henry David Thoreau*, ed. Walter Harding and Carl Bode (New York: New York University Press, 1958), 424.

can call *reality*, and say, This is, and no mistake."[6] In short, one has to look upward or downward according to whether (and perhaps the choice depends on mood as much as on one's philosophical position) the transcendental Grail is an ethereal ecstasy or a gritty bedrock.

But there are other moods still. Possibly more significant and more central to Thoreau's conception of things than the metaphor of direction is that of superimposition. His experience at the Spaulding farm, which he describes in his essay "Walking," generates a metaphor of this kind. The play of light from the setting sun gives him a sense of an alternative world: "I was impressed as if some ancient and altogether admirable and shining family had settled there in that part of the land called Concord, unknown to me,—to whom the sun was servant,—who had not gone into society in the village,—who had not been called on." As in the case of Emerson's moment of gladness to the brink of fear, this vision of the shining family's happy autonomy is merely a glimpse, since it can be preserved only by invisibility ("Their house was not obvious to vision; the trees grew through it"): "They fade irrevocably out of my mind even now while I speak and endeavour to recall them, and recollect myself."[7] Darkness can have a similar impact to that of the sunbeams, producing an effect of adjacent alienness: "Is not the midnight like Central Africa to most of us? . . . medicinal and fertilizing to the spirit."[8]

These images of coalescence and adjacency take us closer to the Transcendentalist perspective than the metaphors of high and low because they bring with them the implication of interconnectedness, and thus the serial principle. The point is that higher and lower, the Spauldings and the sunbeams, day and night, are knitted together in a single system. Thoreau, like Emerson, was primarily concerned with registering these structural connections in visual terms. A political philosopher such as Orestes Brownson could make out of a doctrine of unified opposites a method of historical analysis that famously anticipated Marxism, with periods of materialism and idealism alternating until they finally synthesize into utopia.[9] Thoreau's search for synthesis takes a rather different form. We have already seen his celebration of the thawing sand bank as a generator of the normative leaflike struc-

6. Thoreau, *Walden*, 97–98.
7. Henry David Thoreau, "Walking," in *Excursions*, vol. 9 of *The Writings of Henry D. Thoreau*, 11 vols. (Boston: Houghton Mifflin, 1893), 297–99.
8. Henry David Thoreau, "Night and Moonlight," ibid., 397, 407.
9. Orestes Brownson, *New Views of Christianity, Society, and the Church* (Boston: J. Munroe, 1836), 105.

ture that underpins the almost infinitely baroque variations of the world. In *A Week on the Concord and Merrimack Rivers* he describes sand as "the connecting link between land and water, . . . a kind of water on which you could walk, and you could see the ripple marks on its surface . . . precisely like those at the bottom of a brook or lake."[10] But if sand connects land and water, water itself is seen to mediate between earth and sky, as is evident in a simile Thoreau uses in his Spaulding passage: "The farmer's cart-path, which leads directly through their hall, does not in the least put them out,—as the muddy bottom of a pool is sometimes seen through the reflected skies."[11] He never tires of celebrating such mediation and interpenetration in *Walden*: "It [Walden Pond] is intermediate in its nature between land and sky." In a famous sentence he simplifies this relation into a binary interaction: "Sky water."[12]

If water can be, so to speak, amphibious, in Sir Thomas Browne's sense of providing a link between two planes of being, the same applies, as in Browne, to the human condition itself. Indeed, it is clear that Thoreau's stress on images of in-betweenness in nature is there to help us visualize our own predicament. It is one of the central arguments of *Walden* that man and pond are linked: "It [a lake] is earth's eye; looking into which the beholder measures the depth of his own nature." Thus, in his panegyric on Alcott, Thoreau celebrates his friend's mediating role: "Whichever way we turned, it seemed that the heavens and the earth had met together, since he enhanced the beauty of the landscape." Of course, Alcott is a special case; but in the tradition of Transcendentalist representativeness that status has the effect of making him exemplary rather than anomalous. Moreover, in his use of the organic metaphor Thoreau, like Alcott himself, emphasizes the way in which it balances human nature between the two worlds, the domain of higher and lower law: "The soil, it appears, is suited to the seed, for it has sent its radicle downward, and it may send its shoot upward also with confidence. Why has man rooted himself thus firmly in the earth, but that he may rise in the same proportion into the heavens above?"[13]

As we have seen, Alcott developed his organic metaphor into a *family* tree. Thoreau, though, identifies it with the individual. For him the basic unit of the serial law is a single person. "No doubt," he tells us,

10. Henry David Thoreau, *A Week on the Concord and Merrimack Rivers*, in *Writings*, 199.
11. Thoreau, "Walking," 298.
12. Thoreau, *Walden*, 188–89.
13. Ibid., 186, 269, 15.

"they have designs on us for our benefit, in making the life of a civilized people an *institution*, in which the life of the individual is to a great extent absorbed, in order to preserve and perfect that of the race. But I wish to show at what a sacrifice this advantage is at present obtained, and to suggest that we may possibly so live as to secure all the advantage without suffering any of the disadvantage." Each of us is a country, a world, as he tells us near the end of *Walden*, and these realms all have access to a moral sea:

> Be a Columbus to whole new continents and worlds within you, opening new channels, not of trade, but of thought. . . . What was the meaning of that South-Sea Exploring Expedition, with all its parade and expense, but an indirect recognition of the fact, that there are continents and seas in the moral world, to which every man is an isthmus or an inlet, yet unexplored by him, but that it is easier to sail many thousand miles through cold and storm and cannibals . . . than it is to explore the private sea, the Atlantic and Pacific Ocean of one's being alone.[14]

Here we have another example of the static and dynamic imagery, of the fixity and flow, that lies at the heart of the law of series. The individual is both a country and an ocean, a discrete unit and a component of totality, a hut dweller and the pond itself. Rarely can the scope and possibility (and essential isolation) of the individual have been so tellingly indicated as in that last phrase, "the Atlantic and Pacific Ocean of one's being alone." *Walden* is a work that sets about offering specific advice about ways in which the individual can achieve both microcosmic and macrocosmic fulfillment.

Thoreau first deals with the preservation of the unitary identity of the individual. We saw how the Brook Farmers, from the very start of their project, were preoccupied with role-playing and fancy dress, whether for tableaux or working the land. Thoreau, by contrast, takes a strongly anti-Harlequin stance from the beginning of *Walden*: "All costume off a man is pitiful or grotesque. It is only the serious eye peering from and the sincere life passed within it, which restrain laughter and consecrate the costume of any people. Let Harlequin be taken with a fit of the colic and his trappings will have to serve that mood too. When the soldier is hit by a cannon ball rags are as becoming as purple." Fashion, he goes on to claim, is a matter of "squinting through kaleidoscopes." In other words, it allies itself with the muta-

14. Ibid., 31–32, 321.

bility of the historical process, and therefore disqualifies the wearer from access to the eternal truths of life—and death.[15]

Thoreau progresses naturally from making this point to attacking the manufacturers who pander to the "childish and savage taste of men and women for new patterns," and from there to an attack on the factory system in general. His argument is that the operatives are being exploited like their English opposite numbers, but the chain of association is a suggestive one: plurality in dress being kin to fractionality in labor. Thoreau's objection to the factory system is inevitably that it breaks down individual integrity and holism, subordinating the person to the product. Whereas the Brook Farmers disagreed with the specialization advocated by Adam Smith because they wanted variety of occupation within the coherent structure of the phalanx, Thoreau wants to see his worker operating within the larger rhythms of countryside and weather. Smith saw the individual as subordinate to the function, while the Brook Farmers saw individual and functions as exactly coeval (once the phalanx was up and running). Thoreau, in his sturdily romantic fashion, saw function as subordinate to the individual, as he makes clear in his description of a visit to Sam Barrett's mill in Concord: "You come away from the great factory saddened, as if the chief end of man were to make pails; but, in the case of the countryman who makes a few by hand, rainy days, the relative importance of human life and of pails is preserved, and you come away thinking of the simple and helpful life of the man."[16]

After this discussion of clothing and its industrial implications, Thoreau moves along naturally to the subject of architecture, which he deals with in much the same terms, decrying ornamentation and the creation of external surfaces that fail to reflect the inner core, and at the same time relating this problem to the division of labor: "I never in all my walks came across a man engaged in so simple and natural an occupation as building his house. We belong to the community. It is not the tailor alone who is the ninth part of a man; it is as much the preacher, and the merchant, and the farmer. Where is this division of labor to end? and what object does it finally serve? No doubt another

15. Ibid., 26.
16. Ibid.; Henry David Thoreau, entry for October 19, 1858, in *The Journals of Henry D. Thoreau*, ed. Bradford Torrey and Francis H. Allen, 14 vols. (Boston: Houghton Mifflin, 1906), 11:277. All subsequent references to this edition will be to *Journal*. This edition is being supplanted by a new one edited by John C. Broderick et al., 5 vols. to date (Princeton: Princeton University Press, 1981–). All subsequent references to the latter edition will be to *J*.

may also think for me; but it is not therefore desirable that he should do so to the exclusion of my thinking for myself."[17]

We are back again in the familiar Transcendentalist quest for One Man. Whereas Emerson regretted the Man's collapse into fragments, G. W. Curtis came grudgingly to accept that it was necessary to make the best of this fractional condition: "In one thing well done lies the secret of doing all."[18] Theodore Parker, interestingly, managed to offer a middle course between these two positions. In a sermon on the "universal providence of God," he suggested that the way to regard the human condition was to see man as simultaneously both fraction and integer:

> Each man will be deemed a fraction of society, and so a factor in its product, but also an integer; and both the functions, that of the fraction and the integer, will be sacredly respected. . . . There will be the same blending of the centripetal power of the whole and the centrifugal power of the individual into that cosmic harmony I spoke of before. . . . Then the various persons of the community will work together with as little friction as the planets in their course; with as little waste as the forces which form a rose or a lily.[19]

Thoreau's solution, meanwhile, was to claim that the individual could *replace* the totality. He was One Man in miniature, major man in the minor key.[20] The Fourierists advocated a composite structure as a means of reestablishing human unity and fulfillment, the phalanx, as I have pointed out, being a kind of finite over-soul, a world in itself, containing and fulfilling all passions and proclivities. Thoreau's claim, meanwhile, is that the individual part—the atom as opposed to the molecule—can actually contain the whole. It resembles a miniature phalanx.

His writings are full of gleeful discoveries of examples and images of this truth. In his essay "A Winter Walk" he describes coming across a

17. Thoreau, *Walden*, 47, 46.
18. G. W. Curtis, *Early Letters of George Wm. Curtis to John S. Dwight*, ed. G. W. Cooke (New York: Harper, 1898), 127–28.
19. Theodore Parker, "Of the Economy of Moral Error under the Universal Providence of God," in *Theism, Atheism, and the Popular Theology* (Boston: American Unitarian Association, 1907), 361.
20. The phrase "major man" is Wallace Stevens's. See "Notes toward a Supreme Fiction," in *Collected Poems* (London: Faber and Faber, 1955), 386.

chip of wood left behind by a forester, and suggests interpreting this piece of evidence in the manner of a Transcendentalist Sherlock Holmes: "This one chip contains inscribed on it the whole history of the wood-chopper and of the world."[21] Significantly, the chip has a median identity, representing the point of intersection between an individual and the natural order, and therefore encapsulates within itself the point of balance that has been achieved. In a journal entry for March 8, 1855, Thoreau describes seeing another by-product of the woodsman's task, turpentine globules on logs, which reflect the world with "perfect sincerity."[22] In this case the mediating object is not merely the embodiment of an encounter between man and nature; it also possesses that quality which so fascinated Thoreau of seeming liquid while actually being solid.[23]

The hut by Walden Pond in which Thoreau lived from 1845 to 1847 was obviously an attempt to establish an environment that protected the status of the fraction as integer. If the argument is that students should build their own colleges, that a worker should embody the factory, then the obvious continuation of the logic is that civilization should be established at the level of its ultimate unit, its lowest common denominator, in the form of a device for living and working which can be built by a single person. Such a dwelling represents the original, primeval enterprise of humankind. It can be related to the lodges of the Indians, the cave dwellings of primitive peoples, the first shelters of the original settlers of New England.[24] We are dealing, in short, with a historically validated basic unit of domestic arrangement, whereby the irreducible minimum of the human race, the individual person, builds and inhabits the irreducible minimum of human habitation, the hut.

We saw in the case of the Brook Farmers how their utopian project was vindicated by the revelation of a pattern: Fourier's depiction of the law of groups and series of groups. The Fruitlanders, meanwhile, had access to a similar "given," the circumstantial law as originally formulated by James Pierrepoint Greaves and modified by Charles Lane. Thoreau presents a table of his own—or, rather, not a table exactly but an invoice, the most famous bill of goods in the history of American letters:[25]

21. Henry David Thoreau, "A Winter Walk," in *Excursions*, 211.
22. Thoreau, *Journal*, 7:237.
23. Thoreau, *A Week*, 331.
24. Thoreau, *Walden*, 50–51, 28–29.
25. Henry David Thoreau, *Walden* (Boston: Ticknor and Fields, 1854), 49.

Boards, ...	$8 03½,	mostly shanty boards.
Refuse shingles for roof and sides, .	4 00	
Laths, ...	1 25	
Two second-hand windows with glass,	2 43	
One thousand old brick, . . .	4 00	
Two casks of lime, ...	2 40	That was high.
Hair, ...	0 31	More than I needed.
Mantle-tree iron, ...	0 15	
Nails, ...	3 90	
Hinges and screws, ...	0 14	
Latch, ...	0 10	
Chalk, ...	0 01	
Transportation, ...	1 40	} I carried a good part on my back.
In all, ...	$28 12½	

In its own way it, too, is a formula for the deep structure of the universe. If the individual is the fundamental unit of the human world, and therefore for Thoreau can be seen to replace that world; if the hut is the fundamental unit of the community, and therefore can be seen to replace that community; then this invoice is the fundamental unit of economics, and can be seen (in conjunction with the details Thoreau gives of his earnings from crops and surveying) to replace the whole complex tissue of commerce that has created and sustained civilization itself. Like Ezra Pound, Thoreau sees economics as the fuel of a historical development that has gone awry. Both writers believe that money has somehow taken on a life of its own and as a result has lost contact with the world of things, with the natural order. Since economics is a kind of symbolic language, this loss of contact explains why history has become disconnected from nature in the first place. With usury, Pound tells us, the peasant has no gain from his sheep herd. Thoreau shares, or rather anticipates, Pound's indignation:

It is very evident what mean and sneaking lives many of you live . . . always on the limits, trying to get into business and trying to get out of debt, a very ancient slough, called by the Latins, *æs alienum*, another's brass, . . . still living, and dying, and buried by this other's brass; always promising to pay, promising to pay, to-morrow, and dying today, insolvent; seeking to curry favor, to get custom, by how many modes, only not state-prison offences; lying, flattering, voting, contracting yourselves into a nutshell of civility, or dilating into an atmosphere of thin and vaporous generosity, that you may persuade your neighbor to let you make his shoes, or his hat, or his coat, or his carriage, or import his groceries for him; making yourselves sick, that you may lay up something against a sick day."[26]

The price of liberation from this miserable cycle is $28.12½. "Economy" is the title of the chapter in which this accounting appears. It refers not just to the subject in general terms but also to the strategy that allows escape from its pressures. Just as the Fruitlanders believed that by minimizing circumstances they could purify those that remained, so Thoreau held that by minimizing expenditure one could enable oneself to purchase what was truly significant and necessary.

Like the wood chip, the hut represents a point of intersection between the human and natural worlds, between lower and higher laws. In *The Maine Woods* Thoreau makes a distinction between the historical and political identity of his country on the one hand and its natural identity on the other: "While the republic has already acquired a history world-wide, America is still unsettled and unexplored."[27] Just as the sunbeam family can invisibly coexist with the human occupants of the Spaulding farm, so, generally, the laws of nature can be seen to coexist with, indeed to underlie, those of history, and it is to this world of eternal verities that Thoreau gains access by means of his hut. He concludes his chapter "What I Lived For" with the famous account of penetrating to eternity through the current of time: "Time is but the stream I go a-fishing in. I drink at it; but while I drink I see the sandy bottom and detect how shallow it is. Its thin current slides away, but eternity remains."[28]

The metaphor of fishing is calculated to convey both proximity and difference, interdependence and separateness. The fish of eternity is available within the stream of history, but is an elusive denizen of those waters, only occasionally perceived or caught. The experience is likely to be one of sporadic uplift, in keeping with the angler's triumph, or more profoundly with Tillich's *kairos*. Nevertheless, one can always extrapolate from these glimpses the serene eternal pattern of nature itself. In *The Maine Woods* Thoreau describes fishing for trout in the "clear, swift, shallow stream" of the Aboljacknagesic; the fishermen throw their catch to one member of the party who stands on the shore. His experience is described in the third person, but the lyricism of the passage suggests that the man on shore is Thoreau himself:

26. Thoreau, *Walden*, in *Writings*, 6–7; Ezra Pound, *The Cantos* (London: Faber and Faber, 1975), 229.
27. Henry David Thoreau, in *The Maine Woods*, *Writings*, 81.
28. Thoreau, *Walden*, 98.

While yet alive, before their tints had faded, they glistened like the fairest flowers, the product of primitive rivers; and he could hardly trust his senses, as he stood over them, that these jewels should have swum away in that Aboljacknagesic water for so long, so many dark ages;—these bright fluviatile flowers, seen of Indians only, made beautiful, the Lord only knows why, to swim there! I could understand better, for this, the truth of mythology, the fables of Proteus, and all those beautiful sea-monsters,—how all history, indeed, put to a terrestrial use, is mere history; but put to a celestial, is mythology always.[29]

The contention here is that "mere history" is utilitarian, whereas mythology reflects the static, beautiful, and eternal patterns of nature. As usual the question is one of law versus contingency. As Thoreau puts it in *A Week on the Concord and Merrimack Rivers*, it is not the "countless shoals" that are "so interesting" but "the more fertile law itself, which deposits their spawn on the tops of mountains and on the interior plains; the fish principle in nature."[30] We have, then, the universal on the one hand and the phenomenal on the other, the principle against the shoal, eternity against time.

Like the other Transcendentalists, Thoreau envisages a day when the absolute laws of nature will permeate and finally replace the contingent reality of daily life, when sunbeam will, so to speak, take over from Spaulding, when history and nature will be reconciled and become what he calls mythology. Because he is thinking in individual rather than communal terms, however, he finds it very difficult to see how this occurrence might be part of social development. His version of seriality is structural—"The Maker of this earth but patented a leaf"—rather than progressive. A good index of his problem lies in his attitude toward that substance which so preoccupied the Fruitlanders: manure.

Thoreau is hardly in a position to take Lane's moralistic stance on the subject. He is, after all, a naturalist, a writer willing to acknowledge an impulse to devour a woodchuck raw. Moreover, as we have seen, he is perfectly willing to place "excrements" in the serial scheme he adumbrates upon the thawing of the sand bank. Nevertheless, it is clear that manure causes him problems. It has its structural function in the eternal world of nature, but it also represents the process of process, and can be seen as an embodiment of the wasteful—with the full ambiguity of that adjective—unfolding of history. Thus, in his first year at the pond Thoreau avoided the use of manure, maintaining that it was part

29. Thoreau, *Maine Woods*, 54.
30. Thoreau, *A Week*, 25.

and parcel of the historical continuity represented by ownership: "I put no manure on this land, not being the owner, but merely a squatter, and not expecting to cultivate so much again." Interestingly, he has no problems with the enrichment of the soil through vegetable decay (any more than Alcott does), so long as the historical dimension given by agricultural planning is not involved: "I got out several cords of stumps in ploughing, which supplied me with fuel for a long time, and left small circles of virgin mould, easily distinguishable through the sum-mer by the greater luxuriance of the beans there."[31] The following year he avoided the use of manure again, this time by moving about on the land—in short, by becoming a nomad, the tactic advocated as "Best, for the Spirit Nature" in Lane's circumstantial table. This kind of agri-culture averts its gaze from the historical implications of settlement and farming but tries to reintroduce a husbandry of the immediate need. It is an agriculture that reflected and miniaturized the nine-teenth-century push westward toward new land but was hardly mean-ingful, except in a symbolic sense, in New England. ("When I go out of the house for a walk," Thoreau tells us in "Walking," "uncertain as yet whither I will bend my steps, . . . I find . . . that I finally and inevitably settle south-west. . . . The future lies that way to me, and the earth seems more unexhausted and richer on that side.")[32] Thoreau advo-cates a method of farming designed to cultivate the "present moment; to toe that line."[33]

Toeing the line of the present means in effect opting out of history, and therefore leaves little scope for a reconciliation between the histor-ical process and the crystalline structure of nature. The intersection of lower and higher laws which might be perceived in a thawing railroad cutting or in wood chips or turpentine droplets cannot be multiplied to produce the kind of large-scale pattern that so fascinated the Tran-scendentalist communities. It is true, however, that from time to time Thoreau claims to have an inkling of a grand reconciliation between nature and history. What is perhaps the most reverberant example of this vision occurs at the conclusion of the essay "Resistance to Civil Government," where he outlines a two-stage process. The first, which appears to be the outcome of historical forces, is characterized by the establishment of justice and neighborliness: "I please myself with imag-ining a State at last which can afford to be just to all men, and to treat the individual with respect as a neighbor." Ironically, though, it is the

31. Thoreau, *Walden*, 54–57.
32. Thoreau, "Walking," 266.
33. Thoreau, *Walden*, 17.

individuals who are allowed to *exclude* themselves from this historical and political process who hold the key to the second stage. The imagined state will have developed the maturity to allow those who wish to opt out of it to do so—to opt out of history itself, in fact. It is a state "which even would not think it inconsistent with its own repose, if a few were to live aloof from it, not meddling with it, nor embraced by it, who fulfilled all the duties of neighbors and fellow-men." This group will bring about the inauguration of the *perfect* state, one that obeys the laws of eternity rather than time, of nature rather than history: "A State which bore this kind of fruit, and suffered it to drop off as fast as it ripened, would prepare the way for a still more perfect and glorious State, which also I have imagined, but not yet anywhere seen."[34]

What we have here is a vision not of history arriving at its ultimate destination but of history producing that destination as a kind of by-product. It is only by such an oblique route that Thoreau can connect the dynamic and the static, the seriality of process and that of crystals. There are times when a reconciliation may appear to be effected, as in this sentence from the opening of the chapter in *Walden* titled "Reading": "That time which we really improve, or which is improvable, is neither past, present, or future." In fact, though, he is talking not about the improvement of time at all but about an encounter with absolute truth, and indeed has already made a distinction between the historical and the eternal: "In accumulating property for ourselves or our posterity, in founding a family or a state, or acquiring fame even, we are mortal; but in dealing with truth we are immortal, and need fear no change or accident."[35] Although this philosophy explicitly centers on the individual's status, it makes it almost impossible—since it requires us to sideline history's contingency and endorse the unchanging reality of the absolute—to perceive a meaningful role for an individual to accomplish. There can be no agenda, no program, no course of action to advocate when there is "neither past, present, or future."

The closest Thoreau comes to endorsing individual activism is in his espousal, late in his career, of the cause of John Brown, whom he obviously perceived as a prime candidate for reconciling the gulf between higher and lower laws in the very context in which Webster had made the distinction in the first place: that of slavery. He was a "man of rare common-sense" as well as "a transcendentalist above all"; a New Englander as well as a Westerner; a farmer (with "a rural exterior") but at

34. Henry David Thoreau, "Resistance to Civil Government," in *Reform Papers, Writings*, 89–90.
35. Thoreau, *Walden*, 99.

the same time a hero. Nevertheless, Thoreau is not entirely comfortable in his company: "I do not think it is quite sane for one to spend his whole life in talking or writing about this matter [of John Brown], unless he is continually inspired, and I have not done so. A man may have other affairs to attend to."[36]

Alcott, as we have seen, is a more congenial reconciler of the two laws, precisely because, unlike John Brown, he does not actually *do* anything. As Thoreau says of his friend: "He has no venture in the present."[37] Brown is the man with a historical destiny; Alcott counterbalances him by being (apparently) outside the temporal process altogether. One might almost go so far as to say that it is the very failure of his own utopian community that provides Alcott with utopian credentials in Thoreau's eyes, since what demonstrates his intellectual integrity and significance is his lack of a fixed abode. He is a man "whose fittest roof is the overarching sky which reflects his serenity," one who "should keep a caravansary on the world's highway, where philosophers of all nations might put up." In addition to philosophers, Thoreau associates Alcott with "children, beggars, insane, and scholars," a list of romantic archetypes that closely resembles that given by Emerson at the end of "History," where he designates those privileged beings capable of writing the true, eternal history of nature rather than "this old chronology of selfishness and pride" (i.e., the history of history): the "idiot, the Indian, the child, and unschooled farmer's boy."[38] Emerson does not mention artists in this list, though we know from elsewhere in his writing that there must be a place in it for the poet. Thoreau does not put artists in his list either, but they belong there too, as is evidenced by the story of the artist of Kouroo, which he tells in the concluding chapter of *Walden.* This artist refuses to compromise with time, and as a result is excluded from its processes, so that his task simultaneously lasts eons and "a single scintillation." Significantly, in view of Thoreau's admiration of woodchoppers and his own espousal of life in the woods, much is made of the woodcraft dimension of the artist's art, the search for the stick, the peeling and shaping, the pile of shavings. It is an art that involves the interaction of the human and the natural, and when it is successfully accomplished, the artist discovers he has "made a new system in making a staff."[39]

Thoreau too is an artist. Moreover, he too is an artist in wood. He

36. Henry David Thoreau, "A Plea for Captain John Brown," in *Reform Papers,* 115, 133.
37. Thoreau, *Walden,* 268.
38. Ibid., 269; Ralph Waldo Emerson, "History," in *Essays 1,* 23.
39. Thoreau, *Walden,* 326–27.

lives among the trees; he has built a hut; he writes on paper. The writer is a sort of woodsman. At least, the writer Thoreau was. This art therefore takes its place among those activities that give access to the world of eternal verities, and it is not surprising that just as Emerson was preoccupied by the poet, so throughout Thoreau's work there is a preoccupation with the trade of writing—with meta-writing in fact. Indeed, even Brown, the man of action, is perceived in "The Last Days of John Brown" as a master of language who establishes both "standard English" and "standard American." Perhaps this is his most significant achievement, since "the *art* of composition is as simple as the discharge of a bullet from a rifle, and its master-pieces imply an infinitely greater force behind them." There is only "one great rule of composition," Thoreau goes on to explain, "to *speak the truth.*" This formulation might seem unhelpfully simplistic, but a little later in his essay Thoreau makes up for it by playing wittily with the concept of Brown as a source of language:

> On the day of his translation, I heard, to be sure, that he was *hung*, but I did not know what that meant; I felt no sorrow on that account; but not for a day or two did I even *hear* that he was *dead*, and not after any number of days shall I believe it. Of all the men who were said to be my contemporaries, it seemed to me that John Brown was the only one who *had not died.* I never hear of a man named Brown now,—and I hear of them pretty often,—I never hear of any particularly brave and earnest man, but my first thought is of John Brown, and what relation he may be to him. I meet him at every turn. He is more alive than ever he was. He has earned immortality. He is not confined to North Elba nor to Kansas. He is no longer working in secret. He works in public, and in the clearest light that shines on this land.[40]

The pun on "translation" ("I did not know what that meant") allows Thoreau to exploit to the full the paradoxical adjacency of the alien to the ordinary. Both the Brook Farmers and Bronson Alcott were susceptible to a language coming at them over the Atlantic divide, since its alienness provided a necessary experience of revelation while its compatibility with their own ideas gave it the authority of myth. The divide that is being bridged—translated—on this occasion is the even more oceanic one that lies between life and death. John Brown is special and apart while at the same time remaining, as his name suggests, a representative man.

40. Henry David Thoreau, "The Last Days of John Brown," in *Reform Papers*, 150–53.

But despite the affirmative rhetoric of the passage there is a darker
countercurrent. The pun on "hung," in the context of hesitancy and
wordplay in which it appears, can surely be taken as a reference not
merely to the gallows but also to the sort of lag in linguistic cognition
that nowadays can be identified as Derridean *différance*. It seems to de-
note the separation of discourse from the reality it claims to portray,
the gulf between signifier and signified.[41] As a result, although the
thrust of the passage as a whole appears to be optimistic, we have a
sense of a separation opening up despite the fact that a claim is being
made that a rift has been healed over. In this context we experience
not what Codman calls "an agreeable jog" as we shuttle between torrid
and frigid zones, but that more alienated sensation when the "soft
thing" drops out between. The distinction being made between physical death and spiritual life effectively stresses the idealized vagueness of
the later claim that Brown is now working in public and in the light.
Thus, the gap between the temporal and the eternal is reaffirmed even
as it is overcome.

Perhaps the fundamental irony that lurks behind Thoreau's praise of
John Brown, both here and elsewhere, is that although he purports to
celebrate the fact that this hero shows how language can be converted
into action, what Thoreau is really responding to is how action can be
converted into language—in other words, how we can move away from
the transient world of historical event into the permanent one of written truth. In a letter written in 1856 he makes the distinction between
these two functions of a sentence: "The judge's opinion (*sententia*) of
the criminal *sentences* him & is read by the clerk of the court, & published to the world, & executed by the sheriff—but the criminal's opinion of the judge has the weight of a sentence & is published & executed only in the supreme court of the universe."[42] The prisoner's
sentence, like Brown's, may have the authority of truth behind it, and
may be part of the language of the universe rather than of the "world."
At the same time, the irony of the adverb "only" works both ways. We
are talking "only" about "the supreme court of the universe"; but there
is an implication that in being confined to that supreme level, to the
realm of the higher law, the prisoner's sentence will lack practical efficacy and be disconnected from the lower realm of history. When Tho-

41. See Jacques Derrida, *Speech and Phenomena, and Other Essays on Husserl's Theory of
Signs,* trans. David B. Allison (Evanston, Ill.: Northwestern University Press, 1973), 40.
42. Henry David Thoreau, *Correspondence,* 320, letter of January 21, 1854. A revised version of this passage (which has lost some of its sting) is in "Slavery in Massachusetts,"
Reform Papers, 98.

reau celebrates the transcendent power of language, whether here or in his account of the death of John Brown, one always senses his fear that its very transcendence separates it from our daily concerns. Moreover, his play on words such as "translation" and "*sententia*" has the effect of problematizing language and depriving it of that transparency he claims to seek. For example, in *A Week on the Concord and Merrimack Rivers* he describes a universal language that clearly has a relationship to Emerson's doctrine of the over-soul: "In the mythus a superhuman intelligence uses the unconscious thoughts and dreams of men as its hieroglyphics to address men unborn." Our task, he suggests here, is to try to emulate this superhuman intelligence in achieving a universal discourse: "The wisest man preaches no doctrines; he has no scheme; he sees no rafter, not even a cobweb, against the heavens. . . . Your scheme must be the frame-work of the universe; all other schemes will soon be ruins."[43]

To read Thoreau, however, is to encounter a perpetual interaction between the terse and the oblique, the proverbial and the paradoxical. Despite his apparent desire to achieve an ultimate linguistic architecture, he can not bear to relinquish the sprawling complexity of the contingent world. It is true that he claims to repudiate news on the grounds that once you've heard one item you've heard them all: "If we read of . . . one cow run over on the Western Railroad, or one mad dog killed, or one lot of grasshoppers in the winter,—we need never read of another. . . . [I]f you are acquainted with the principle, what do you care for a myriad instances and applications?" Nevertheless, part of the fascination of his writings is precisely his eye for the particular, his meticulous recording of detail. He will talk of perch and pouts, shiners, chivins, or roach, "a very few breams," and conclude with a recollection "of a little fish some five inches long, with silvery sides and a greenish back, somewhat dace-like in its character."[44] So much for the "fish principle in nature." The journals, as William Howarth points out, reveal an ever-increasing concern with the details of the natural world, and their concluding sentence can be seen as an acceptance of contingent reality: "Thus each wind is self-registering." In the penultimate sentence Thoreau has advocated not a transparent eyeball but simply "an observant eye."[45]

The trajectory that Howarth plots for Thoreau's last years is, iron-

43. Thoreau, *A Week*, 61, 70.
44. Thoreau, *Walden*, 94, 184.
45. Thoreau, *Journal*, 14:346, entry for November 3, 1861. See William Howarth, *The Book of Concord* (Harmondsworth: Penguin, 1983), 211.

ically, one from nature to history—that is to say, from a view of nature as the unchanging patterned world we have become familiar with in the thinking of the New England Transcendentalists to a historical view of nature, a nature subject to the winds of change. This development is hardly surprising, given that the decade of the 1850s was to culminate in the publication of Darwin's great exploration of natural evolution, *The Origin of Species*. But there were other factors at work besides developments in natural science itself, and Thoreau's increasingly empirical stance can be related to the courses followed by other members of the movement during this period: to Emerson's shift, as monitored by scholars such as Stephen Whicher, from freedom to fate, or Parker's increasing commitment to the anti-slavery platform, to Alcott's modulation from paradise planting to gardening, or Ripley's espousal of journalism after the failure of his utopia.[46]

The reasons for this more or less general movement from the idealistic to the pragmatic (and Brownson's flight to the Catholic Church provides its own reverse testimony to the process) are manifold and relate to the psychologies of the principals involved, to their career needs, to the urban and industrial developments taking place in New England and the United States in general, and to the gradual slide toward civil war. But my purpose has been to demonstrate that the New England Transcendentalists were conscious throughout their careers of the need to reconcile "natural" patterning and historical contingency, so to see these terms simply as successive is to distort the intellectual drama that lay at the heart of the movement. Although it is true that perceptions of the relationship between nature and history altered with time, the project from the beginning was to find a way of balancing these two factors, and thus to achieve a utopia in which human society conformed to the laws of the universe itself, in short, to reconcile lower with higher law. The way Thoreau attempted to achieve this point of balance—and the element of defeatism implicit in his solution itself marks him as a second-generation member of the movement—was by building, in effect, *two* huts, one that exists for a time in the historical realm of the lower law, the other that exists, presumably forever, in the eternal realm of the higher one.

In the conclusion of *Walden* Thoreau takes leave of hut number one in the name of historical pluralism: "Perhaps it seemed to me that I had several more lives to live, and could not spare any more time for

---

46. See Stephen Whicher, *Freedom and Fate: An Inner Life of Ralph Waldo Emerson* (Philadelphia: University of Pennsylvania Press, 1953).

that one."[47] The actual wooden dwelling on which he spent his $28.12½ soon disintegrated and disappeared. A year after Thoreau's death his friend Bronson Alcott went on a little pilgrimage to the site of his experiment: "Abby walks with me to Walden. We find the old paths by which I used to visit [Thoreau] from 'Hillside,' but the grounds are much overgrown with shrubbery, and the site of the hermitage is almost obliterated." A little more than a decade later he describes another visit with some companions: "After bathing we contribute severally our stone to Thoreau's cairn." The hut has turned into a monument. Nowadays, with the site marked out by a chain-link fence, it rather appropriately resembles a grave. But Alcott is quick to suggest a distinction between the temporariness of historical endeavor and the permanence of art. He goes on: "The pyramid is insignificant as yet; but could Thoreau's readers add theirs the pile would rise above the treetops to mark the site of his hermitage."[48] In the early editions of *Walden* a little engraving of a hut in the woods, from a drawing by Thoreau's sister Sophia, appears on the title page. It is as a text, an artwork, that Thoreau's project will participate in the structural permanence he associates with nature. The shingles, windows, hinges, and screws may have perished or dispersed with time, but their itemization survives in the book *Walden*, interrupting the flow of narrative like one of the extracts from poetry that coexist with gritty details in the chapter titled "Economy." The structure may fail, but the formula lives on. The purchases soon disappeared, but the bill of goods has become part of American literature. Just as in the case of John Brown there is a delay between action and meaning, a period in which the significance of Brown's life was left hanging like his body from the gallows, so there is a difference between Thoreau's sojourn in the woods and its literary resurrection nearly a decade later.

Even as a conversationalist Thoreau was notable for the way he would extract words from the continuum, so to speak, and give them autonomy—at least if the testimony of Emerson (whose own designs on language were similar) is to be believed: "H.[enry]'s conversation consisted of a continual coining of the present moment into a sentence & offering it to me."[49] Certainly Thoreau's artistic procedure consistently demonstrated his desire to remove his experience from historical time and give it permanence, most obviously by accommodating it

47. Thoreau, *Walden*, 323.
48. *The Journals of Bronson Alcott*, ed. Odell Shepard (Boston: Little, Brown, 1938), 358, entry for September 27, 1863; ibid., 452, entry for June 28, 1874.
49. Emerson, *Journals*, 9:101–2.

to a self-consistent diurnal or seasonal cycle. "The day is the epitome of the year," he tells us in *Walden*. "The night is the winter, the morning and evening are the spring and fall, and the noon is the summer." In his account of his trip on the Concord and Merrimack rivers, he compresses two weeks' experience into the self-contained unit of one, while in *Walden* itself he "reduced all of history to one year, the solar cycle that shapes all measured time."[50] Ocasionally he can show some unease about the process, as in this almost Jamesian passage describing how immediate experience is given the hard, cold substantiality necessary for it to endure in the museum of culture:

> From all points of the compass from the earth beneath and the heavens above have come these inspirations and been entered duly in such order as they came in the Journal. Thereafter, when the time arrived, they were winnowed into Lectures—and again in due time from Lectures into Essays—And at last they stand like the cubes of Pythagoras firmly on either basis—like statues on their pedestals—but the statues rarely take hold of hands—There is only such connexion and series as is attainable in the galleries. And this affects their immediate practical & popular influence.[51]

It is worth noticing here the way in which the carefully balanced organic metaphor—the "earth beneath" and the "heavens above" producing a harvest that can be "winnowed" into lectures—is displaced by forms that are geometrical and forbidding, as Thoreau goes on to state quite explicitly that "connexion and series" are consequently of a reduced and specialized kind.

The imagery in the penultimate paragraph of *Walden*, which features the anecdote of the bug, has a slightly more optimistic tendency. Thoreau leads up to his fable by talking about the present generation's inclination to see itself as the culmination of history. The context suggests that Thoreau is here envisaging discourse itself as a cause of imprisonment and entombment: he talks of "deep thinkers," sermons, psalms, and after-dinner conversations, of science as a record. But in defiance of all these intellectual structures, a living bug does finally manage to escape from the "made" environment in which it had been imprisoned for sixty years or more, "hatched perchance by the heat of an urn," that very repository of death, or in Keatsian terms of the

50. Thoreau, *Walden*, 301; Howarth, *Book of Concord*, 93.
51. Thoreau, *J*, 2:205–6, entry for summer 1846.

deathly stasis of art. "Who knows," Thoreau asks, "what beautiful and winged life, whose egg has been buried for ages under the many concentric layers of woodenness in the dead dry life of society, deposited at first in the alburnum of the green and living tree, which has been gradually converted into the semblance of its well-seasoned tomb"—and, given the seasonal organization of *Walden*, one can imagine these words referring to the tomb of the text itself, particularly as the evidence of the bug's escape is the *sound* that it makes in doing so—"heard perchance gnawing out now for years by the astonished family of man, as they sat round the festive board,—may unexpectedly come forth from amidst society's most trivial and handselled furniture, to enjoy its perfect summer life at last!"[52]

This perspective has some points in common with that adopted by Fourier in "Le sphinx sans Oedipe." Thoreau too seems to be relying on the irony that a suspended language, a discourse that is conscious of its own *différance*, might through its very belatedness correspond to the slow rhythms of nature. He does not, like Fourier, sneer at his generation for not having been able to read this ultimate text earlier—"THE BOOK," he calls it, in the Journal for 1855—but he does feel that the readership may be restricted: "I do not say that John or Jonathan will realize all this," the principle of inclusion being simply our own receptivity. As in the case of the John Brown conclusion, the rhetorical uplift is modified by the negative, and this countercurrent is given additional force by the imagery of loss of eyesight ("The light which puts out our eyes is darkness to us"), that very capacity to witness (or to read), which is the essential feature of revelation. And we are left waiting. "Only that day dawns to which we are awake."[53] Perhaps one day the text will meet up with external reality, the living bug will crawl out of the tomb of the book. Thoreau claims that the signifier can in some way generate the signified—as he puts it in one of his letters, "What can be expressed in words can be expressed in life"[54]—but at the end of the book we are inevitably left hanging, waiting for history to be redeemed. It is a conclusion, therefore, that reestablishes the gulf between higher law and lower law, that emphasizes the separation of the crystalline and dynamic structure of the law of series, that shows a perception of the fundamental incompatibility of series as structure and series as serial.

52. Thoreau, *Walden*, 333.
53. Howarth, *Book of Concord*, 107; Thoreau, *Walden*, 333.
54. Thoreau, *Correspondence*, 216, letter of March 27, 1848.

One could argue that this impasse is the inevitable outcome of Transcendentalist individualism. A communal experiment, whether on a biggish scale like Brook Farm or on a more limited one like Fruitlands, can be seen as having the capacity to engage with the prevailing social order, and therefore as having a potential for transforming it—a potential that could not be available to Thoreau in his hut by Walden Pond—even if in the case of Brook Farm and Fruitlands that potential was finally unfulfilled. Although there is a certain logic in identifying the individual as the smallest and therefore the most fundamental unit of society, it can also be argued that he or she is not a unit of society at all, since society is intrinsically plural. Certainly both Emerson and Thoreau can be seen as most fulfilled in the roles for which they express the most praise, those of poet and artist, happiest when they have stepped outside the social network altogether.

Theodore Parker is a rather different case, and it is worth looking briefly at his thought for an example of how a Transcendentalist who espoused individualism could in fact reach an accommodation with the historical process without conceding his utopian vision. Certainly he is a thoroughgoing individualist. "Individuals are the monads, the primitive atoms, of which society is composed," he tells us in his sermon "The Three Chief Safeguards of Society," which he preached in the Melodeon on July 6, 1851. Society's "power, its perfection, depend primarily on the power and perfection of the individuals, as much as the weight of a pendulum or of Mount Sheehallin depends on the primitive atoms thereof. Destroy the individuality of those atoms, human or material, all is gone. To mar the atom is to mar the mass. To preserve itself, therefore, society is to preserve the individuality of the individual."[55] Some years earlier in a letter of March 18, 1844, he tells Convers Francis that "I rejoice very much in the *Fourier* movement" but expresses certain fundamental reservations. "Three things are needed to make a complete revolution," he claims (with a Fourieristic precision of his own): "the sentiment, the idea, the action. I fancy their sentiment is not far from right, but if their idea be wrong, so must their action be. I see no cure for the evil but this, to give each individual clear views of the right, and then leave it to him to do what he thinks best."[56]

In one of his *Sermons of Religion* Parker explains how the individual

55. Theodore Parker, "The Three Chief Safeguards of Society," in *Sins and Safeguards of Society* (Boston: American Unitarian Association, 1907–8), 54.
56. Theodore Parker to Convers Francis, March 18, 1844, quoted in *Theodore Parker: An Anthology*, ed. Henry Steele Commager (Boston: Beacon Press, 1960), 272.

contribution can have its effect. He says, "All the good qualities you give example of" have a personal immortality in your life beyond the grave, but also "a national, even a human immortality on earth."[57] To substantiate this claim he refers to the virtue of the great men of antiquity. It is worth reminding ourselves of the Transcendentalist context of this contribution to the debate on heroism. Carlyle, as we have seen, considered great men the necessary exception to the run of humanity, whereas Emerson, by contrast, claimed the typicality or averageness of the great man, who sums up the general tendency of the human race. Charles Lane took issue with Emerson's doctrine of representativeness, despite the paradoxically anti-individualistic individualism at its heart, on the grounds that "a few intense spots of wealth, learning, or heroism" require "an endless range of poverty, ignorance, and degradation" for their very definition.[58]

Parker offers yet another perspective. He tells us that the great men of the past did not merely set an example—which would leave them isolated in their own time and place, with a merely iconographic significance—but "raised the temperature of the human world. For, as there is a physical temperature of the interstellar spaces, betwixt sun and sun, which may be called the temperature of the universe, so there is a spiritual temperature of the interpersonal spaces, a certain common temperature of spirit, not barely personal, not national alone, but human and of the race, which may be called the temperature of mankind. On that in general we all depend, as on our family in special, or in particular upon our personal genius and our will."[59]

There is a serial connection between the individual, the family, the nation, and the race, which takes us from "personal genius" to "interpersonal spaces." This is, of course, simply an aspect of the principle of connectivity that runs throughout the universe: "Everywhere in the world there is a natural law, there is a constant mode of action, which seems to belong to the nature of things, to the constitution of the universe; this fact is universal." This particular passage comes from one of Parker's most important and interesting pieces, the sermon "Of Justice and the Conscience," which he published in his collection *Ten Sermons of Religion* in 1852. He goes on to discuss the apparent diversity of nature's operations, the point being that there are "different departments" in the total scheme of things, and within each the same "mode

57. Theodore Parker, "Of Truth and the Intellect," in *Sermons of Religion* (Boston: American Unitarian Association, 1908), 28.
58. Charles Lane, "Social Tendencies," pt. 1, *Dial* 4 (July 1843): 72.
59. Parker, "Of Truth," 28.

of action" is called "by different names, as the law of matter, the law of mind, the law of morals, and the like."[60] These words anticipate the claim made by Brisbane in his autobiography: "*Law is unchanging*: but there is infinite variety in its manifestations;—such manifestations being as rich and complex as are the varied spheres or departments of the universe."[61]

In the material world, Parker tells us, the law manifests itself in the guise of "the great general law of attraction, which binds atom to atom in a grain of sand, orb to orb, system to system, gives unity to the world of things, and rounds these worlds of systems to a universe." He experiences the usual Transcendentalist glee at discovering a chain of continuity that connects the little with the big:

> Looked at in reference to this globe, an earthquake is no more than a chink that opens in a garden-walk of a dry day in summer. A sponge is porous, having small spaces between the solid parts; the solar system is only more porous, having larger room between the several orbs; the universe yet more so, with vast spaces between the systems; a similar attraction keeps together the sponge, the system, and the universe. Every particle of matter in the world is related to each and all other particles thereof; attraction is the common bond.

When he moves from external space to "the spiritual world, the world of human consciousness," he claims that

> there is also a law, an ideal mode of action for the spiritual forces of man. To take only the moral part of this sphere of consciousness, we find the phenomenon called justice, the law of right. Viewed as a force, it bears the same relation in the world of conscience, that attraction bears in the world of sense. I mean justice is the normal relation of men, and has the same to do amongst moral atoms,—individual men,—moral masses,—that is, nations,—and the moral whole,—I mean all mankind,—which attraction has to do with material atoms, masses, and the material whole.[62]

There is therefore a structure, a chain, which allows particular acts of virtue to spread indefinitely through time and space. "Those great men," he tells us in his sermon "Of Truth and the Intellect," "added

60. Theodore Parker, "Of Justice and the Conscience," in *Sermons of Religion*, 50.
61. *Albert Brisbane, A Mental Biography*, ed. Redelia Brisbane (Boston: Arena, 1893), 258.
62. Parker, "Of Justice," 51–52.

wisdom to mankind, brought spiritual truths to consciousness, which now have spread throughout the enlightened nations of the world, and penetrate progressively the human mass, giving mankind continual new power." At this point Parker introduces the image of magnetism in order to demonstrate that this process is a law of nature like any other: "So shall you see an iron bar become magnetic; first it was a single atom of the metal which caught the electric influence, spark by spark; that atom could not hold the subtle fire, whose nature was to spread, and so one atom gave the spark to the next, and soon it spread through the whole, till the cold iron, which before seemed dead as stone, is all magnetic, acquires new powers, and itself can hold its own, yet magnetize a thousand bars if rightly placed."[63]

It is interesting to compare the meticulous way in which Parker balances out the relationship between the one, the group, and the totality with this passage from John Sullivan Dwight, which also makes use of the imagery of electrical series:

> An individual is nothing in himself. . . . We are real *persons* only enter-ing true relations with all other human beings; we enter into our own life and find ourselves just in proportion as we realize and make good those relations. Only so far as the electric chain of sympathies which God threw round us all, in sign that we are *one* . . . is kept entire and unobstructed . . . can we be said to live; and most men live, like old trees that are dying, only in a few branches, an incoherent, fragmen-tary, partial life; nothing continuous, fresh, and whole about it. It takes the life of all mankind to make our single life complete. . . . So far as each lives not in the whole, does he lack life; so far as he is indifferent to any, does he miss a portion of himself.[64]

Here Dwight modulates from the electrical to the organic metaphor, and although he uses the latter to refer to the individual, he has a basically corporate perspective that reflects his communitarian ap-proach: "An individual is nothing in himself." His emphasis on the "electrical chain" is not on the empowering role of the single atom but on the necessity for keeping the series unobstructed. One can see how logical it was to move one stage further along from such an analysis and advocate, as W. H. Channing ultimately did, a doctrine of individ-ual self-sacrifice for the common good.

63. Parker, "Of Truth," 28–29.
64. John S. Dwight, "The Idea of a Divine Social Order," *Harbinger*, February 19, 1848, 122.

Parker, by contrast, insists that the individual must preserve his own identity and achieve a balance between his interests and that of the totality: "He must keep his personal integrity and discreteness of person, and not be lost in the press and crowd of other persons." This, he tells us in his sermon "Of Love and the Affections," is achieved by self-love, "the lesser cohesive attraction which keeps the man whole and a unit, which is necessary for his consistency and existence as an individual. It is a part of his morality, and is to the man what impenetrability is to the atoms of matter, and what the centripetal force is to the orbs of heaven." This centripetal force is balanced by "the expansive and centrifugal power" of love, "the greater gravitation which unites me to others . . . that extends my personality, and makes me feel my delight in others, and desire them to have theirs in me." The delicate balance between these forces can be knocked off kilter, either by selfishness— "no longer merely conservative of myself, I become invasive, destructive of others, and appropriate what is theirs to my own purposes"—or its opposite, neglect of that "natural and well-proportioned self-love" which is necessary to create the counterforce at the basis of the whole structure: the impenetrability of the individual, "the natural concomitant of attraction." Parker sees the achievement of this equilibrium as the outcome of a process of rational adjustment and experiment, the ultimate result of which will be a world of utopian harmony:

With man there is this greater gravitation of men into masses; which, without doubt, is at first as instinctive as the groupings of bees or beavers; but man is capable of modifying the action of this gregarious instinct so, on the one side, as to form minute cohesions of friendship, wherein each follows his private personal predilections, his own elective affinities; and also, on the other, to form vast associations of man gravitating into a nation, ruled by a common will; and one day we shall, no doubt, group all these nations into one great family of races, with a distinct self-consciousness of universal brotherhood.[65]

Parker devotes little space in his writings to speculating about the utopian outcome of the social development he describes. In the early "Thoughts on Labor," which he published in the *Dial* in 1841, he makes the Fourieristic observation that in a "rational and natural state of society," the "diversity of gifts would be quite equal to the diversity of

65. Theodore Parker, "Of Love and the Affections," in *Sermons of Religion*, 81–82, 85, 87–88.

work to be done."[66] In the sermon "Of the Universal Providence of God," written some years later, he elaborates this point, claiming that each of us will be able to do the "normal work which he can do best"; moreover, he or she will be able to achieve "normal personal freedom" because our personal needs will mesh exactly with the demands of society, so that a perfect balance will have been struck.[67] Despite its "normality," however, this prospect is not an imminent one. True, the image of electrical series could in itself suggest instantaneous or, in the Emersonian sense, magical transformation. Nevertheless, the question of scale makes a gradualist perspective seem more convincing. "It is only a little that any of us can do—for anything," Parker says in a sermon titled "Poverty," but goes on to look at the bright side: "Still we can do a little; we can each do by helping towards raising the general tone of society: first each man raising himself by industry, economy, charity, piety; by noble life. So doing, we raise the moral temperature of the whole world, and just in proportion thereto."[68] In "Of Justice and the Conscience," Parker compares the achievement of the ordinary person—"you and I"—with that of "little insects" who "lay the foundation of firm islands." In just the same way, we "in our daily life, in house, or field, or shop, obscurely faithful, may prepare the way for the republic of righteousness, the democracy of justice, that is to come." Although Parker identifies with those who "look for a great social revolution," he thinks the associationists are mistaken in assuming that their projects are anything more than part of a long line of such enterprises. His own belief is that private property, for example, will not be abolished in the near future: "I think it will linger for some ages to come. Like the snow it is to be removed by a general elevation of the temperature of the air, not all at once; and will long hang about the dark and cold places of the world."[69]

In the broadest sense Parker can be viewed as a utopian, though one who sees the good society as the end product of the historical process: it is a long way off. Ultimately, therefore, his position is that of optimistic radicalism rather than of the millennialism that characterized Brook Farm and Fruitlands. Parker became increasingly engaged with the processes of a painfully evolving American society, throwing his energies into the abolitionist movement and playing his part in elevat-

66. Theodore Parker, "Thoughts on Labor," *Dial* 1 (April 1841): 501.
67. Theodore Parker, "Of the Universal Providence of God," in *Theism*, 301.
68. Theodore Parker, "Poverty," in *Sins and Safeguards*, 287.
69. Parker, "Of Justice," in *Sermons of Religion*, 76; "Poverty," in *Sins and Safeguards*, 279–80.

ing the temperature of the air. In his case we are not left with a philosophical impasse as we seem to be at the end of *Walden*. Rather, the utopian solution is deferred to the point where its distinctive Transcendentalist identity fades away, leaving Parker's activism to be associated with long-term, large-scale reforming programs in general. The question is not whether John or Jonathan will realize all this. None of us will, for generations to come, since what is on offer is not a means of perceiving the true nature of the world, but an opportunity to play our small individual parts in bringing into being that true—or, to use Parker's word, that "normal"—ordering of things whereby history will ultimately keep its rendezvous with natural law.

A year after the publication of *Walden*, the first edition of Walt Whitman's *Leaves of Grass* appeared, and the law of series made its appearance in another context. There is a certain appropriateness about concluding this study of New England thought by glancing at the work of the great New Yorker, for we have seen that the tendency in the later stages of the Transcendentalist movement, as faith in specific, local solutions to the universal problem waned, was to engage with the dilemma on the universal level. Thus Brown the man is no longer confined to Kansas; Thoreau's wooden hut is transmuted to an engraving, a book, a cairn; and the law of series can become the determining principle of the great American poem:

The nearest gnat is an explanation, and a drop or motion of waves a key,
The maul, the oar, the hand-saw, second my words . . .
And to glance with an eye or show a bean in its pod confounds the
    learning of all times,
And there is no trade or employment but the young man following it
    may become a hero,
And there is no object so soft but it makes a hub for the wheel'd
    universe . . .[70]

A year after this, the new edition of *Leaves of Grass* included the poem later titled "Crossing Brooklyn Ferry," where the last and perhaps strangest of the Transcendentalist utopias makes its appearance. In this poem Whitman provides a memorable depiction of the double perspective that Santayana identified as characteristic of Transcendentalism: the mythic, whereby the world is incorporated by the subject, and

70. Walt Whitman, "Song of Myself," in *Leaves of Grass*, ed. Harold W. Blodgett and Sculley Bradley (New York: New York University Press, 1965), 85–86.

the methodical, whereby that world is perceived afresh. Whitman writes:

The impalpable sustenance of me from all things at all hours of the day,
The simple, compact, well-join'd scheme, myself disintegrated, everyone
   disintegrated yet part of the scheme,
The similitudes of the past and those of the future,
The glories strung like beads on my smallest sights and hearings, on the
   walk in the street and the passage over the river,
The current rushing so swiftly and swimming with me far away,
The others that are to follow me, the ties between me and them,
The certainty of others, the life, love, sight, hearing of others.[71]

In the first line the poet depicts himself as feeding upon the surrounding world, like an etherialized version of one of Hawthorne's porkers. This organicism is replaced by its opposite, as Whitman shows himself "disintegrated" into part of a patterned overall structure. We switch back to a vision of him walking along the street or crossing the river and carrying the little epiphanies of his experiences like a necklace; then suddenly he is a small figure himself, being washed away on the river of time. But because he is simultaneously the whole of which everything else is a part, and a part of the great whole, because in short of the miracle of seriality, he can express faith in the links between himself and the rest of the race to follow: the pattern can be reconciled through time.

When, a little later, he comes to depict himself on the Brooklyn ferryboat, he uses the strategy we have seen in Thoreau for reconciling the larger and smaller cycles of time, and thereby giving a sense of eternity. His crossing takes him from winter to summer, from the "twelfth-month seagulls" to the "reflection of the summer sky in the water," and at the same time through a single day, from the oblique light of early morning, through the brightness of noon, toward the violet of evening. During this journey Whitman is both a subordinate part of the scheme ("Had my eyes dazzled by the shimmering track of beams") and its very source ("Look'd at the fine centrifugal spokes of light round the shape of my head in the sunlit water").[72] The latter vignette is oddly reminiscent of that description Alcott gives us of the effect achieved by the application of cold water and flesh brush, when electrical series took a literal form: "I shook flames from my finger

71. Walt Whitman, "Crossing Brooklyn Ferry," in ibid., 160.
72. Ibid., 161.

ends, which seemed erect and blazing with the phosphoric light. The
eyes, too, were lustrous, and shot sparkles, whenever I closed them."

The secret of the ferry is that it is both a place, because people
congregate on it, and a vehicle, because it moves. Thus, it has the
necessary attributes for reconciling the static and the dynamic, for providing an embodiment of what Emerson called "the flying Perfect."
Moreover, as it shuttles between two fixed points, it offers an experience that can be shared by all and will persist unaltered through time:

Just as you are refresh'd by the gladness of the river and the bright flow, I
    was refresh'd,
Just as you stand and lean on the rail, yet hurry with the swift current, I
    stood yet was hurried,
Just as you look on the numberless masts of ships and the thick-stemm'd
    pipes of steamboats, I look'd.[73]

The ferry is a public conveyance which for Whitman has the capability
of taking its passengers to a utopian destination, like the omnibuses
and the Richmond steamboat that were to carry members of the public
to Alcott's London meeting "for the promotion of the great end." The
synthesis that the Transcendentalists were looking for between static
pattern and historical movement could hardly be more concisely
phrased than in that description Whitman gives of himself aboard the
ferry: "I stood yet was hurried." He is part of an impromptu community, made up of a random concatenation of his fellow citizens, each
one ordinary yet uniquely important: "Crowds of men and women at-
tired in the usual costumes, how curious you are to me!"[74]

For Whitman the ferryboat is also quite clearly the poem itself. Its
lines too shuttle between fixed points across the page. It too moves as
the reader's eyes follow the words, yet remains fixed as each individual
word stays in its allotted place. This enterprise is different from those
undertaken by Ripley, Alcott, and their colleagues a decade earlier.
The terms of the equation are no longer nature and history but art and
history. The ferry itself is a sort of art object, the product of human
craftsmanship. Language and reality, the poem (as vessel) and the vessel (as poem), thus operate simultaneously. There is no suspension or
différance.

The Brooklyn ferry—as a civic facility, as the embodiment of a collective need, both a thing and a trajectory—was able to persist through

73. Ibid., 160–61.
74. Ibid., 159.

time in parallel with the poem that celebrated it, for a while at least. It maintained the course mapped out in Whitman's poem until the opening of the bridge that superseded it as both a practical and an imaginative resource, and in turn became the subject of another poem in which America's mission was explored and defined, Hart Crane's *The Bridge*.

Eventually, then, Whitman's poem was to outlive the ferry it celebrates. The interaction that can be perceived in his work, as in Thoreau's, is ultimately between the eternal world of art on the one hand, and the historical world on the other. In their different ways both Thoreau and Whitman come to perceive nature as part of the historical world in any case: Thoreau as he became more sensitive to its particularity, its intricate detail, its shifts and changes, Whitman as he broke down the romantic distinction between the urban and rural environments. Both moved toward a Darwinian perspective, Thoreau through his groundbreaking studies in what we would now call ecology, Whitman in his robust acceptance of the part played in the natural cycle by death and decay: "And as to you Corpse I think you are good manure, but that does not offend me."[75] (One could imagine how Alcott and Lane would have felt about such a claim!) The effect is to put both history and nature on one side of the equation and the book on the other. In "Crossing Brooklyn Ferry" the passengers, the ferry, Whitman himself are all transformed into the poem, just as Thoreau's hut was turned into text. Whether a bug can be hatched to make the *opposite* journey is left unclear. What is certainly true is that the synthesis between nature, regarded as the embodiment of eternal law, and history, the story of human mutability, which constituted the utopian mission of the first generation of New England Transcendentalists was by now no longer a valid enterprise.

Hardly surprisingly, at our greater historical distance, it is not easy for us to understand the urgency of that task for the generation that undertook it, and it is even less easy for us to appreciate the millennial fulfillment that offered itself as a reward for its successful accomplishment. It has been my purpose in this book to make that noble project a little more comprehensible, and to shed light on the serial law, which, as I see it, was the key to the whole intellectual, imaginative, and social endeavor.

75. Whitman, "Song of Myself," 87.

Index

Note: Abbreviated forms (used for a few titles of volumes and collected editions that have been cited throughout this book) are given in brackets, and the first page reference includes a footnote giving full publication details.